RECOLLECTIONS
of Early Texas

Personal Narratives of the West Series

John Holland Jenkins and Mary Jane Foster Jenkins, ca. 1848

RECOLLECTIONS
of Early Texas

The Memoirs of
JOHN HOLLAND JENKINS

Edited by
JOHN HOLMES JENKINS, III

Foreword by J. FRANK DOBIE

AUSTIN
UNIVERSITY OF TEXAS PRESS

International Standard Book Number 0-292-77037-5
Library of Congress Catalog Card Number 58-7234
© 1958 by the University of Texas Press
Printed in the United States of America

Second Paperback Printing, 1990

Requests for permission to reproduce material from this work should be sent to Permissions, University of Texas Press, Box 7819, Austin, Texas 78713-7819.

∞ The paper used in this publication meets the minimum requirements of American National Standard for Information Sciences—Permanence of Paper for Printed Library Materials, ANSI Z39.48-1984.

TO MOTHER AND DAD

WHO DID NOT KNOW

OF MY PREPARING THIS BOOK

YET WITHOUT WHOSE UNWITTING AID

IT COULD NEVER HAVE BEEN COMPLETED

WITH ALL MY LOVE

Foreword

JOHN HOLLAND JENKINS was thirteen and a half years old when the Alamo fell in 1836 and he became a soldier of the Texas Republic under General Sam Houston. He and his family had been in Texas about eight years. It was not until 1884, when he was past sixty years old, that he began writing down for publication in the Bastrop *Advertiser*, the weekly newspaper of his county, the reminiscences that, as now put into book form, light up for whoever will read the earliest days of early English-speaking Texas.

Jenkins' memories of what happened in his boyhood world are as specific, though not so elaborately detailed, as the childhood and boyhood recollections of W. H. Hudson, Maxim Gorky, Leo Tolstoy, Serghei Aksakoff, and other singular recorders of the Far Away and Long Ago in their lives; but Jenkins, so far as his recorded reminiscences go, had no childhood or boyhood. If he recollected any gleams of magic before the light of common day faded them out, he failed to transmit even one of them. He revealed not self but the society of cabin-dwellers, Indian fighters, and buffalo hunters that he belonged to. His reminiscences are the stuff of narrative history concerned with the purely physical but not of the novel that would sound deep into the thoughts, emotions, and sensory experiences of human beings—whether on a frontier of vast vacancies or in a great city outwardly dominated by masses of people and machines.

However that may be, it is something extraordinary to have at this late date a contemporary of one and a third centuries ago speak in fresh accents of those forever vanished times. The cedar logs for the Jenkins cabin, built about forty miles down the Colorado River from where Austin was later to be established as the capital of Texas, were "cut with axes and dragged up with horses." The boards for roof and siding were hand-hewn, from that curious island of pines for which the Bastrop area remains botanically distinguished, and brought by hand and horse to the cabin site and placed without nails. Without mills, the home-raised corn was hand-ground for bread and the high-priced coffee beans were roasted in a pan and then "tied in a piece of buckskin and beaten upon a rock with another rock" to make them release their virtue in boiling water. In the absence of corn, the settlers at times substituted the dried breasts of wild turkeys for bread, eating unsalted venison for meat. There was no money crop and there was virtually no money for these first settlers. A family farm consisted of about ten acres planted by hand in corn, with maybe a dozen rows of cotton, to be cleaned of seeds by hand and home-spun for clothes.

Eli Whitney's body had been moldering in the grave only about three years when the Jenkins family set out from Alabama for Texas. Eli Whitney's cotton gin, invented in 1792, was making planters over the South rich and slaves high and was ginning out the Civil War like the loom of destiny, but such outposts of settlers as the Jenkins community had hardly felt the first breath of industrialization before Josiah Wilbarger was scalped, in 1840.

Texas was still country-living and frontier-minded in 1889, the year that J. W. Wilbarger's *Indian Depredations in Texas* was published and became a household book over the land. Wilbarger made use of the materials now gathered into *Recollections of Early Texas*. He would have been derelict not to have made use of them. The Wilbarger and Jenkins families were old neighbors, friends, and fellow warriors. If *Recollections of Early Texas* had appeared in book form in the 1880's it might have raced *Indian Depredations in Texas* for popularity; the two books are of the same kidney.

They carry one back to the generations of old-timers who considered themselves as having virtually nothing to say unless they could give a firsthand account of an Indian scrape—or of a few killings, preferably involving John Wesley Hardin, Ben Thompson, or some other notability among bad men. The bad men came after the Civil War. Not a single white man killing, unless it has escaped me, occurs in these Jenkins reminiscences of bloodshed and also of white-skinned brutality as naked as any red-skinned. There was hardly another area in Texas that during the process of being "redeemed from the wilderness" suffered so long and so often from Indian molestation, unless it was the Sabinal Canyon country, celebrated by A. J. Sowell in his *Early Settlers and Indian Fighters of Southwest Texas* (1900), and the Parker–Palo Pinto counties area west of Fort Worth.

The man Jenkins made no bones about his preference for Ed Burleson as a leader over Sam Houston. His account of Houston's cursing him is one of the characteristic outright honesties of the book. The feelings between Houston and Burleson were fierce and deep and they were shared by partisans of both leaders. The historical value and interest of this narrative lies to no small extent in the sidelights it throws not only on personalities but on certain vivid episodes—the Runaway Scrape, the Mier Expedition, the Santa Fe Expedition, Texas Ranger campaigns, etc.

John Holland Jenkins had little schooling, but a human being's congenital intelligence, memory, and proclivity for observing are not dependent upon schooling. Frequent quotations from classical writers show that Jenkins had read and remembered. He was aware of style in written histories and defined his own purposes in writing. "Little incidents here and there," he observed, "these touches of reality, are necessities in historical narration, just as salt, pepper, and sauce are essential to the right flavoring of soup, roast, and vegetables." Moreover, he felt an inner urge to add to what he entitled "The Treasury of Truth."

Of course, every narrator, whether of fiction or fact, whether writer or talker, knows the effect of detail, for good detail never loses freshness or power to illuminate life. One would have to go no further than the details in this book, cumulative in effect, concerning horses to realize that on the frontiers, as the saying went, a man on foot was no man at all, and that a man on a good horse had the advantage over both nature and enemy.

There was the "Duty Roan," a horse about which tantalizingly little is told. There was Jonathan Burleson—brother to the great Ed—hemmed up by Indians on a bluff "nearly thirty feet high," but he was riding a good horse, the horse made the tremendous leap, and horse and rider got to safety without a scratch. On one horse raid, Indians stole General Ed Burleson's "celebrated" Scurry, a present to him from one Richard Scurry, manifestly an "American" horse in contradistinction to the low-priced mustang breed. Burleson and eight or ten men took the trail of the horse thieves, but when they caught up with them the General was severely handicapped for want of a horse that could run. One of his party named Spaulding rode the best horse of the lot and when the chase began, across a prairie, Burleson yelled out, "Twenty-five dollars for Scurry, Spaulding!" A little farther on, in a louder voice, Burleson yelled again, "Fifty dollars for Scurry, Spaulding!" And then, as the chase grew hotter, it was, "One hundred dollars for Surry, Spaulding!" Burleson got Scurry back, but whether Spaulding got the hundred dollars Jenkins does not say.

How the bodies of slain bee hunters were buried in the hollow stump of a bee tree they had cut down, for the discoverers of the bodies had no way of transporting them to a settlement; how the comrades of another man who died far out dug his grave with the "blade bone" of a buffalo and covered him up; how the prairie bottoms were covered with "wild rye," while "sage grass" (little and big bluestem) was high enough for Indians to hide in—these and many other details transport us to the times. Jenkins' prowess as a bee hunter calls up that classic of bee-hunting days, T. B. Tharpe's *The Hive of the Honey-Bee,* in which the hero avers that he could course a bee in the air "a mile away easy." The last sentence in the Jenkins narrative sums up the sympathy for the life with which it is written: "And now, after sixty years of the best hunting, I believe I would ride twenty-five miles [on horseback, of course] to see a fresh bear track."

My people never did believe in voting for a Confederate veteran for public office solely because he was one-armed, one-eyed, half-witted, or possessed of some other defect calculated to influence the majority of voters. When I became acquainted with Johnny (John Holmes III) Jenkins (born March 22, 1940), he was just past fifteen and was doing the research and editorial work that now add much to his great-great-grandfather's *Recollections.* I do not vote for Johnny Jenkins because he became an editor so young but because he has edited so ably. Many a Ph.D. thesis shows less scholarship and less intelligence than Johnny's editorial work and is not nearly so interesting. Some of his notes are for students; some will add to the comprehension of readers in general.

The biographical dictionary at the end of the book is an

achievement in usefulness and handiness that might well be adopted by editors of various historical narratives. Like his ancestor, Johnny Jenkins seems to consider it his duty to put down the truth whether it is complimentary or not. As he searches on into the ever-receding Beyond, he will learn that in the realm of thought—perhaps the highest, though not necessarily the most delightful, realm that a historian enters— a great many conclusions based on irrefutable evidence are not patriotic according to politician standards and are not complimentary at all to what Mark Twain dubbed "the damned human race."

J. FRANK DOBIE

Preface

IN MARCH OF 1836 Texas was in an uproar. Independence from Mexico had been declared, one Mexican Army had already been driven from Texas, and preparations were being made for the full-scale war which was undoubtedly soon to come, for an army of six thousand regular Mexican soldiers under Antonio Lopez de Santa Anna had captured San Antonio, and laid siege to the little mission San Antonio de Padua, commonly known as the Alamo. Inside were 187 valiant Texans, under Colonel William B. Travis.

At the town of Gonzales, a few miles away, men from all over the state were banding together to form an army which would attempt to defeat the Republic of Mexico and the self-styled "Napoleon of the West." Among the recruits from the little village of Bastrop was a boy named John Holland Jenkins. Although only thirteen years old, he was remarkably tall and stout and could easily pass for a man. The outcome of the siege at the Alamo had particular importance for him —his stepfather was one of the Texans in Colonel Travis' band. On March 7 tidings came that the Alamo had fallen; every one of the Texans had been killed by the Mexicans. The cries of anguish from the wives and children of the thirty-two men from Gonzales who had been killed left a deep and lasting impression on the youthful mind of John Jenkins.

In a few days the Commander-in-Chief, Sam Houston,

arrived, organized the army, and began the retreat which
ended with the Battle of San Jacinto and victory for the Republic of Texas. Jenkins did not participate in the battle,
however, because he had been detailed by Colonel Burleson
to return home and move his now twice-widowed mother
and his brothers and sister to safety. Thus at the age of thirteen John Jenkins became the man of the family, but he was
equal to the job.

After the Texas victory and capture of Santa Anna, Jenkins took his mother and family back to their home in Bastrop County, and successfully protected them through all the
hardships and dangers of pioneer life. Bastrop then was actually beyond the frontier. There was as much danger of
Indian attack from the east as from the west—and the little
settlement received far more than its share of raids and thefts
from the hostiles.

The story of those Indian depredations and the Mexican
invasions is recounted in this book. After Texas became a
thriving and populated state of the Union, and Jenkins had
retired with his wife to a quiet life on his farm, he was requested by his children and neighbors to set down his recollections of early Texas. He began by writing, with the help of
his daughter-in-law, a series of articles made up of his own
personal reminiscences of life in pioneer Texas. These were
published in the Bastrop *Advertiser* during 1884 and 1885.
He then began to collect the reminiscences of other old
Texans—Captain Rufus Perry, John Morgan, Captain Dan
Grady, Captain Claudius Buster, William Clopton, Captain
Samuel Highsmith, Judge N. W. Eastland, and many others.
Most of these were published by the *Advertiser* at various
times between 1884 and 1889. Jenkins' death on November
30, 1890, ended his research, but he had already contributed
much toward the preservation of historical data of colonial
Texas.

John Holland Jenkins was born on September 16, 1822, near Demopolis, Marengo County, Alabama. At the age of six or seven he moved with his parents, Edward and Sarah (Parrent) Jenkins, to Texas as members of Stephen F. Austin's Third, or Little, Colony. The family first lived with the William Bartons on Barton Creek, near Rosanky, while Edward Jenkins and Thomas H. Mays were surveying a league of land for the Jenkinses, which was granted to each emigrant family. In the spring of 1830 they began their new life on their league, which lay on the west bank of the Colorado River, about thirty-five miles below Austin.

Indian depredations were constant, and young John frequently saw the savages skulking about. Occasionally a band of Indians claiming to be friendly would appear to trade with the colonists, but more often than not it would be found the next day that some livestock or other property was missing. Then, in 1833, while working out in a field, Edward Jenkins was murdered, supposedly by marauding Indians, although no conclusive proof was ever found. This left the widowed mother, who was four months' pregnant, with three defenseless children. She was forced to move into the town of Bastrop with friends and sell half of her husband's land.

Bastrop then was a thriving settlement. It was one of the largest towns in Texas, for at that time Houston, Austin, and Dallas had not even been laid out. Located where the Old San Antonio Road crossed the Colorado River, it was in one of the most fertile and beautiful areas in Texas. Stephen F. Austin, speaking of the Bastrop area, recorded in his journal:

Tuesday, August 7 (1821). Came to the Colorado River—poor, gravelly ridges and near the river heavy pine timber, grapes in immense quantities on low vines, red, large, and well flavored, good for Red wine. The Colorado River is sometimes less than the Brazos, banks very high—generally clear of overflow—bottom and banks gravelly, water very clear and well tasted, current brisk, the river very much resembles Cumberland River, except that there are no rocks and it is some larger.

The bottom where the road crosses is about five miles, mostly high prairie, clear of overflow, land rich, timber Pecan, Ash, Oak, Cedar, abundance of fish.*

The town of Bastrop was established about 1829, when Martin Wells settled there with his sons, and grew steadily until 1839, when Austin was laid out and made capital of the Republic. From that time on, progress in Bastrop was small.

In 1835 Mrs. Jenkins remarried—to James Northcross, a Methodist minister from Virginia. They had one son.

After Northcross' death in the Alamo, John Jenkins took his mother and the rest of the family back to their half-league of land across the river from Bastrop, where he cared for his mother until her death in 1840, and raised his younger brothers and sister. On October 29, 1845, he married Mary Jane Foster, daughter of another old pioneer family. They had six sons and one daughter.

Much of the material in the Jenkins reminiscences has appeared in other works, usually without acknowledgment, but the memoirs themselves present such an interesting and enlightening view on pioneer life in early Texas that publication in full is long overdue.

The book has its shortcomings. The original reminiscences are rough and loosely connected, words and names are frequently misspelled, and there are some confusing grammatical errors. It seemed desirable, however, to preserve the original flavor of the narrative; hence revision has consisted mainly in correcting spelling and grammar and rearranging the

* E. C. Barker (ed.), "Journal of Stephen F. Austin on His First Trip to Texas, 1821," *Texas Historical Quarterly*, VII.

articles for the sake of continuity. Critical and explanatory notes have been added.

Noah Smithwick was used as much as possible for comparison of accounts, rather than John Henry Brown, Frank Brown, James DeShields, or J. W. Wilbarger. Smithwick moved to California in 1861 and lived there the rest of his life. Hence there is little chance of his narrative having been influenced by Jenkins, who was first to attempt to assemble a history of the Indian hostilities in Texas. The two Browns, DeShields, and Wilbarger, however, used Jenkins' reminiscences freely and many of their narratives are exact repetitions of the Jenkins accounts. Wilbarger, particularly, quotes Jenkins word-for-word without acknowledgment.

It is hoped that the succeeding pages will not only be of value to the historian as a reference but will also prove as entertaining and as exciting to those who are interested in understanding and reliving the lives of their forefathers as it has to this young Texan.

JOHN HOLMES JENKINS, III

Beaumont, Texas

Acknowledgments

MY SINCERE and grateful thanks are due to many persons throughout the state who assisted me in the preparation of this book. First, I give my most heartfelt thanks to my great-aunt, Mrs. W. T. Decherd of Austin. She it was who showed me the Jenkins reminiscences and who, instead of laughing at the thought of a fifteen-year-old writing a book, encouraged me to do so. Fostering the love of Texas and of history in general which I share with her, she gave much of her time telling what she knew of her grandfather and her mother, who copied by hand the original memoirs.

Next I thank Miss Claire Andrews, Mrs. Harriet L. Willis, and my Grandmother Lila of Beaumont, who helped me make this book a surprise for my mother and father.

In Bastrop, Texas, Tignal Jones allowed me the use of the probate and deed records, and Hartford Jenkins spent much time showing me the exact location of many of the places mentioned in this book. Misses Grace and Nell Fitzwilliam permitted me to use material belonging to the Bastrop Historical Society, as well as their own personal data on Bastrop County.

An important necessity in writing a book is a place to work without interruption and where books and papers may be scattered about without danger of their being "straightened" or put in neat little stacks by some helpful elder. For arrang-

ACKNOWLEDGMENTS

ing such bachelor quarters for me, my love and thanks go to my Gran and Grandaddy Chalmers of Bastrop.

Essential material was gathered during two summer vacations at the Archives Collections of the University of Texas Library and the Texas State Library. The Archivists of these two libraries willingly gave me much helpful information. I especially appreciate the trust that they reposed in me and the liberties they granted me in the use of their invaluable source material relating to Texas history.

I also thank Mrs. Carl Swanson of the Austin Public Library for the use of the Frank Brown papers and for trusting me with other valuable Texas books.

I received constant encouragement and valuable advice from Mr. J. Frank Dobie, who very graciously wrote the foreword to this book. Words cannot express the deep appreciation I feel for the time he gave to me.

Contents

Illustrations

RECOLLECTIONS
of Early Texas

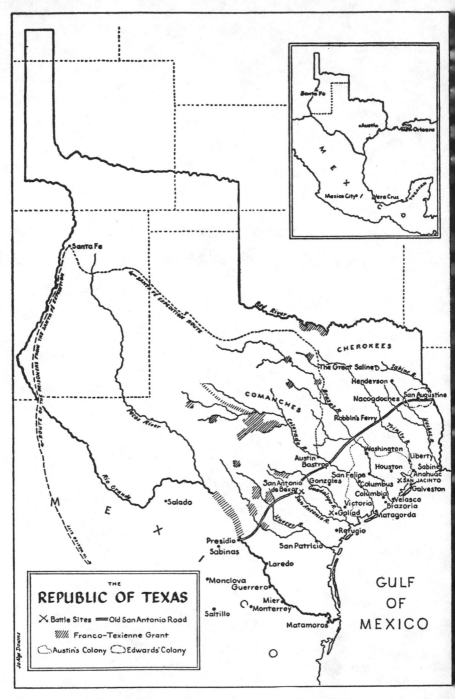

REPUBLIC OF TEXAS. *From Stanley Siegel,* A Political History of the Texas Republic, 1836–1845, *1956*

CHAPTER I

Austin's Little Colony

ABOUT THE MIDDLE of October in the year 1828[1]
my father left his old home in Alabama and came
west, intending to grow up with the new country—at least
in a financial point of view.

I was then a mere child, but the scenes and incidents of
those early times are very clear and distinct in my mind even
now, although more than fifty years with many and great
changes have worked upon my life since then, and I look
around me in vain for those who accompanied us on our
journey westward.[2]

One by one they have tired upon the journey of life and

[1] There is some confusion regarding the date of the Jenkinses' emigration to Texas. The deed records in the county courthouse at Linden,
Marengo County, Alabama, show that both Edward Jenkins, Sr.,
and his wife Sarah (Parrent) Jenkins were at that place on June 11
and August 8, 1829, when they sold two eighty-acre lots to Glover &
Gaines of Alabama. The Register of Spanish Archives, IV, 630, however, tends to substantiate the statement that they left in October of
1828. Later references in the first chapter of these memoirs intimate
that Jenkins was incorrect by a year concerning the early events of his
life. It must be remembered that he was only six or seven years old
when his family moved, and his reminiscences were written forty or
fifty years after the events occurred.

[2] A search of the Marengo County records shows that Benjamin,
Elisha, and William Barton sold their land in that county about the
same time as the Jenkins family. All three of these men settled at
Bastrop and may have been members of the Jenkins party.

have gone to their long rest, until no signs of the old stirring times are left, except here and there an old man recounts to his children and to his children's children the many thrilling experiences of the old Texans.

Standing now and viewing the populous and thriving cities, together with the vast expanses of fields and pastures wrought by man's hand in this half-century, a description of our State as those early settlers found her seems as a "tale that must be told."

The broad prairies covered with rich grass and wild rye and her dense forests teeming with game are indeed a thing of the dead past. Memory recalls her as a proud and happy queen, holding forth her rare treasures of grand and beautiful scenery, and bright prospects to those hardy children who came thus upon her virgin soil, facing so many hardships, deprivations, difficulties, and dangers.

Surrounding our small band of pioneers was one vast and magnificent solitude with no sight nor sound of human kind, except the wandering tribes of Indians in their raids against each other and against the slow but sure inroads of civilization—which had driven them from their native hunting ground. I can recall many tales of horror concerning Indian cruelty and treachery upon the eastern portions of the Republic of Texas, and as we journeyed we found substantial proof of their truth. Near Captain James Ross's[3] on the Colorado River, thirty-five miles from Bastrop, which was

[3] Captain James J. Ross, one of Stephen F. Austin's Old Three Hundred colonists, led the attack mentioned against the Indians early in 1829, giving further evidence that the Jenkins family emigrated in that year rather than 1828. James T. DeShields, *Border Wars of Texas* (1912), 47–48 (hereafter cited as DeShields, *Border Wars*); Worth S. Ray, *Austin Colony Pioneers* (1949), 199, 274; Andrew Jackson Sowell, *Early Settlers and Indian Fighters of Southwest Texas* (1900), 15–16 (hereafter cited as Sowell, *Early Settlers*); Andrew Jackson Sowell, *Rangers and Pioneers of Texas* (1884), 23 (hereafter cited as Sowell, *Rangers and Pioneers*).

then called "Mina,"[4] we found human bones lying "grim and ghastly on the green grass." Upon inquiry they were found to be the skeletons of Indians who had come to Captain Ross's, first under pretense of peace and friendliness, then growing more and more aggressive until they gradually revealed false and murderous designs, until at last for self-protection the whites collected and killed them.

While here, we heard of a murder by Indians of rather recent date. An old man by the name of Tumlinson*[5] was at

[4] When the town was formally established on June 8, 1832, it was given the name of Bastrop, in honor of Philip Hendrik Nering Bogel, Baron de Bastrop, who had materially aided Stephen F. Austin to obtain the grant for the first American colony in Texas.

In 1834 while Stephen F. Austin was in prison in Mexico, under suspicion of working for the annexation of Texas to the United States, Texans were trying desperately to prove their loyalty to the Mexican government, so that Austin would be freed and the reforms for which Austin had been sent to plead would be granted. On April 3, 1834, Oliver Jones, a close friend of Austin, introduced a bill in the legislature of the State of Coahuila and Texas proposing that the town be renamed Mina, after Francisco Xavier Mina, a national hero and a martyr to the cause of liberty in Mexico. The bill also proposed that a new municipality be created out of the area surrounding the town, to be called the Municipality of Mina. The bill became a law on April 24, 1834, and by August 18 of that year the ayuntamiento (the Spanish equivalent of our modern city council) had been established with Robert M. Coleman as alcalde, or president.

After Texas had won her independence, however, Mexican authority was no longer feared and Mexican heroes no longer honored. On December 18, 1837, James Seaton Lester introduced a resolution to the Second Session of the First Congress of the new Republic of Texas changing the name of the town and county of Mina back to Bastrop. This joint resolution passed the Senate and the House on the same day, and President Houston approved it that afternoon. Both the town and county have had that name ever since. Charles A. Bacarisse, "Baron de Bastrop," *Southwestern Historical Quarterly*, LVIII, 319–330; Grace Fitzwilliam, "From Bastrop to Mina to Bastrop," *In the Shadow of the Lost Pines* (1955), 41.

[5] Names marked with an asterisk indicate that further information is given in the Biographical Notes, where the names are listed alphabetically.

work, tanning or dressing hides some distance from the home. A party of Comanches, finding him there alone and helpless, killed and scalped him with the relentless cruelty which characterized this tribe. Coming on to Woods' Prairie,[6] we found similar bones, bleaching and seeming to point to coming strife, and possible death. Besides, the few families who had preceded us and were in a measure settled there, could give accounts of many deeds of bold and unwarrantable cruelty by the Indians, who were most evidently resenting the coming of white men upon their hunting grounds. All this would naturally fill the minds of the women and children with terror and alarm, which increased as we came farther westward—for we knew full well that the frontier settlers would be most exposed.

Continuing on in face of all these tales of danger we at last reached our first home, which was situated on Barton's Creek, about forty miles below Austin. Here we began life in the Republic of Texas, squatting out on the raw prairie, where never a stick of timber had been hewn, and deprived of many things generally regarded as being among the very necessities of life.

Our absolute need gave birth to invention and energy, however, and all hands—men, women, and children—went to work with a will to make our new quarters as comfortable as possible. When we think of families without houses, wagons, milk, or even nails, far removed from any communications or exchange with the world—when we think of them thus situated, it is natural to wonder what could be done.

<hr/>

[6] Woods' Prairie, named after Zadock Woods, is near West Point, ten miles west of La Grange. Zadock Woods's residence was used as a fort for protection against Indian attacks between 1828 and 1842. *Monuments Erected . . . to Commemorate the Centenary of Texas Independence* (1939); Walter Prescott Webb and H. Bailey Carroll (eds.), *Handbook of Texas* (1952), II, 933 (hereafter cited as *Handbook of Texas*).

But it is surprising how much can be done when bone, sinew, and muscle are used with a will upon any material—however meager and insufficient. The change wrought upon the wilderness and the solitary place would have seemed almost like magic work to one who simply looked upon the scene as we came upon it, and then in a few days upon the huts, which stood ready for us to enter. And very comfortable quarters these were—log cabins covered with pine boards, all of which had to be cut, hewn, brought to hand, and built in shape, without wagons, nails, or any kind of machinery.

The cedar logs were cut with axes and were dragged up with horses, while the pine boards for the roofs were split about a mile and a half distant and then brought up by the men, who carried them on horseback.

Having completed and taken possession of the cabins, we settled into habits of life no less primitive and destitute of modern advantages than the cozy little huts that sheltered us, and few people of these modern times can imagine the ten thousand difficulties with which we had to contend. Mother, as well as the other wives of those pioneers, must have possessed rare tact and common sense, however, and been willing and ready to adapt herself to all circumstances, for although our home life was destitute of the most common necessities and conveniences, we never seemed to suffer for anything.

Beginning with bread, it seems difficult to understand how corn could be ground into meal without machinery of some kind; then we had no sieve, and no oven, but our old mortar and pestle was a first-rate grist mill, though very tedious as compared to present processes. Our sieve consisted of a wooden hoop, over which buckskin was stretched, and this in turn was perforated with a red-hot steel or wire. Upon our "Johnny Cake" boards, as they were called, was baked as good bread as was ever taken from oven or stove.

Our coffee was tied in a piece of buckskin and beaten upon a rock with another rock.

As soon as possible corn was planted, for our bread supply was getting very slim, and neither corn nor salt could be obtained nearer than the Brazos River. Once we were out of both, and we were compelled to live a while on dried turkey breast for bread, while our meat was unsalted venison. Our hard life, as is usually the case, was a very healthy one, and we were quite comfortable in our new home, despite all these hardships, and the prospect of Indian attacks staring us in the face.

Very soon we received our first visit from Indians, which, by the way, was an entirely new experience in our lives—it being the very first time I had seen one of these red men of the woods. I remember full well what a wild picture the band formed—forty Comanches on the warpath under the leadership of the famous "Buffalo Hump," who was then young, and a magnificent specimen of savage manhood. The warriors were almost without exception large, fine-looking men, displaying to the very best advantage their erect, graceful, well-knit frames and finely proportioned figures, being entirely naked, with the exception of a small apron attached to a belt or girdle, which was made of cloth of all textures and colors, with fringes and tassels at the ends. They had keen black eyes without lashes, and long plaits of coarse black hair hanging from their bare heads down to the very ground behind them. All this peculiarity of costume, combined with their no less peculiar color, and their arms consisting of bows, arrows, lances, and carbines, made a rare picture of wild, untamed beauty, which could not be viewed without interest, and once seen could never be forgotten.

They could speak only the Spanish language, which was entirely unknown to our party, except one Mrs. Woods, whose husband had been forced on account of Indian depredations and dangers to take his family from their home in Woods' Prairie, four miles below us, and had come to us for protection. Though understanding their language, "Mrs. Betsy" was very bitterly opposed to serving as interpreter—regarding the savages with the most intense fear, hatred, and suspicion. Under the circumstances she was obliged to act as interpreter, however, and Buffalo Hump, being chief, was also spokesman.

He first asked, "Where is your Captain?"

She answered that he had gone hunting that morning, and would soon be back. He then proceeded to state their business, saying they meant no harm to the whites, were hunting Tonkawa Indians, were in great hurry, were hungry, and must have meat.

In the few months of our stay here we already had gotten a small start of cattle, so we proposed to let them kill a yearling. To this they cried, "No, must have *big* beef. If white man come to Indian hungry, Indian kill big mule or horse—have no cows."

So, without more ado, they killed one of our finest cows and before it was thoroughly dead were eating its raw liver most ravenously, while the warm, red blood trickled from their mouths and down their chins. Father and Mr. [William] Barton, who, as Mrs. Woods informed them, had gone hunting that morning, now arrived with venison, of which they immediately took possession, eating portions of that raw also.

There was one warrior among them, the peculiarity of whose appearance and position caused us to especially notice and remember him. He was very slender, indeed was much smaller than the Comanches, as well as different from them in form and feature—besides, he occupied the position of slave to the chief. By their own account he was a captive Tonkawa whom they had raised from infancy. While there he ran a footrace with one of the Comanches, and such running we had never before seen. The Tonkawa came out ahead and was pronounced winner, but both were most wonderfully fleet, nimble, and light, the race being one hundred yards.

This visitation was the beginning of a long and aggressive series of depredations, which gradually increased in effrontery first—then culminated into theft and murder and brought about fierce struggles and terrible loss of life, which characterized the history of our frontier settlements in their early days. For a time, bands of Indians would be seen passing to and fro in their warfare against other tribes and in search of game; always, however, seeming to assume the most friendly attitude toward us.

At length, one morning we awoke to find every horse gone, and upon examination there were moccasin tracks and other signs, plainly showing that the Indians had made us a visit during the night and had driven our horses away. The discovery naturally created great excitement, and there was a general uprising and preparation on the part of our men to pursue the thieves, and if possible regain our horses. Upon going a very short distance, however, they were much relieved to find the horses all quietly grazing on the prairie. The Indians had evidently reconsidered the matter, and for some reason had concluded not to take them. We afterward learned that a band of Coushattas in their rovings had mistaken our horses for those of some other Indians, their enemies, and had started off with them, but daylight revealed their mistake, and they turned them loose. This was a kind of initiatory step, however, and seemed to cast a shadow of coming events.

Very soon other little things of a suspicious character occurred. A band of Caddoes next came constantly in and out, pretending to be hunting and trying to seem friendly and honest; but Messrs. Monte Woods* and John Cooke,* old settlers, who had been here some time before us and had acquired considerable knowledge and experience of Indian treachery and cunning, as well as a personal acquaintance with the various tribes, warned us that their coming and maneuvers meant no good and probable mischief. Of course this warning put our men upon the alert, and careful note was taken of every new or unusual circumstance connected with their visits, which were all the time becoming more frequent.

Sometimes they would be joined by two or three other tribes, and would linger in the vicinity as if hesitating upon some question or meditating some new project. At last they commenced stealing, going to Woods' Prairie, where the families had crops growing, and stealing corn until serious damage was done.

Immediately ten or twelve settlers collected, and arming themselves went into their camps to see about it. The Indians assembled in council, and proceeded to business. Our men informed the Caddoes that the thing must be stopped, and at the same time let them know that they had come for that purpose—to stop it. The cool bravery and determination of our men had a telling effect upon the thieves, who at once acknowledged the theft and gave us a mule by way of compensation, then made all manner of concessions and promises for the future. One of our party, Mr. Jeff Prior [or Prayor], used every power of effort and persuasion to induce the whites to attack and kill the Caddoes without delay or mercy, but the proposition was overruled by a unanimous vote.

The apology of the thieves was accepted and a treaty of peace made. But the Indians would not consent to the departure of the whites till all had formed a circle about the campfire and smoked the calumet, or pipe of peace, together. The smell or taste of tobacco always made my father deathly sick, and he tried to be excused from taking part in this ceremony, but they would not be satisfied until all had taken a whiff from the calumet.

Constantly in the fall and summer of 1829 [1830] we would have additions to our small band of settlers—men, old and young, from all parts of the United States, coming to try, or look at, Texas. These newcomers were very welcome, for we were not only glad to get news direct from the great world of commerce now so remote from us, but we were also glad to be strengthened in numbers, in view of probable assault by the roving bands of savages, whose visits were constantly growing more frequent and more aggressive.

This summer marked the coming of some of the first settlers of West Texas, now known as Bastrop County. Martin Wells* came from Alabama, and was the first man who settled where the town of Bastrop now stands. Then, too, one Moses Rousseau* stayed a week with us, and then moving on settled first and alone west of the Colorado River on the Old San Antonio Road, opposite Bastrop. But most prominent, as well as most welcome among these newcomers, were old James Burleson and his sons, who came as strangers, but soon were at home with their new-found friends.

Finding my father to be a brother of one of his best friends back in Tennessee, their meeting was the beginning of a life-long friendship. Ah! How we learned to look to the kind old soldier for council and comfort. His manly, genial bearing, his extensive experience, and his sound judgment soon won the confidence and love of our entire party.

Little did we know as we enjoyed these visits of father and sons how the boy Edward would serve Texas in the constant and severe struggles through which she was destined to pass. I have often wished for the pen of a ready writer that I might show forth his bravery and fidelity to his adopted state in fitting manner. Thrall, in his *History of Texas*,[7] has been the

[7] Homer S. Thrall, *A Pictorial History of Texas* (1879), 507–511.

first and only historian who has paid anything like just tribute to Edward Burleson. If I could, I would force upon the world a fact of which I am fully persuaded—that, although partial or prejudiced minds may decide that the laurels mainly belong to Sam Houston, in justice and in gratitude, Texas owes to Edward Burleson the *fairest, most enduring* monument which she can erect, for among her many brave and devoted advocates and heroes, he was not only the most faithful, but the most useful. Especially is this the truth with regard to western Texas—along the Colorado, for in the days when this vicinity was in most peril, he stood guard as it were, and was ever ready to meet any danger, or endure any hardship that our state might demand.

A peculiar chain of circumstances was linked and ran through the record of the family history of these Burlesons which is not without interest. In Tennessee, they were neighbors to a band of Cherokee Indians, who by a persistent course of stealing, finally exasperated them to such an extent, that the old father with his sons and nephews went into the Indian village to adjust matters. The visit brought on a little skirmish, which was the beginning of a feud that followed them through life, so that even here in the new country chance or fate brought them constantly and unexpectedly together.

I have heard the old man give a detailed account of the difficulty, and have seen a scar across his breast which was left by the knife of the Cherokee chief, "Bowles." Jim Burleson was old in all the "tricks and trades" of war—especially versed in Indian warfare, having served under General Andrew Jackson in the early days of the frontier troubles, and the entire family seemed to consider that they owed a debt of vengeance to all Indians. This vindictive hatred was not entirely without cause, for many friends and even members of the family had perished at the hands of Indians.

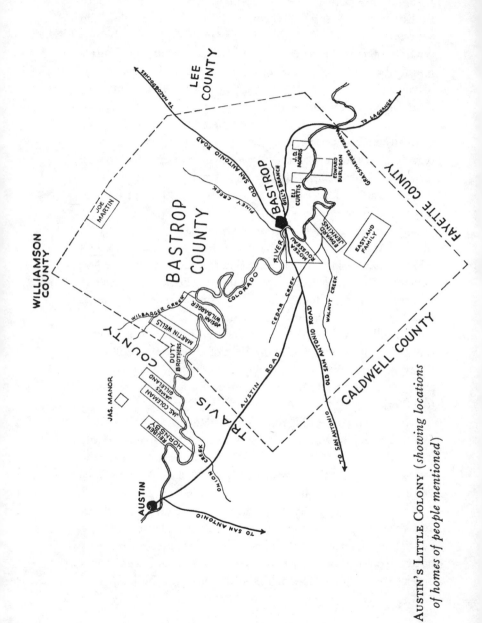

AUSTIN'S LITTLE COLONY (*showing locations of homes of people mentioned*)

BASTROP 1837

1. HUGH M. CHILDRESS
2. ANDREW MAYS
3. L. C. CUNNINGHAM
   (First Courthouse)
4. S. V. R. EGGLESTON
5. D. C. BARRETT
6. WALKER WILSON
7. J. L. LYNCH (City Hotel)
8. JOHN BERRY (Gunsmith Shop)
9. GREENLEAF FISK
10. L. W. ALEXANDER
11. JESSE HALDERMAN
12. JAMES R. PACE
13. STOCKADE
    (Site of Present Courthouse)
14. WILLIAM MAGILL
15. THOMAS H. MAYS
16. BARTHOLOMEW MANLOVE
17. AMOS ALEXANDER
    (General Store)

BASTROP, TEXAS (*showing location of homes in 1837*)

Upon moving to Texas it was natural to suppose that the old trouble was left at the old home in Tennessee, and the Burlesons settled in the western portion of our state. Gradually, the sons by their bravery and fidelity became "soul and center" of the defensive work which our country required from 1833 to 1845. Considerable trouble between the Indians and whites arose over in East Texas, around Angelina and Tyler Counties, and an appeal for help came to Edward Burleson, who now held command of quite a strong force from the Colorado.

Of course, he obeyed the call, being always ready at a moment's warning to act even unto death in behalf of Texas and her settlers. The Indians, whose depredations had given rise to this appeal to Burleson, proved to be none other than the old family foes—the Cherokees under Chief Bowles. They had moved to East Texas, and true to the inherent greed and treachery of their past lives, had become unendurable and dangerous to the white settlers, who everywhere learned to look to Edward Burleson for help and protection amid the suffering and dangers to which they were exposed. The Cherokees were defeated, and their old Chief Bowles was killed, so they struck out westward—still changing locality, but never changing character or habits.

Our frontier being a constant scene of trouble and danger from invasion and theft, Burleson concluded to make an invading raid against the invaders, and marched with his men to the San Saba—again never dreaming of coming in contact with the old Cherokee foes. He had a few Tonkawa Indians in his company, and through their native intuition they soon discovered Indian signs, whereupon they were sent out under Jonathan Burleson* to find the camps. Soon they came upon a solitary Indian, who at first would not venture near, but was finally decoyed by the Tonkawas to talk with them. Seizing him, they took him to Burleson, who made him lead the way to their camps.

On Cherokee Creek, a branch of the San Saba, they found encamped a strong force of Cherokees under young Bowles, a son of the old chief—and the old foes met again. Burleson did not act hastily, however, but first sent the captive Indian into the Cherokee camps, bidding him to say to them that the whites did not come to fight the Cherokees— indeed would not harm them, unless they first made war. As soon as Burleson's company came within gunshot, however, before the Indian could deliver his message, the Cherokees fired upon them, instantly killing Captain [John L.] Lynch,* one of Burleson's men. The fight was a close one, but again the Cherokees were defeated—their young chief Bowles was killed and the entire Bowles family was captured.

Thus ended a feud in which circumstances seemed to combine in always bringing together the parties at enmity.

I will now return to our own lives in the new country. In the fall of 1829 [1830] we moved to what is still known as the "Jenkins League" of land—then called Jenkins Prairie, now known as Hills Prairie,[8] situated five miles south of Bastrop, and west of the Colorado.

A half-covered log cabin with a dirt floor had already been prepared for us by my father, and very near we had the luxury of a fine spring. Building cowpen, lot, and such things first busied the men, then the small stock of cattle was brought on from our first home on Barton's Creek.

Ah! What a country was West Texas then. It almost

[8] Hills Prairie was named for Abraham Wiley Hill, who bought the east half of the Jenkins League from Sarah Jenkins in 1835. *Handbook of Texas,* I, 816.

"flowed with milk and honey," and in truth nothing could be more beautiful than the broad plains covered with wild rye and the finest grass the world ever afforded. Feasting upon such luxuries the faithful old cows gave an abundance of milk the whole year round, and now when summer's drought or winter's blight comes upon us, and our stock suffer so much, despite every effort we make, it is no wonder that we wish for the *good old days,* when the land stood "dressed in living green."

Our only neighbors were the two citizens whose coming I have already mentioned, Martin Wells, who lived where Bastrop now stands, and Moses Rousseau, from the Colorado, five and six miles distant from us.

Before we had been there long a message came from Barton's Prairie, our former home, that Indians were growing very troublesome, stealing horses, etc. Immediately the men all collected and went to see about it. They were gone about three weeks, but all efforts to catch the thieves or regain the horses were unsuccessful, though they trailed them to the mountains, and from grains of coffee and other signs of civilization, they concluded the thieves belonged to the same band of Caddoes who had stolen corn from Woods' Prairie the previous year, as that tribe was less savage than most others who came through here at that time. They were very cunning and skillful in their thefts and retreats thereafter, and in this case fired the grass behind them as they went, thus destroying all trace.

CHAPTER II

Valuable Additions Arrive

FROM NOW until 1833 our new lives were comparatively quiet, so that we were gradually growing accustomed to the realities of the "western wilds." The simplicity
and limit of our farming operations in those days would at
least be suggestive of rest and peace to the poor farmers of
the present, who are trying so hard to make money under
the rule of *King Cotton*. Our farms were comprised of about
ten acres in all, most of which was planted in corn, with just
a little cotton, only about ten or twelve rows!

In the meantime, the flow of immigration continued and
up to date we had several new neighbors. Three families,
those of [Reuben] Hornsby, [Solomon] Duty, and Dr.
[Thomas J.] Gazley, had settled in Mina, and that of
Major Robert M. Coleman on the east bank of the Colorado,
a mile or two from the river. In that house more than fifty
years ago I heard the first sermon ever preached in Bastrop
County.

One evening in the spring of 1833, Martin Wells and son,
riding a short distance out of Mina, returned in great haste,
reporting Indians to be lurking in the hills, evidently intent
upon mischief. After a brief council, the citizens planned to
trap and catch the Indians. They were to stake horses on
Gill's Branch, just out of Mina, where the Indians had been
seen, then hide, and watch for them to try to steal the horses,

at which time their capture would be an easy matter. A nice plan if well executed, but by a little heedlessness or want of prudence they were caught in their own net. Having staked their horses, they imprudently left them without guards, and returned to Bastrop to eat supper, thinking the Indians would not attempt to take them until later in the night. They were greatly surprised upon going out after supper to find all the horses gone! The thieves in ambush had seen and seized their first opportunity. This theft left the little village almost destitute of horses, for nearly every horse owner rode his mount out to aid in the scheme. Being therefore on foot, the citizens made no pursuit, and the savages went on their way unmolested.[1]

Early in this year Col. James Neill, an old soldier under Jackson, came from Alabama and settled where old Mr. [Hugh King] McDonald* now lives. His bravery and experience won for him a hearty welcome in our midst, and he was of great service to us in subsequent years.

I come now to the first and most bitter experience in my life—my father's death—sudden, mysterious, and cruel. It is painful even to touch upon the calamity, which came like a pall over my whole life, so that, even now, when old age is creeping on, the memory of my father's death still looms up before me as most sad and harsh.

He was fast getting a comfortable start, owned a good many cattle; our home was being improved and we were just beginning to enjoy life when he was murdered—cruelly and unjustly. He was found by friends, killed and scalped under a large pecan tree out in a cornfield. It was said that Indians committed the dastardly deed, but no positive clue to the

[1] Noah Smithwick [*The Evolution of a State* (1900), 241–242] also recounted this incident, with the same details. He added that, having been thus outwitted, most of the men burst out laughing. The only one who remained silent was Wells, who had devised the scheme.

real murderers was ever found.[2] I, the oldest male relative, was but a boy ten years old, and nothing was ever done to detect or bring to justice the killers. Suffice to say, Mother with her helpless family had to settle into a new life without my father, as best she might.

About now occurred the first scouting raid ever made by Edward Burleson against the Indians. An old man, Amos Alexander,* and his son were coming to these parts with a load of goods when they were waylaid and killed on the Gotier [Goacher] Trace where their bodies were found a few days afterward. Burleson raised a squad of men and after burying the bodies of the unfortunate father and son proceeded to examine the ground and everything near the scene in order to learn all he could as to the strength of the assaulting party and the direction of their flight.

From all signs the band had been quite small and on foot, but after trailing them about one hundred miles every trace was lost. The company was at a loss as to what course they should pursue. They were in camp deliberating matters when Bayt [John Bate] Berry, with one or two others, went out hunting. In the course of this hunt Berry found a solitary Caddo Indian whom he immediately brought to Burleson. The captive warrior claimed to be entirely honest and friend-

[2] This was indeed a most mysterious murder. According to family legend, Jenkins was killed by the half-Negro, half-Indian slave of Moses Rousseau. Edward Jenkins had killed Rousseau in a knife fight a year before and there are no records of Jenkins's ever being brought to trial. Matters of that sort were generally handled by the families or friends of those involved. Rousseau's slave was semicivilized, wore moccasins, and was known to be able to handle a bow and arrow. General Burleson, it is said, told John Jenkins this when he reached manhood. The general had wisely wished to avoid any more murders on that account and since the slave was never again heard of in civilized circles, it was supposed he joined the Indians or was killed by them. Edward Jenkins was buried in a small graveyard on the Benjamin Barton league near Smithville, supposedly near where he was killed.

ly, at the same time informing General Burleson that his friends in band were camping near. He was at once ordered to lead the way to their camps and very soon they came to an encampment of eight or ten warriors. The approach of Burleson's men caused terrible confusion and alarm amongst them and two of them started off apparently in great haste. Seeing this, Burleson dispatched men to follow them. They were led to two horses which being well shod and cared for were evidently horses belonging to citizens—Indian horses were seldom well shod or cared for in any respect.

Burleson captured the entire band, having considerable evidence that they were the murderers of the Alexanders and a strong suspicion that the horses were stolen from our citizens although they claimed that they had been hired to find and restore them to their rightful owners. A vote was taken as to what should be the fate of the captives and seven were killed. The eighth was a notorious glass-eyed Caddo who had before been caught with thieving parties. He was brought to Mina, where he was held under guard a while until his identity could be fully proved, and finally released.

Many on the Trinity and Brazos rivers, who had known these Caddoes only on their trading and hunting raids, censured Burleson for their being killed, but if they had known all the circumstantial evidence pointing to them as not only horse thieves but the wretches who murdered the Alexanders, they would have acquitted him of all the blame.[3]

[3] John Rabb and John Henry Brown state that Canoma, the glass-eyed Caddo referred to, presented a written certificate from the citizens of Robertson's Colony, who had hired him to recover some of their lost horses. Burleson was satisfied of his loyalty, but the men, already angered at finding shod horses, believed that the other seven Indians had betrayed the Robertson citizens and were on their way to the mountains. They voted 40 to 22 to kill them, and Robert M. Coleman and a few men volunteered to do the deed. The Indians were scalped and one had the skin torn from his back by a Texan to be used as a razor strap. When the true facts about Canoma's band

Soon after this, Major Coleman raised about eighteen men and made a raid over on the Navasota River, near Parker's Fort, where was situated a village of Waco Indians. A scheme was laid whereby the entire village might be taken. Under cover of darkness they crawled up into the very midst of the Indians, and there lay concealed, waiting for daylight.

Jessie Holderman [Jesse Halderman*] was appointed to give the signal for action. But matters were somewhat hastened. Some dogs commenced barking, and one of the Indians arose and walked out to see what was the matter. He soon showed that he discovered the concealed whites, so Holderman, realizing their danger, fired, thereby giving signal for the fight to begin. It was a fierce and heavy fight,[4] although Coleman's eighteen men were struggling against an entire tribe. He was at last forced to retreat; three men—Holderman, Bliss, and Wallace being badly wounded, and one Mr. Wallace being killed.

Soon after this defeat, Edward Burleson and Col. John H. Moore* raised a good force of men, and made another raid

were learned, they "were ever lamented by the chivalrous and kind-hearted Burleson." The rest of the Caddo tribe declared an unconditional war on the Bastrop colony, but remained friendly to the Robertson colonists. John Henry Brown, *Indian Wars and Pioneers of Texas,* quoted in John Henry Brown, *History of Texas from 1685 to 1892* (1892), I, 285–287 (hereafter cited as Brown, *History of Texas*); John Rabb, "Story of an Indian Experience in the Early Settlement of Texas," *Texas Monument,* August 27, 1841.

[4] The battle took place in July of 1835 at Tehuacana Spring in Limestone County. The first name of neither Bliss nor Wallace is known. Jenkins is the only source found to give even the last names of those wounded and killed. The Indians were Tawakonis not Wacoes. Coleman retreated to Parker's Fort, where he was joined by three other companies under Robert M. Williamson, Dr. George W. Barnett, and Captain Coheen. John H. Moore was elected to command the force as colonel and James C. Neill was elected adjutant. Brown, *History of Texas,* I, 287–288; *Handbook of Texas,* I, 371–372; J. W. Wilbarger, *Indian Depredations in Texas* (1889), 218–219.

against the Waco village, which they found lone and deserted, the Indians having evidently left in great fright, leaving the finest kind of corn crops growing in their fields.

Following their trail from the village for more than one hundred miles, they came upon a small encampment of Wacoes. They immediately opened fire and killed three, taking five or six captives. From these they learned that the main Indian force was encamped some distance on. It was already too late to see distinctly, so they concluded to wait until morning to pursue the trail. Starting at early daylight, they soon found, as the captives had stated, what had been the encampment of a large tribe, who had evidently left camp in great haste, for there were their own stake ropes *cut*. They would not tarry long enough to untie their horses! Men and horses were almost worn out, so it was thought best to come home, rest a while, and then make another effort.

So the men commenced their homeward march, bringing their captive Wacoes with them. Among these was one squaw with a bright little girl about three years old. This Indian child was much noticed and petted by the men, as she was not only bright, but very pretty. One night, while encamped on the Brazos River, a horrible incident occurred, which seems almost incredible. This savage mother, having by some means obtained possession of a knife, first killed her little daughter, and then attempted to kill herself. She was almost dead the next morning when first noticed, and there being no time for delay, Burleson called for a volunteer to kill her. Oliver Buckman came promptly forward, and volunteered to commit the deed, seemingly a brutal one, but in reality a mercy to the wretched woman, whose death was only a question of time. Taking her to the water's edge he drew a large hack knife, which he had made himself. As she gazed unflinchingly into his face, he severed with one stroke her head from her body, both of which rolled into the water beneath.

As they came on homeward, they discovered two Indians on foot about a half-mile from them. The Indians were making for a timber which was still a half-mile further on. Some of the company were well mounted, and they instantly put out at full speed in pursuit. The young warriors outran the horses and reached the timber in time to conceal themselves before their pursuers came up. The whites partially surrounded the thicket, while some were sent in on foot to "drive" it. Soon they found and shot one, and all were busy hunting the other one. At length, Smith Hornsby, seeing him, shot, but missed him! The Indian then shot and wounded him in the shoulder. Having only a discharged gun and suffering from his wound, he started from the brush, at the same time calling out, "Here's the Indian!" One of the surrounding party, William Magill,* in his excitement and haste, mistook Hornsby for the missing Indian, shot, and tore the unfortunate man's arm literally into pieces. A physician who belonged to the company, after an examination, declared that amputation of his arm was his only chance for life. He positively refused to submit to the operation, declaring he preferred death to losing his arm. So, after lingering along in great pain for a day or two, he died and was buried according to the custom of the times.

The earth was packed and smoothed above the body until perfectly level, then a fire was kindled upon the spot and left burning. Thus our dead slept in peace, concealed by a seeming campfire. This precaution was observed in order to prevent Indians from digging up the bodies and taking their scalps.

On this raid, Colonel Neill adopted a singular, if not barbarous, method of sending destruction upon the Indians.

Having procured some smallpox virus, he vaccinated one of the captive warriors, and then released him to carry the infection into his tribe! Nothing was ever heard as to the success or failure of this project.

The subsequent history of one of these captives, a squaw, is not only interesting, but somewhat remarkable. After living in town a while, she seemed to have a growing and abiding horror of Indians, so that when a treaty and exchange of prisoners were made, she pleaded with tears to be allowed to remain with the whites. Sometime afterward, a Mr. [Sumner] Bacon preached in Bastrop, and never having before seen a congregation or heard preaching, she imagined that the whites were holding a council to kill her, and although several tried to quiet her she ran away that night and was never heard of again.

Our settlers now had a short period of peace, the past raid having resulted in five or six captives, besides driving the thieves far from their accustomed haunts. But the quiet was of short duration and once more our citizens were aroused to extreme indignation and horror by Indian cruelty. Josiah Wilbarger, Stranuther,[5] [Thomas] Christian, and two others [James Standifer* and ——— Haynie[6]] from Bastrop went above Austin and around Brushy Creek on a hunting and reconnoitering excursion. One morning in the course of their rambling they came upon the track of one Indian, which was evidently just made. They felt sure that this solitary warrior

[5] Since no man named Stranuther participated in Wilbarger's fight, Jenkins was probably referring to William Strother, and nothing is known about him prior to his death while with the Wilbarger party. He was survived by his wife, Mary B. Strother, who must have been previously married to a man named Litton, for she had a son named John Litton. Mrs. Strother died in 1859. Probate Records, Bastrop County, File S-1.

[6] Haynie came from Missouri and was perhaps a relative of John Haynie who later settled in Bastrop.

was not far off, and pursuing his trail far enough to find signs of other Indians, they concluded to retrace their steps and get home. Four miles from Austin they camped for dinner, and while eating were attacked by a large band of Waco Indians—about thirty in number. Only two of the horses had been tied, while the other three, having been turned loose to graze, were out of sight. At the appearance of the savages, the two hunters whose horses were at hand mounted and fled, leaving their three companions above named to their fate. Each of these in their extremity took to a tree, Indian fashion, and prepared to defend himself as best he could, though against fearful odds.

Wilbarger, from his position, could see only the hip of one of the warriors, but taking aim, fired at that, the shot taking immediate effect. A shot aimed at Christian only took his powder from him, and having procured powder from Wilbarger, he was trying to make his way back to his first hiding place when he received a shot in the thigh and was forced to retreat. At the same time, Stranuther received a shot in the bowels, and retreated, vomiting as he went. Mr. Wilbarger had his finger on the trigger ready to shoot, when a ball struck him on the back of the neck, "creasing" him, as it is called. He realized that the Indians were scalping him and fainted just as Christian fired.

Upon returning to consciousness, his ears were greeted by loud yells and piercing wails, demonstrations of wrath and grief, which he supposed was caused by the death of one of their warriors. Those who stood over him went to join in the lamentations, leaving him for dead. He now had a short time in which to collect his wits and try to save the life which the savages thought they had taken. He lay very still, feigning death, and soon they returned as if to ascertain whether or not he was really dead. In their excitement they were deceived and left him without further harm. Cautiously, he raised his head and watched them, as they caught the loose horses and disappeared. Then, almost dead from pain in neck and head, he dragged himself into a hole of water nearby, lying there a day and night, alone and in excruciating pain—twenty miles from home and friends, and in constant fear of again falling into the hands of the Indians. His suffering needs no comment, and words of description cannot touch a situation so terrible.

In the meantime the two who had escaped made all possible speed to Bastrop, where they reported their three comrades as killed, having heard the shots and knowing the strength of the Wacoes. Of course, these tidings created the greatest excitement, and immediately a crowd of citizens went out to find and bury the bodies of the unfortunate men, who only a few days before had gone out from their midst in good health and hopes, never dreaming of what horrors awaited them in the near future.

A short distance from the scene of the brief but desperate struggle the company first found Wilbarger, scalped and crippled, covered with mud and blood, and sitting under a tree, resting after having toiled himself along a few yards toward home. Poor man! It is shocking to imagine what intense agony he must have suffered, for in his wounds worms were already at work, seeming to anticipate dissolution which seemed so near. Hurriedly some of his friends brought him home, while the crowd went on to find the other two victims, of whom he had seen nothing since the last shot of Christian, which he heard just as he fainted. Very soon and without difficulty they found both killed and scalped near the scene of the encounter.

Having buried the bodies as decently as circumstances would allow, they then took to the trail of the Wacoes. Very soon they found the body of a warrior who had been shot through the head. He was carefully wrapped in a buffalo skin and concealed in a dense thicket, which they were led to search by seeing the sky above thick with buzzards. It was doubtless the death of this warrior which caused the yelling and lamentations that saved Wilbarger's life. They also found hanging on a tree one of the scalps—the Indians having probably found some objection to it, and thus discarded it. The trail was very old and obscure, and having little encouragement to pursue it, the company at length came home. Wilbarger survived this escape several years, but his scalp wound was never entirely healed, and finally caused his death.[7]

Later on in the same year a young man by the name of Harris came to Bastrop from Alabama, and was soon well known in our community as a constant and most devoted hunter. Out on a buffalo hunt alone, he once discovered fresh Indian signs, and hearing a shot prudently came home. In a day or two he started again, accompanied by two of his friends, McDonald and Blakey, all still intent upon hunting buffalo below Austin. Coming to a steep bluff, two of them dismounted and were leading their horses, when a band of Indians came upon them, killing Harris and McDonald, who, being on foot, were entirely at their mercy. Blakey, however, saw the danger in time and having never dismounted escaped, bringing home the news of the violent death of his friends. Immediately a small squad of men hastened to the scene, where they found both men killed and

---

[7] This version differs materially from that of J. W. Wilbarger, Josiah's brother, which has been accepted as the most reliable account. See Bastrop *Advertiser*, August 29, 1935; J. Frank Dobie, *Tales of Old-Time Texas* (1955), 34–41; Margaret Belle Jones, *Bastrop* (1936), 10; Mary Ann McDowall, "A Little Journey through Memory's Halls" (unpub. ms., Bastrop Historical Society), 61–63 (hereafter cited as McDowall, "Journey"); Anne Doom Pickrell, *Pioneer Women in Texas* (1929), 58–68; *Telegraph and Texas Register* (Houston), August 12, 1840.

scalped. In addition to the scalp of McDonald, the savages had also carried off one of his arms, which was cut off at the elbow.

Finding their trail the whites followed them some distance, at length finding where a large band had been encamped on Onion Creek. Here they found the arm of McDonald, which the savages had cooked to sufficient tenderness, and then removed one small bone, from which they constructed a peculiar signal whistle, much used by them in battle and in hunting.[8]

Again there were two brothers, Furnash by name [sons of Charles Furnash*], who had settled on the Brazos, and together with a Mr. Gleason had gone in pursuit of some horses stolen from them by Mexicans. Finding the thieves with their horses out near San Antonio and having thoroughly "quirted" or chastised them, they started home with the horses. Late one evening, just as they were ready to camp for the night, they killed some buffalo, and it has been thought the report of their guns attracted the Indians. At any rate, it being very cold, they built a large fire and lay down to sleep. About daylight a party of Indians crawled up in gunshot, unperceived, and fired upon them, breaking the arm of Gleason and mortally wounding the elder Furnash brother. Jehu, the younger of the brothers, a boy only sixteen years old, alone escaped unhurt. Seeing the three men rise after their attack, and not knowing whether any were hurt, the Indians immediately retreated.

Amid the extreme danger of his position young Jehu lingered to saddle all three horses. Then, after trying in vain to help his brother to mount, the poor fellow being too nearly dead to ride, Jehu was at last persuaded by him to take Gleason and escape if he could, assuring him that he

[8] According to Wilbarger, this happened in the fall of 1836 and not in 1833. Wilbarger, *Indian Depredations in Texas,* 259.

31

VALUABLE ADDITIONS ARRIVE

was beyond help. So, with Gleason and his brother's horse, he came on to old Judge Smith's place,⁹ a mile east of the Colorado, and collecting four or five men he immediately started back to find and bury his brother. It was most remarkable how an inexperienced boy in a strange country under such conditions, could with unerring accuracy and without hesitation take, as it were, a beeline almost to the very spot where his brother lay dead. This was but one instance, however, out of many which had made Jehu Furnash well and widely known as a most extraordinary and almost supernatural woodsman.

About now our State entered upon a series of constant and severe troubles from the oppressions and innovations of Mexico on one hand and frequent thefts and murders by the Indians on the other, so that while Burleson held a force at San Antonio, which was comprised mostly of our men, our frontier was thereby left almost defenseless.¹⁰ The Indians were growing more and more troublesome, and Captain John Tumlinson raised a minute company of the few men and boys left at home. These held themselves in readiness for protecting the homes and families of the soldiers who were doing valiant service against Mexico. Very soon after the organization of this company a man by the name of Hibbans was traveling with his family just below Gonzales, when some Indians came upon them, killed him, and captured his wife with two children. They lashed Mrs. [Sarah] Hibbans* to a

⁹ Judge Smith's cabin was located at the north end of Montopolis in the eastern edge of the present city of Austin. Aloise Walker Hardy, "A History of Travis County, 1832–1865" (Master's Thesis, University of Texas, 1938), 44.

¹⁰ This must have been in November and December of 1835, when Edward Burleson was in command of the Texas volunteer army at the Siege of Bexar.

horse, where she was forced to travel three days without rest or food, except small portions of raw buffalo tallow. It is painful to think of what the poor woman must have suffered apart from her great physical pain and fatigue, in beholding first the cruel death of her husband, and then that of her youngest child, her baby, of whom the savages grew tired and dashed his brains out against a tree.

They camped one night on the Colorado, just below where Austin now stands, and the Indians, as if to tantalize her, told her that "heap of Mexicans live just down the river a piece." She silently put her wits to work to devise or find some means of escape, just as soon as possible. That night after the warriors were all asleep, she left her little four-year-old boy, knowing that to take him would render her escape impossible. The night was very dark, and the woman had to grope her way from the midst of the sleeping savages. While wandering still near the camp, she heard her child calling her. For a moment she hesitated. Her child was in distress, and her first impulse was to go to him and comfort him. Then thinking of finding friends who might aid her in rescuing him, she trampled under foot all the anguish of a mother's heart and moved resolutely onward.

Following the river down as well as she could, she at length came to some cows feeding on the prairie and concluded to try to drive them to their homes, thus hoping to find friends. She halloed at the cattle and fortunately their owner, Reuben Hornsby, was out after them, and hearing her voice went to her and took her to his home. As good luck would have it, Captain Tumlinson and his men were there upon arrival, and having heard the woman's tale, they immediately mounted and hastened to the well-known Indian passway— intending to intercept them there.

They came upon them just as they had finished supper. Already the captive boy was lashed to a mule, and they were in the act of resuming their journey, when Tumlinson's men charged upon them, killing one and causing the others to stampede, leaving stolen goods, horses, child, and all. The little boy had more than one narrow escape that day, for in the skirmish, a Mr. [Conrad] Rohrer,* mistaking him for an Indian, raised his gun and tried to shoot him, but it refused to fire. Two of the whites were wounded, one, Elijah Ingrum,* had his arm shattered, and four or five years afterward, while out on a surveying excursion, was killed by Indians.

Some time about then, Bat Manlove* and John Edwards* started to Cole's Settlement in Washington County. They were riding leisurely along on the Gotier Trace when, upon turning a short bend of the road, they found themselves face to face with ten or fifteen Comanches. Extending their hands as they approached, they said, "Howdy, howdy." Bat Manlove, knowing their friendly overtures could not be trusted, warned Edwards not to shake hands with them, at the same time dashing right through their midst, and made his escape. Edwards, not heeding the warning, was killed instantly.

Then too [1850], John Wilbarger,* a Mr. Neal, and Dock Sullivan belonged to a company of Rangers on the Rio Grande, and having been home on a furlough were returning to their company. Riding along near the Nueces River they discovered four or five Indians approaching. Not fearing so small a force they dismounted and made ready to fight. What was their surprise and dismay to see a large band come on just behind them, and thus they were almost surrounded! The situation was truly a desperate one. Dock Sullivan was killed instantly on the spot. Wilbarger was also killed after a race of four miles, but from all signs he must have made not only a desperate run but a brave fight for his life.

Neal alone escaped. He was on foot and running with all his might when one of the Indians riding after him asked in good English, "Which way are you traveling, sir?" Not wasting time or breath in a reply, he ran on, whereupon the Indian fired. The shot stunned him and he fell, apparently dead. His pursuer, after scalping him, left under the impression that he was dead. In a little while his consciousness returned to him and he made his escape, and according to latest accounts, he still lives to describe his *hairbreadth* escape.

CHAPTER III

Mexican Invasion

W E COME NOW to the fall of 1835, when without reservation or mercy Mexico threw aside all obligation involved in the treaty of 1824[1] and became so despotic in her dealings with Texas, as to venture to seal her authority even by force of arms at Gonzales. This unwarrantable piece of tyranny and oppression of course aroused every loyal Texan, and there was a general rallying to arms and preparation for war.

I was a boy in my fifteenth year,[2] but was remarkably large and stout for my age. Besides, by constant practice, possessing by nature a good eye and steady nerves, I was an extraordinary shot, and as our citizens one after another took up arms and left home to face the Mexicans, I began to use every effort to gain my mother's consent for me to enter the army. It was all in vain, however, and she positively refused to give ear to such a thing until the siege of the Alamo, when a new call came for men. Then, with several friends to intercede in my behalf, we finally overcame her scruples and objections, and she consented. Since I have grown older, I know it must have been a trying ordeal for the lone woman to give up her oldest boy.

[1] This was the Mexican Constitution of 1824.

[2] Actually Jenkins was thirteen years and four months old when he joined Billingsley's company, and he has been called the youngest soldier in the army during the Texas Revolution.

I enlisted in Captain Billingsley's company,[3] which was organized about ten miles below Bastrop, at what is now known as the "Old Burleson Place."[4] About the first of March, 1836, we struck out for the appointed rendezvous, which was Gonzales. Ah! As I found myself among old friends and acquaintances, with all of a growing boy's appetite for good beef, bread, and adventure, I thought there had never been such fun as serving as a Texas soldier marching against Mexico.

Reaching Gonzales, we joined Edward Burleson's regiment, which was already encamped there and awaiting recruits. In about two weeks our commander-in-chief, General Sam Houston, came, marking quite an era in my life. I thought I had never seen so perfect a model of manliness and bravery, and my admiration knew no bounds.

[3] The "Mina Volunteers," as Jesse Billingsley's company was called, was organized on September 28, 1835. Under Captain Robert M. Coleman the company was kept in reserve during the Siege of Bexar, December 5 to 10, 1835. On December 16, Coleman resigned and the next day the company disbanded and returned home. When Santa Anna began his invasion of Texas the company reorganized and on February 28, 1836, elected Jesse Billingsley as captain, Micah Andrews as 1st lieutenant, and James A. Craft as 2nd lieutenant. Edward Burleson joined the company as a private, but was soon elected Colonel of the 1st Regiment of Volunteers. The company marched to Gonzales where it was mustered into the army as Company C of the 1st Regiment. It participated in the Battle of San Jacinto on April 21, 1836, under Colonel Edward Burleson and was disbanded June 1, 1836. Jesse Billingsley Papers (Archives Collection, University of Texas Library); *Handbook of Texas*, I, 162, II, 554; L. W. Kemp, San Jacinto Roll; William Preston Johnston, *The Life of Gen. Albert Sidney Johnston* (1878), 65–66; *Monuments Erected . . . to Commemorate the Centenary of Texas Independence* (1939), 164; Ray, *Austin Colony Pioneers,* 61, 309.

[4] This was the home of General Edward Burleson and his uncle, Joseph Burleson. It was located on the Colorado River, two miles west of Smithville. The cabin, which recently collapsed, is still owned by the Burleson family. Burleson, Aaron Burleson II; Ray, *Austin Colony Pioneers,* 342–345.

Calling the men together at DeWitt's tavern in Gonzales, he delivered a short speech setting forth in stirring words the complications of troubles that threatened our Republic, finally closing with a rousing appeal to every Texan to be loyal and true in that hour of need and peril.[5] I yet consider him about the finest looking man I ever saw, as he stood over six feet tall, in the very prime of mature manhood. Things began to wear a more serious aspect now that I comprehended more fully the situation in all of its bearings, and in the still hours of the night as we lay and listened to the low ominous rumbling of cannons at San Antonio, I felt that we were engaged in no child's play. I now began to take in all of the responsibility, danger, and grandeur of a soldier's life.

While at Gonzales awaiting recruits, tidings came to us of the fall of the Alamo on the 6th of March, and of the terrible loss of 180 men, besides the band of 27 Texans who during the siege made their way into the fort and were *all* slain.[6] Many of the citizens of Gonzales perished in this wholesale slaughter of Texans, and I remembered most distinctly the shrieks of despair with which the soldiers' wives received news of the death of their husbands. The piercing wails of woe that reached our camps from these bereaved women thrilled me and filled me with feelings I cannot express, nor ever forget. I now could understand that there is woe in warfare, as well as glory and labor. Immediately after

[5] Houston arrived on March 11, 1836. His speech consisted mainly of the reading of the Declaration of Independence and the order of his appointment as major-general of the volunteer army, which he was to organize and command. Andrew Jackson Houston, *Texas Independence* (1938), 153.

[6] Travis' force consisted of 145 men plus a number of San Antonians. He was reinforced on March 1 by 32 men from Gonzales, making a total of 187 men who died in the siege. The Mexicans lost about 1,544 men. Amelia W. Williams, "A Critical Study of the Siege of the Alamo and of the Personnel of Its Defenders," *Southwestern Historical Quarterly*, XXXVII.

these tidings we were removed to the east side of the Guadalupe River, where the soldiers were at once set to work throwing breastworks and making every preparation for battle.

A heavy gloom seemed to settle upon our men after the fall of the Alamo, and the oldest, most experienced soldiers could be found at all times collected about camps discussing the situation of affairs, and it would have been amusing to note the widely different views of the various questions under consideration, if they had not been of such vital importance to our Republic and her citizens.

It was a generally conceded point that the oncoming of the Mexican army was simply a question of time. Some thought Houston's most prudential course would be a retreat, while others more daring and impatient, clamored to "stand and fight unto death! Never retreat!"

One evening Mrs. Almaron Dickinson was sent to our troops from San Antonio—she and her child were the only white persons who were spared in the terrible massacre at the Alamo. She came to warn us to be in readiness for the advance of the Mexican army. Our spies corroborated her testimony by stating that they had seen three or four hundred cavalrymen approaching.

Houston at once dispatched a reconnoitering party to discover how strong and how near were the approaching forces. At the same time, collecting our men, he proceeded to draw them out in battle array. Here and now I first took my stand in the ranks for impending action, and the prospect of immediate battle had but the effect of increasing my ardor. I felt equal to any charge with my big rifle, and grew more eager for the conflict as it seemed nearer. I remember I stood beside Sampson Connell,* an old soldier who had weathered the storms of many years and had stood at the front in many struggles. He had served under Andrew Jackson back in revolutionary times, giving from personal experience and observation all the details of the famous Battle of New Orleans and others. I can never forget the expression of countenance and the tone of voice with which the veteran soldier addressed me. Looking down almost pityingly upon me in all of my boyish inexperience, he said, "John, you are too young for this kind of business! You ought not to be here. You stay in camp and take care of the *baggage!*" I felt that this appeal was almost an insult to my dignity as a soldier, and looking him straight in the face, I answered zealously, "No, sir, I am here to fight, and would sooner die than leave my place in the ranks."

The preparations were in vain, however, and my courage for the time being remained untested. The reconnoitering party, after a short absence, returned and reported the alarm entirely false. A large herd of beef cattle, which were being driven beyond the reach of Mexican invasion, had in the distance assumed the appearance of an advancing army. Houston now made another short speech to his men, and I can recall the ring of confidence contained in its closing words, "Why," he said, "three or four hundred Mexicans would be as nothing to this force of Texans!"

Between ten and eleven o'clock that night, we were ordered to get us a day's rations and make ready for retreat. After a very brief period of bustle and confusion, each soldier fell in line with "knapsack on back and rifle on shoulder." My knapsack consisted of about two pounds of bacon wrapped in a large Mackinaw blanket. We took the road leading into what is called the Burnham neighborhood in Fayette County, and after a tedious march camped the first night on Peach Creek only about ten miles from Gonzales. Now, after one day's steady march, carrying rifle, ammunition, and rations, tired and sleepy, I began to realize what endurance and fortitude are required in a soldier's life. Immediately after early breakfast the next morning we were once more formed in line of battle and then ordered to fire, prime, and reload our arms, whereupon we again took up the line of retreat.

Here occurred my first disappointment in General Sam Houston, and some may regard it a small matter, but the sensation of surprised and wounded pride, mingled with indignation returns to me even now, when I recall the circumstances. I suppose he must have noticed how very young I was, and how tired I seemed, for having a Negro riding along behind him, he ordered him to dismount and told me I could ride a while, at the same time bidding me to ride immediately in advance of the army and not get too far ahead. Ah! Being tired and footsore, I mounted the horse and felt that I would be willing to die for Houston, who was thus proving himself not only a great general, but also a kind friend to his men. The horse was very spirited, and I, becoming absorbed in the scenery and my own thoughts, allowed him to go a little too fast, and was rudely aroused and shocked by the voice of my hero saying, "God damn your soul! ! ! Didn't I order you to ride right here?" Of course he had cause to rebuke me, and I was thoroughly aware of the culpability of my carelessness when it was too late, but his passionate harshness and curse insulted and outraged my self-respect, young as I was. Turning and dismounting, I gave the horse to the Negro's charge, declaring that I would rather die than ride him another step; at the same time I again took my place in the ranks.

With those few harsh words, General Houston completely changed the current of my feelings toward him, and my profound admiration and respect was turned into a dislike I could never conquer. In the subsequent history of our State, when he was candidate for her honors, my vote was never cast in his favor, for memory was ever faithful in bringing back that loud curse and my feelings as I listened.

After a steady march of three days, on the evening of the fourth day we reached our destination, the Burnham neighborhood, where we lay encamped, still ever and anon receiving recruits. General Burleson occupied a twofold relation to me, being not only my commander, but also he had been my guardian since my father's death.[7] After a few days' stay there, he detailed four of us: Greenleaf Fisk,* Edward Blakey,* Walker Wilson* and myself to come back to Bastrop and look after the families, which had been left there, and among which was my mother. At the Grassmeyer place[8] we met eight or ten families, others having already gone on. Here I set in as a regular hand, driving cattle and helping in all the "ups and downs" of refugee life. And a terrible life it was, especially to the women and children. Exposed to the most disagreeable weather, wading by day through mud and water over the very worst of roads, and tentless at night, it was tedious and hard beyond description.

In Washington County on the Brazos River we met some of our neighbors, who having left the families safe at old Washington were on their way back to Bastrop County to collect and run off stock from the invading Mexicans. Sam and Andrew Neal,[9] Bob Pace, and old Hugh Childress* composed the party, and they brought word from my mother that I had best turn back and help them.

I was relieved to try anything new, for the work of moving the families was not only hard, but exceedingly monotonous.

[7] There is no record of General Burleson's being made guardian of John Holland Jenkins, but this may be explained by the fact that there are no minutes of the probate court in Bastrop County until late in 1837.

[8] The home of F. W. Grassmeyer, who ran a ferry where the Colorado River crosses the Bastrop–Fayette County line. Remains of his house can still be seen.

[9] Andrew Neal is not to be confused with Captain Andrew Neill, who did not arrive in Texas until after the Battle of San Jacinto.

We came in great haste to Bastrop, fearing we might find Mexicans already there. We found Colonel [Robert McAlpin] Williamson,* or Three-legged Willie, as he was called, with a small company of men, stationed there for its protection. I remember my shoes were worn almost entirely out when we reached Bastrop, and Colonel Williamson presented me with a pair of good boots which were indeed acceptable.

We crossed the Colorado and collected all our cattle at Judge Smith's place, a mile west of the river, then they went back to the town, leaving only Andrew Neal and myself to guard the stock. We felt the full danger and responsibility of our position and kept a close watch around us, to be ready for any emergency. Very soon we saw a man whom we decided was a Mexican spy coming on the Old San Antonio Road—just the right direction for the advance of the Mexican army. We shut the doors and pulled out a chink in order to see and to shoot if necessary. Soon we saw five or six more men and what seemed like a large Mexican force approaching. We left the house and broke for the river bottom. Immediately the army seemed to charge or rush after us, and lo, upon a nearer approach our Mexican spy proved to be a Delaware Indian who had been trapping out on the San Saba and again the advancing army was a herd of cattle being driven beyond the reach of invasion. The Delaware was fresh from the woods and knew nothing of the existing war. He had a horseload of beaver hides, the first I had ever seen.

Our men soon came on from the prairie with the balance of our cattle, and next morning we swam the river, and moved on with them. I recall a remark of Hugh Childress here, which while it was a droll and original one, seemed almost prophetic in the light of subsequent events. He called out to us in a hurry, "I smell the Mexicans now." Sure enough, we just did get away in time, for the very next day

Cos's Division ran Williamson's company out of Bastrop, taking possession of all cattle and everything that had been left there.[10]

This, the "First Runaway Scrape," as it was justly called, ruined the prospects of our people and left us literally broken up. In the first place, most of the men were in the army and wagons or ways of transportation were very scarce indeed.

When we reached the families[11] at old Washington-on-the-Brazos with our cattle we found them in great alarm and confusion, having heard that the Mexicans were at Bastrop. Immediately the work of moving commenced, and such moving! That spring of 1836 was the wettest I ever knew. First, after crossing the Brazos, we had to raft across

[10] The Texans pulled out of Bastrop in such a hurry when Cos's 600 men were discovered that they almost forgot the sentry, James Curtis, who had been placed at the river ford. Noah Smithwick happened to think of him as they were leaving and ran back to get him. Curtis was sitting under a tree with a bottle of home brew. "Hello, Uncle Jimmy," Smithwick called, "Mount and ride for your life. The Mexicans are on the other side and our men all gone!" "The hell they are! 'Light and take a drink," was the reply. "There's no time for drinking. Come—mount and let's be off. The Mexicans may swim the river and be after us any moment!" "Then," Curtis persisted, "Let's drink to their confusion." And thinking it the fastest way to get him going, Smithwick drank with him. Then they struck out for Three-Legged Willie's command. (Editor's note: Abridged from Smithwick, *Evolution of a State*, 126–127, with dialogue quoted from Smithwick.)

[11] Among those known to have gone from Bastrop in the Jenkins party were the families of James Burleson, General Edward Burleson, Walker Wilson, Nancy Blakey, and probably the Wilbargers and McGehees. The Jenkins family consisted of Mrs. Sarah Jenkins Northcross, whose second husband, James Northcross, had been killed in the Alamo a month before, her children Edward Jenkins, Jr., William A. J. Jenkins, Elizabeth Jenkins, and her newborn baby, James Northcross, Jr.

Jonathan Burleson and a son of Chief Placido were helping to move the Burleson family. Edward Blakey was escorting his widowed mother and sisters. Bastrop was completely deserted until Jesse Billingsley disbanded his company there on June 1, 1836.

two or three bayous, and all along we worked to our knees in mud and water. It was pitiful and distressing to behold the extremity of the families, as sometimes a team would bog down, and women with their babies in their arms, surrounded by little children, had to wade almost waist deep in places. One very large lady, Mrs. Wilson, bogged completely down and could not move until pulled out by others.

It took us a whole day to traverse that Brazos bottom, a distance of only *four miles!* As soon as we reached dry land, we camped, and after one day's rest, struck out for the Sabine—getting near the United States. The road was simply terrible, and upon reaching the Trinity River at Robbins' Ferry,[12] we found that stream five miles wide and the bank was literally lined with families waiting to be crossed over, there being only one small ferryboat. Following the old, just rule of first come first serve, we had to wait a week before our turn came to be put across.

Just as we were getting on the ferryboat, we heard news of the Battle of San Jacinto on the 21st of April, but doubts were entertained as to its truth, there being so many false alarms flying through the country all the time. Going on five or six miles farther, however, we learned the particulars of the battle—the capture of Santa Anna, etc., which relieved us from present dread of Mexican troubles. After a week's rest, the refugee families scattered, some going farther east, while a few, among whom was my mother, came back to our same old home in Bastrop County on the Colorado. We had a pretty hard struggle getting along about then; two houses in the town had been burned and the country was sacked of everything except a few hogs.

It was now about the first of May, but the settlers hustled

[12] Robbins' Ferry, named for Nathaniel Robbins, was established in 1821 by Joel Leakey where the Old San Antonio and La Bahía roads crossed the Trinity River. *Handbook of Texas,* II, 482–483.

45

MEXICAN INVASION

around and soon had good prospects for a late crop. Then we occasionally had good beef. Some of the settlers, among whom were the Hornsby, Duty, and Rogers families, moved out of Bastrop and on to their respective localities above, and were trying to make a late crop. But now after a singular session of quiet in that quarter, Indian troubles began once more. The first tragedy occurred in the Hornsby neighborhood.

Messrs. Williams, Haggett, and three Hornsby brothers were at work in a field about a half-mile from old Reuben Hornsby's house. Williams and Haggett were working some distance apart from the Hornsby brothers, and seeing a band of ten or fifteen Comanches riding up, were naturally alarmed, but as they came nearer they saw that the warriors bore a white flag, which was always a token of friendly intentions. They therefore stood and were brutally shot down, after which the wretches made a rush for the Hornsby brothers, who ran for dear life, swam the river, and lay concealed in the bottom until dark, then crawled cautiously up to their home, expecting to find the inmates all dead, and Indians perhaps still there. Upon their approach, they found everything quiet. Fearing some trick, they hesitated a moment, then by way of a venture threw a stick at the house, whereupon their father spoke, and upon going in there was indeed a joyful meeting, for all were safe.[13]

[13] The men in this fight were John Williams, Howell, Haggett, Malcolm Hornsby, Billy Hornsby, Reuben Hornsby, Jr., and one Cain, not mentioned by Jenkins. Williams, Haggett, and Cain were detailed by Captain Tumlinson, before the Runaway Scrape, to stay and help move the families in Bastrop County to safety. They afterward returned with the Hornsbys and stayed to help with the crops.

The Indians, according to Wilbarger's account numbered about one hundred, but this is an exaggeration and Jenkins is more nearly correct. The fight took place in May, less than a month after Santa Anna's defeat. Reuben Hornsby, Sr., his wife, Miss Cynthia Castner, and the youngest children, back at the house, saw the Indians ap-

Immediately after this a second murder occurred, equally cruel and unprovoked, and of course, the excitement and alarm increased among our citizens. Reuben Hornsby, in moving back to his home after the Runaway Scrape, had thoughtfully taken a supply of ammunition and it became generally known; the neighbors would frequently go to him for ammunition. Jim Craft,* Joe Rogers,* and another man had been there for ammunition and were on their way home. Within a mile of Joe Duty's house,[14] they looked back and saw a band of Comanches charging in full speed upon them. There was a terrible race and they, at length, overtook Joe Rogers and killed him with a lance, in sight of the house.

Again, Conrad Rohrer went out to saddle his horse and was shot at his own gate[15] by an Indian who had crawled up and awaited his opportunity. At the firing of the gun thirty or forty Indians ran off. The excitement became so intense and the Indians so bold in their outrages that all the families again left their homes and got together in Bastrop. Men went out from town in armed squads, and worked their

---

proach. Reuben took his gun and those of Howell and Haggett and started to their assistance. Seeing them being shot down by the Indians, however, he returned to the house. The women dressed in men's clothes, and all three paraded about the yard with the guns, giving the appearance of a good-sized force. The Indians stole some cattle and departed.

The three Hornsby brothers, aged nineteen, seventeen, and twelve, and Cain, aged eighteen or nineteen, saw Haggett and Williams from a distance, but thought they were being attacked by Mexicans. De-Shields, *Border Wars,* 199; Probate Records, Bastrop County, File W-1; Wilbarger, *Indian Depredations in Texas,* 255–260.

[14] This house was situated on the Joseph Duty league just below Reuben Hornsby's home on Hornsby's Bend of the Colorado.

[15] Actually, Conrad Rohrer was killed on June 8, 1836, while saddling his horse at the house of Thomas Moore, not his own house. Frank Brown, "Annals of Travis County," IV, 59–60; Probate Records, Bastrop County, File R-1; Smithwick, *Evolution of a State,* 209; Wilbarger, *Indian Depredations in Texas,* 226.

farms together, still tugging away at their late crops. Even this did not afford security from the savages, however, who seemed constantly on the alert.

Matthew Duty* and Mike Hornsby were driving cattle into Bastrop, when, noticing the cows in front raise their heads and give sign of seeing something unusual, they suspected that Indians were coming, and just did get home in time to escape a band of Indians who were pursuing hard behind them. Soon after this, Matthew Duty, who belonged to a squad working the Duty neighborhood, rode out one evening to look over the crop. He was just out of sight when guns were heard and in a minute his horse was seen coming back at full speed, without his rider. Blood on the saddle corroborated the dark truth suggested by the shots, and runners springing upon their horses broke for Bastrop. A squad of men went out and found him killed and scalped.

In the midst of all the excitement and horror of these Indian outrages, news came to us of another Mexican invasion. A fresh panic at once seized the families, and we had the Second Runaway Scrape. All of the families had gone in this escapade except the Woods, Berrys, and Harrises,[16] and they had crossed the river and camped at the Cunningham place,[17] about fifteen miles below Bastrop. At sunrise the next morning eighteen or twenty Comanches stampeded the horses, running them off, and one of our men, Alex Harris, barely escaped being taken by them. Realizing the danger of

[16] These were families of Zadock Woods, John Berry, and Isaac Harris. The group totaled at least ten grown men, including John Berry, Sr., John Bate Berry, Andrew Jackson Berry, Joseph Berry, Alexander Harris, Henry Gonzalvo Woods, Norman B. Woods, Montraville Woods, and Zadock Woods. It is not known whether or not Isaac Harris was alive at that time.

[17] This was on the Jonathan C. Cunningham headright league on the east side of the Colorado. The league started opposite Grassmeyer's Ferry and ran up the river several miles.

the route, they decided not to go on by the Gotier [Goacher] Trace as first intended, but to come back and go down the river to La Grange. Arriving at the Barton place, three men, among whom was Monte Woods, had to go back to the Cunningham place for some stock or something that they had left behind. When about three-quarters of a mile from the house, they heard loud calling and screaming from their friends, and looking back, they found that the Indians were behind them, having come between them and the house. Now came a race for life, and a rough race it was, too, for the ground was just newly plowed. Several shots were fired, though nobody was hurt.

We suffered a good deal of uneasiness concerning some friends, Mr. Grassmire [Frederick W. Grassmeyer*] and Mrs. Orkenbor, who had already gone down the river in a flat boat, taking what plunder they could to La Grange. We thought the savages would surely find and kill them, but somehow they, too, escaped and reached their destination in safety.

Some of the Crafts had moved their families into the Cole's settlement in Washington County and were on their way back to their farms in Craft's Prairie. In three miles of home, coming to what is known as the J. D. place, a small cabin situated on a bluff belonging to J. D. Morris, they stopped to have lunch. While eating they heard a low peculiar hum of a song, but could not tell from whence it came. It aroused them, however, and they got their guns, when lo, a band of about eighteen Indians came up the hill. They evidently were not expecting to find white men there, for upon seeing them, they whirled and retreated in double-quick time. Old Captain Jim Craft shot and one warrior fell, or pretended to fall, then jumped up and ran on, whereupon there was a hardy laugh among them. They stopped across the creek in the prairie and a few shots were exchanged; then, seeing the

Indians were too strong for them, the white men retreated.
There was a half-mile run through an open prairie, then
seeing the savages in pursuit, they dodged into a thick post
oak country and escaped unhurt.

The Second Runaway Scrape did not affect us as much
materially as did the first, for it was not so wet, and when
in fifteen or twenty miles of Washington-on-the-Brazos, we
received news of Mexico's interior war, or war on herself,
which quieted our fears from that source, and having brought
our cows with us, we stayed awhile very comfortably. At
length, however, Coleman and Billingsley brought companies
up the river to protect the families, and we came on to Bastrop with Coleman's company.[18]

Once more the families stopped in town while the men
came out into the prairie planting and working the farms,
again in squads. In the fall of 1837 three families—the
[Elisha] Bartons, Allens, and ours, the Jenkinses [Sarah Jenkins Northcross*], moved across the river back to our old
homes, where we found good crops awaiting us.

And still Indian assault and murder constantly threatened
us. About now a man was moving a family of Negroes to
Bastrop by way of the Gotier Trace, which lay through a
perfect wilderness. When in about a day's travel of the
Cunningham place, seeing some Indians and becoming
alarmed, he drove very hard to get to the settlements that
night. Failing, however, they had to camp on the Gotier
Trace. They used every precaution, to be ready for the
Indians, first tying their horses, and he or a Negro standing
guard. Sometime in the night an Indian was discovered
behind a tree with a bearskin extended, which he would

[18] This was Robert M. Coleman's regiment of Texas Rangers. The
company was organized after the Texas Revolution, and included
Tumlinson's Rangers. *Handbook of Texas,* I, 372; Smithwick, *Evolution of a State,* 153.

shake, trying to get the Negro to fire off his gun at that. But the Negro was too smart, so the Indian finally concluded to kill him. Again he was foiled, however, for the Negro being wide-awake noted his every move and fired at the same time, both shots taking effect, the Negro's arm and the Indian's thigh being broken. All ran off and left an old Negro woman asleep in the wagon. Coming on, they reported the attack. General Burleson took a squad of men and hastened to the scene. They found the woman unhurt, but the wagon plundered. Striking the trail, they followed it a short distance, when they were startled by a gun snapping near them. Looking around they found the wounded Indian, who was pluck to the end. Killing him they came home, without further pursuit.

Robert M. Coleman along now held a small fort[19] on Walnut Creek, and one night from this fort our men saw a bright fire blaze up, away over on the west side of the river, near where Austin now stands. Immediately our light was put out. The soldiers knew the hill from which the light gleamed and after watching shadows come and go between them and the fire, they decided to go and investigate the matter, being very certain that the light was an Indian campfire. Lieutenant Wren, with a few men, was dispatched to the hill, near which they came upon eighteen or twenty horses staked out. Now came a dilemma. Of course, they knew Indians were very near, but in the deep, still darkness, who could tell where? Having secured their own and the

[19] Fort Coleman, also known as Fort Colorado, was located on Walnut Creek about four miles below Austin. It was built in June, 1836, by Colonel Coleman's Rangers for protection against Indian raids. The fort consisted of a cluster of log cabins enclosed by a heavy stockade with two block houses at opposite corners. It was abandoned in November of 1838. Smithwick, *Evolution of a State,* 153–154.

Indian horses, they commenced crawling around, looking for the sleeping warriors. As good luck would have it, an Indian coughed in his sleep and thus revealed their whereabouts. Wren then got his men together and crawling near waited for daylight. Just at dawn, before it was light enough for action, these savage children of the woods lay and answered the hoot of the owls and the whistling of the birds, all unconscious of their impending danger. Suddenly, as if suspecting or hearing something, one of the Indians arose to his feet and seemed listening. Joe Weeks had been appointed to fire and signal for attack, and an Irishman, Tom McKarnan, thinking it time to shoot, said in a loud stage whisper, audible all around, "Plug him, Weeks!"

Seeing they were discovered, Weeks did "plug" him, whereupon all fired and the Indians broke for a thicket close by. Just as they were entering the thicket one of the warriors, turning, fired one shot, which struck one of our men right in the mouth, killing him instantly. This ended the skirmish and bearing their dead man, our men came home without further action.[20]

Burleson, having heard nothing from the Gotier family in some time, grew uneasy, and went to see about them, fearing Indian assault. A terrible sight met his eyes upon arriving there. Five members of the family lay dead, and the rest gone, supposed to be prisoners. I will give the particulars of the

[20] This skirmish took place in the spring of 1837. Lieutenant Nicholas Wren and fifteen men volunteered to attack the Indians. Wren, Joe Weeks, and Noah Smithwick formed the advance until the Indians were found, at which time Wren detoured to the left and Smithwick to the right, each with a party of men. The Indian that Weeks shot was seriously wounded, but managed to escape. The Texan killed, Philip Martin, was buried on the north side of Fort Coleman. Joe Weeks was killed soon afterward in a private difficulty. Smithwick, *Evolution of a State*, 160–163.

horrible affair just as they were given to me by a surviving son, who was among the captives and still relates the tragic story.

Old James Gotier [James Goacher*] and two sons were at work in the field a short distance from the house. Mrs. Jane Crawford, a widowed daughter of Gotier, was in the house while the old lady was rendering out lard in the yard; the children were at play nearby. She sent a little boy and girl to the creek after water and very soon she saw an Indian coming from the creek holding the girl by the throat to prevent her from screaming. They had choked the girl until she was bleeding at the nose. The old lady screamed to Mrs. Crawford, "Jane, the Indians have got your child!" and running into the house she seized one of the guns, which the men had very carelessly gone without. Jane begged her mother to let the gun alone, knowing that if the Indians saw her with it, they would kill her, but she raised the gun to fire and was killed in the act. The men in the field, hearing the gun, rushed in upon the scene unarmed and were also killed. The Indians then captured Mrs. Crawford, two brothers, and a little girl three or four years old, and struck out on foot for their village, making the captive woman carry her child and a bundle of salt. She became so tired that she concluded she would have to leave her child, and putting her down, started on, but hearing her call, and looking around, she saw the little one tottering along, trying to follow her. She turned to go back, and the Indians whipped her with quirts, or bow-strings, to her child and back, literally cutting the flesh with their blows.

They kept the unfortunate woman with her two children for several years, often treating her most cruelly. At last, however, deliverance came for them. An old trapper by the name of Spaulding found her, bought all of the family from the

Indians, and married Mrs. Crawford—bringing them all back to Bastrop.

I will now give another little Indian raid, merely as an illustration of Indian cunning and running ability. Thirty or forty Wacoes and Tawakonis made a raid on the Ebbins neighborhood about twelve miles below Bastrop and robbed the house of J. D. Morris, who would doubtless have been killed if he had been at home. Burleson, with fifteen or twenty men, took their trail, soon tracing them to a cedar brake on Piney Creek, about four miles above Bastrop. He then sent three men, Jonathan Burleson, Hutch Reid, and another man ahead as spies. The first thing they knew, they rode right into the Indian encampment, and were fired upon. They wheeled to run, but Jonathan Burleson was hemmed on a bluff nearly thirty feet high and made his horse leap the tremendous height. They all made their escape and got back to General Burleson "without a scratch." They reported the Indians too strong for our small force and said they were in a cedar brake only three miles from town.

Burleson at once sent out runners for more men, and in a short time a few recruits came in. The trail was very easily found and followed. The men rode at half-speed sometimes and in a lope all the time except over bad hollows.

On the waters of Yegua Creek, about an hour and a half by sun, they came in sight of the Indians, who stopped in a steep hollow, tied a horse they were leading, and pretended to make ready for a fight. A shot or two were exchanged. Our men were ordered to dismount and get into the hollow just above them. They struck down the hollow, expecting every minute a volley of shots. Upon coming to the spot where the savages were first hid, they found nothing—all were gone. They mounted immediately intending to pursue them, but could find no sign of a trail anywhere, only here and there a moccasin track, showing where one had been running, and no sign of their ever coming together again could be found. Mrs. Spaulding, formerly Mrs. Crawford, who was at the time a prisoner with this band, afterward told us that nearly all of these warriors died upon coming into camps. They had killed and eaten some fat hogs on that trip and that, together with their terrible run, had killed them.

The next Indian raid was a very bold one. A band of Comanches came in daytime and rounded up about fifteen horses belonging to our citizens. As many as could secure horses mounted and started after them. Following them about eight miles, they came upon the thieves just in the act of changing horses, i.e., riding the stolen horses and resting their own. Immediately a running fight commenced, and the Indians were at last forced to run off and leave their own horses, which we secured. Nobody was hurt on our side, although Dick Vaughn's* horse was killed beneath him. It is strange that men could be so careless and could neglect matters of such vital importance. It might almost be called criminal carelessness, for knowing the dangers to which the families and property were exposed, they never held themselves in readiness. In this particular instance men were charging upon Indians with rusty guns that would snap and flash and fail entirely. Out of a company of ten or fifteen men only two could fire! Hugh Childress ran right on an Indian who was riding a fat pony and his gun snapped, and he had to see horse and thief go together. Why, sometimes, when a call for men came, they would find themselves compelled to *mold* bullets before they could move!

In 1838, William Clopton went hunting in the pine hills near Bastrop, and found unmistakable and recent signs of Indians—saw where they had killed and cleaned a deer. Coming back to town immediately, he tried to raise men to see about it, but could get no help, some claiming to be too busy, while others were too indifferent even to render an excuse. That night Indians *came into town* and shot two men, Messrs. Hart and Weaver. *Then* men roused Clopton and were loud in their talk of following the murderers when it was too late, as he very justly reminded them. No effort was made to catch the wretches, and the unfortunate men being buried, the citizens pursued the even tenor of their way, ignoring the fact that such deeds of violence if unnoticed would pave the way for others of greater daring.

Very soon after this Samuel Robertson and a man named Dollar were out making boards on the Old San Antonio Road, about three miles from Bastrop. They had stopped to rest a while, when suddenly about fifteen Indians charged upon them, killing Robertson, who fell over on top of Dollar, giving him a terrible shock or jar. The Indians then chased him to a steep hollow near the river, where they hemmed him in. Jumping from his horse and swimming the river, he made his escape. The poor man was *fortunate* only to be *unfortunate,* it seemed, for he was doubtless killed by Indians, or by someone soon afterward. Determined to leave this country and go back to his old home in Tennessee, he bought a horse and disappeared, and was never more heard of, but through letters from Tennessee, we learned that he never reached home.

Robertson was buried, and still men took no pains to find and punish the murderers.

CHAPTER IV

Brushy Creek and Plum Creek

IN THE SPRING of 1839 old Mr. Gideon White,* with two or three neighbors, went out on the head of Wilbarger's Creek to kill buffalo. Finding many fresh Indian signs they came into town and reported it. A squad of fourteen men met at the Wilbarger place, and just as they were starting, received news of the murder of Mrs. Coleman. The particulars were substantially as follows: She and her little boy five years old were in the garden, while the rest of the family, consisting of three children, were in the house. A force of one hundred and eight Indians came up and dividing, one band went to Dr. Robertson's house nearby, while the other division came on to Mrs. Coleman's house. The first thing she knew, the savages were right at her. She started to run, but upon seeing her child and stopping to help him along, she received an arrow in the throat, which killed her.

She lived, however, to reach the house, help her son bar the door, and then sit down on a chair and die, without a word. The Indians captured the five-year-old boy who was with her in the garden, but still there were three children in the house, the oldest of whom, Albert Coleman, a lad of fourteen, deserves to have his name enrolled among the heroes of those bloody times. With two helpless little sisters, he stood above the dead body of his mother, and succeeded in keeping the savages out of the house. They must have supposed there were armed men in the house, which was natural judging from the number and effect of Albert's shots. He had a breech-loading "yorger" and as they came up, shot, then said, "I killed one!" Reloading, he wounded another. They shot into the house at him, striking first the breech of his gun, shattering it and scattering the lead all over the faces of the little girls, who stood around him, and at last killed the young hero; whereupon his little sisters ran under the bed. The Indians went around the house and poked their lances through the cracks, trying to kill them. A loud yelling from the other division called them away, and the little girls left the house and took to the river bottom and escaped. The loud yelling was at the running of a Negro, who got away from them.[1]

Our men went right on and took their trail. Captain [John J.] Grumbles was commander of the small company. After following the trail four or five miles, he overtook them. The Indians halted and prepared for fight. Although the force was entirely too strong, consisting of over one hundred warriors, some of the little force of fourteen wanted to attack them. Grumbles very wisely ordered a retreat, and coming

[1] This fight took place near Webberville on the Colorado on February 18, 1839. The Indians numbered between two and three hundred. Dr. Joel W. Robertson was in Austin visiting his brother-in-law, Colonel Henry Jones. Seven Negroes were captured at Dr. Robertson's house. Mrs. Elizabeth Coleman was the widow of Robert M. Coleman, who had drowned two years before. Thomas Coleman was captured while James Coleman and a man named Rogers escaped to Fort Wilbarger. Albert Coleman killed at least four Indians before he died. The two girls, aged nine and eleven, were found by John D. Anderson, who took them to George W. Davis' house, where several families had gathered. Brown, *Indian Wars*, 61–62; Harriet Smither, *Journals of the Fourth Congress of the Republic of Texas, 1839–1840, to which are Added the Relief Laws* (n.d.), III, 112–113; Sowell, *Rangers and Pioneers*, 54–56; Wilbarger, *Indian Depredations in Texas*, 146–148.

back, runners were sent in every direction for men. Soon forty or fifty men under command of Jacob Burleson, brother of Edward, were on the trail of the savages, which they had no trouble following.[2] The Indians were evidently not afraid, and had made no effort to conceal their whereabouts, doubtless feeling confident in their own strength.

Burleson's force overtook them at Brushy Creek. Dismounting, he attacked them immediately. The Indians then charged and Burleson ordered a retreat. Coming right on, the savages were very near overrunning some of our men before they could reach their horses. Jonathan Burleson,[3] another brother of Edward Burleson, was killed, but no one

[2] Twenty-five men from Wells' Fort under Jacob Burleson and twenty-seven under Captain James Rogers from Fort Wilbarger joined forces. Brown, *Indian Wars,* 61–62; Wilbarger, *Indian Depredations in Texas,* 148.

[3] This was Jacob Burleson, not Jonathan Burleson. All of the Burleson brothers—Edward, Jacob, John, Jonathan, and Aaron were in this fight, hence the confusion. Captain Jacob Burleson ordered his men to dismount and charge the Indians. He, Winslow Turner, and Samuel Highsmith did so, but as there were only twelve men in the whole group, the other nine deemed the chances too great and turned and fled, leaving their comrades to face the Indians. Seeing the rest of the men deserting, Captain Burleson and the other two fired and started to mount, but one, a boy about fourteen years old, jumped on his horse without untying him. The captain ran back and untied the boy's horse but was shot in the back of the head when he started to remount.

The savages, thinking that he was General Edward Burleson, the Texan they hated most, cut off his right hand and right foot, took out his heart, and scalped him. Jacob Burleson had come to Texas in 1832 with his brother John. He served in the Texas Revolution from February 28 to June 1, 1836. He settled on his league and labor of land in Burleson County, where his wife Elizabeth and their five children lived after his death. Brown, "Annals of Travis County," V, 44–47; John Burlage and J. B. Hollingsworth (eds.), *Abstract of Land Claims* (1859), 604; Sowell, *Rangers and Pioneers,* 54–56; Wilbarger, *Indian Depredations in Texas,* 148.

else was hurt. On their return march, when they buried Burleson, they found that the savages had cut out his heart. Thus another of our bravest men was sacrificed.

About four miles back on the retreat they met General Edward Burleson with reinforcements, and at once turned for a fresh charge. In the meantime the Indians had secured a fine position in a hollow, and could not be drawn from cover. Some of them were well armed and fine sharpshooters. The fight continued until dark, and might be termed a drawn battle, but during the night the Indians retreated. Ed Blakey, John Walters,* and Parson [James] Gilleland,* three more of our best citizens, were killed here, leaving dependent and defenseless families.[4]

In the meantime, William Hancock had charge of a small squad of recruits, to which I belonged.[5] We were just behind Burleson's force, and were making all possible speed to overtake them. About sundown, as we were riding along in couples, considerably scattered, we saw to our left a band of men moving about, and thinking they were Burleson's force we turned aside to join them, not dreaming of danger until they charged upon us and we saw that we had approached a band of Indians.

We retreated to a mot of timber where we awaited an attack for some time, but for some reason they gave up the charge and we waited in vain. In the meantime, we were

[4] The Battle of Brushy Creek was fought in February of 1838 near the present town of Taylor in Williamson County. Brown, "Annals of Travis County," V, 44–47; Brown, *Indian Wars,* 61–62; Sowell, *Rangers and Pioneers,* 54–56; Wilbarger, *Indian Depredations in Texas,* 146–150.

[5] This company was probably the one organized by the city council of Bastrop to scout daily and protect nightly the town of Bastrop. Each member of the twenty-man company was to receive $20 a month, but had to furnish his own mount and gun. Minutes of the Corporation of Bastrop, January 6, 1839.

much perplexed as to the whereabouts of Burleson's force. Finally, after a short deliberation, deciding it to be dangerous for so small a party to be riding about in the face of such odds, we returned to the settlements.

The Indians kept the little boy of Mrs. Coleman until he was almost grown, when our men bought him from them. He had, however, been so imbued with their ideas and habits that he went back to them, never feeling satisfied among the whites.

In Burleson's battle with the large force one man was wounded, besides the four killed. He received a slight wound in the mouth from a rock, which some thought was shot, while I believe, with others, that a bullet knocked the rock up. That night men were stationed in and around Bastrop as guards. Late in the night, having neither seen nor heard sign of danger, they had just gone in, when old Mr. [Stephen V. R.] Eggleston,* hearing an unusual noise, went out to see about it, whereupon he was shot through the bowels with an arrow, inflicting a wound from which he died the next day.

Thus ended the Battle of Brushy Creek. Next came the largest, most horrible raid ever made by Indians upon Texas, which resulted in the famous battle of Plum Creek. A large band of Comanches under the notorious chief, "Buffalo Hump,"[6] took possession of Victoria, then came on down

[6] This seems to be the only account of the Victoria and Linnville raids which states that the Comanches were under the command of Buffalo Hump. Accounts of the Battle of Plum Creek tell of Indians who wore buffalo horns on their heads, which may have caused them to be confused with the real Buffalo Hump. The raid on Victoria took place on August 6, 1840, and the attack on Linnville on August 8. The Indians numbered close to one thousand.

On August 6, 1840, Dr. Ponton and Tucker Foley were attacked by twenty-seven Indians just west of Ponton's Creek near Halletsville. At the very moment of their attack the Rev. Z. N. Morrell was traveling as fast as his ox team could carry him to warn the settlers of the Indian raid. Ponton saw the wagon pass but was afraid to call out.

Peach Creek, through a sparsely settled country, burning houses and killing until they came to Lynnville. They were supposed to have been guided by Mexicans.

On their way they came upon Mr. [Tucker] Foley* and Parson [Dr. Joel] Ponton,* who were going across the country to Gonzales. Foley was riding a very fine race horse, while Mr. Ponton's animal was old and slow. They saw the Indians about a quarter of a mile off and whirled to run. The race horse soon bore Foley far in advance of Ponton, who was fast losing ground. The first Indian swept past him without even turning his head. Foley on the race horse was evidently the prize upon which he was bending every energy.

The next night Ponton returned home and gave the alarm. Captain Zumwalt and thirty-six men returned to the scene, buried Foley, and went in pursuit of the Indians.

Mrs. Crosby, granddaughter of Daniel Boone, was captured with her child at Nine Mile Point near Linnville. Mrs. Watts was the wife of Major H. D. Watts of Linnville. Others killed besides Major Watts and Mr. Crosby were Colonel Pinkney Caldwell, a Dr. Gray, Varlan Richardson, William McNuner, a Mr. Daniels, a Mr. O'Neal, and six Negroes.

Tumlinson and sixty-five men attacked the Indians on August 9 and a Mr. Mordecai of Victoria was killed. Tumlinson was joined by Ben McCulloch and twenty-four men, Adam Zumwalt and thirty-six men, Clark L. Owen and forty men, and other single recruits. McCulloch took command. Morrell who had driven his ox team thirty miles in twelve hours to La Grange, rode from there to General Burleson's home, giving the warning along the way. He and Burleson rode to Bastrop to raise a force of volunteers.

Burleson held a council in Bastrop and sent Morrell to Austin to do the same. Eighty-seven men volunteered to go. Jonathan Burleson was sent with an urgent message to Tonkawa Chief Placido for aid. Placido and thirteen of his braves went back on foot with Burleson. Placido put his hand on the side of Burleson's horse and ran without stopping thirty miles to join General Edward Burleson at Plum Creek, where the Texans planned to fight the Indians. Frank Brown, "Annals of Travis County" (Archives Collection, University of Texas Library) V, 44–47; Brown, *History of Texas*, I, 168n.; Brown, *Indian Wars*, 78–82; Z. N. Morrell, *Fruits and Flowers from the Wilderness* (1872), 205–207.

The second Indian came on, and in passing, struck him on the head with a spear—he, too, intent upon overtaking Foley. A third drew his bow as he came and shot, the arrow striking Ponton's leather belt with such force as to knock him from his horse. He lay as if dead, and pondered whether or not he should shoot, his double-barreled shotgun being still at his side. He wisely concluded to be still, and the rest of the Indians passed him without a pause, doubtless thinking him dead.

As soon as the last one had gone by, he sprang up and crawled into a thicket and there lay hidden until they came on back with Foley, who had made a brave run but was caught at last. They had chased him to a little creek, where they had hemmed him in and as a last resort, he had dismounted and tried to hide in a water hole. From the signs they had roped and dragged him out, and brought him on to the spot where they had left Ponton, whom they had thought dead. Finding him gone, they made Foley call him, but of course no answer came. The cruel wretches then shot and scalped Foley and, when he was found, the bottoms of his feet had been cut off and he must have been made to walk some distance on the raw stumps! The cruelty of those Comanche warriors knew no bounds. The Rev. Ponton himself gave me an account of this race, and its attendant particulars, and I think I can vouch for its truth.

At Lynnville the Indians burned a few houses, killed a few more citizens, and then went on unmolested. They took two captives, Mrs. Crosby and Mrs. Watts, whose husbands were killed in the fight, and started back on their incoming trail. It is strange, but true, that all this was over before we had heard any of the circumstances. Captain John Tumlinson immediately raised a squad of forty or fifty men, and taking their plain trail came upon them on their way out—

a large force of between four and five hundred Indians. Our captain was nothing daunted, however, and ordered our men to fire a charge at them. He was brave, cool, and deliberate, and I have always believed would have whipped them, if a misunderstanding among the men had not forced him to draw off, with the loss of one man. The Indians charged upon the rear of our force, which was composed of Mexicans, who came near stampeding, and thus brought great confusion into our ranks. Tumlinson then followed along at a distance, receiving recruits constantly.

By this time, the news having been well ventilated here around Bastrop, General Burleson had raised all the men he possibly could and started out, anxious to intercept them at Plum Creek. Every now and then we met runners, who were sent to bid Burleson to come on. We rode until midnight, then halted to rest our horses. Very early the next morning we were again on the warpath, still meeting runners at regular intervals beseeching us to hurry.

We fell in with the Guadalupe men in the edge of Big Prairie, near Plum Creek, about two miles from where Lockhart now stands. We were now ordered to dismount, lay aside every weight, examine our arms, and make ready for battle. [Gen. Felix] Huston's men had gotten in ahead of the Indians, and were lying in a little mot of timber, when they heard the Indians coming, they being seemingly ignorant of our close proximity to them, for they were singing, whistling, yelling, and indeed making every conceivable noise. Here, while awaiting the Indians, we of Burleson's force joined them. A double-filed line of march was formed, Burleson's forces from the Colorado marching about one hundred yards to the right of Huston's men from the Guadalupe, and in sight of the Indians.

Four men were sent ahead as spies and the rear guard of

the Indians, consisting of four warriors, turned and rode leisurely back to meet them. Slowly and deliberately they came on, making no sign or move for fight. When within twenty steps of our spies, Colonel Switzer[7] raised his gun and killed one, whereupon the others beat a hasty retreat for their main force. Burleson ordered us to "spur up," and we rode very fast. We saw confusion in the Indian ranks, which we could not understand. A squad of men seemed to retreat in the face of a pursuing band of Indians. They were evidently divided against themselves or pursuing some other body of men.

At length, however, we were discovered by the main force of Indians, who immediately formed a line between us and their pack mules, stolen horses, and other plunder, and awaited our attack. When in one hundred and fifty yards of this line, we were ordered to dismount; one man of the double file held both horses, while his comrade shot.

It was a strange spectacle never to be forgotten, the wild, fantastic band as they stood in battle array, or swept around us with all strategy of Indian warfare. Twenty or thirty warriors, mounted upon splendid horses, tried to ride around us, sixty or eighty yards distant, firing upon us as they went. It was a superstition among them, that if they could thus run around a force they could certainly vanquish it. Both horses and riders were decorated most profusely, with all of the beauty and horror of their wild taste combined. Red ribbons streamed out from the horses' tails as they swept around us, riding fast, and carrying all manner of stolen goods upon their heads and bodies.

There was a huge warrior, who wore a stovepipe hat, and another who wore a fine pigeon-tailed cloth coat, buttoned

[7] Dr. Alonzo B. Switzer was one of the men from Gonzales. Jack W. Gunn, "Ben McCulloch, a Big Captain," *Southwestern Historical Quarterly,* LVIII, 7; Sowell, *Rangers and Pioneers,* 207.

up *behind*.[8] They seemed to have a talent for finding and blending the strangest, most unheard-of ornaments. Some wore on their heads immense buck and buffalo horns. One headdress struck me particularly. It consisted of a large white crane with red eyes.

In this run-around two warriors were killed, and also a fine horse. We were now ordered to reload, mount, and charge. They at once retreated, though a few stood until we were in fifteen steps of them before starting. In the meantime, the same warriors played around us at the right, trying to divide our attention and force, while the main body of Indians retreated, firing as they went. Soon, however, they struck a very boggy bayou, into which all of their pack mules and horses bogged down. A number of men halted to take charge of these, and such a haul they were making! The mules were literally loaded with all manner of goods, some even carrying hoop-irons to make arrow spikes. They bogged down so close together that a man could have walked along on their bodies *dry*.

Still the Indians retreated while the whites advanced, though the ranks on both sides were constantly growing thinner, for at every thicket a savage left his horse and took to the brush, while every now and then a horse fell under one of our men. About twenty warriors kept up their play upon our right, while an equal number of our men kept them at bay. In this side play, Hutch Reid [Hutchinson Reed*] was wounded. He undertook to run up on an Indian and shoot him. As he passed, his gun snapped, and before he could check his horse, an arrow struck him just under the shoulder blade, piercing his lungs and lodging against his

[8] This Indian is mentioned in all accounts of the Battle of Plum Creek. He wore a high silk top hat, leather gloves, a broadcloth coat worn backward, an Indian shield on his breast, and carried an open umbrella. Wilbarger, *Indian Depredations in Texas,* 31.

breast bone. Then one of the most daring and best mounted of the warriors was killed by Jacob Burleson,[9] who was riding the notorious Duty roan, the race horse which a while back bore Matthew Duty to his death and which finally fell into Indian hands. This broke up the side play. Burleson, with about twenty-five men, pursued them to within a mile of the San Marcos River, where they separated, so we retraced our steps.

One instance of the hardness and cruelty of some men, even though not savage in form and color, was shown us on this raid. As was often the case, some squaws were marching in Indian ranks, and one of them had been shot, and lay breathing her last—almost dead, as we came by. French Smith,* with almost inhuman and unmanly cruelty, sprang upon her, stamped her, and then cut her body through with a lance. He was from the Guadalupe; indeed, I do not think there was a single man from Bastrop who would have stooped to so brutal a deed. Ah! Men almost forgot the meaning of love and mercy and forbearance amid the scenes through which we passed in those early days.

While halting to rest our horses, we heard a child cry, and upon going into the thicket, a Mr. Carter found a fine Indian baby, which had been left in the retreat.

Joe Hornsby* and I were riding about two hundred yards in front of Burleson's main army, watching for Indian signs and trails as we went. Suddenly we came in sight of about thirty Indians some distance ahead. At first Joe said they were Tonkawas, who were a friendly tribe living in our midst. Upon seeing their shields, however, we knew they were hostile. I galloped back to notify Burleson, while he kept his eye upon them. When we came up they immediately shied

[9] This was one of the other Burlesons, probably John or Aaron. Jacob had been killed in the Battle of Brushy Creek, nearly a year before. The "Duty roan" was ridden by the Indian, not by Burleson.

off. We cut in ahead of them and advanced upon them. In thirty steps of them, Burleson ordered us to fire, and the action was simultaneous, though no one was hurt and only two horses killed. At one time here, I felt as if my "time" had come, sure enough. We had fired one round, and I was down loading my gun when I saw an Indian approaching me with gun presented. At this critical moment Joe Burleson[10] shot, killing him instantly. We discovered afterward that the Indian's gun was not loaded, and he was playing a "bluff."

We had a hot race after another warrior on foot, who was unarmed except bow and arrow, but would turn and shoot as he ran. General Burleson rushed at him with pistol presented, when an arrow from the Indian would have killed him if he had not stepped back. Then the warrior made another shot at [Thomas] Monroe Hardeman,* which missed him, but was driven eight inches into his horse. The hardy warrior made a brave and persistent fight, and even after he was knocked down, drew his last arrow at me, the man nearest to him. I killed him just in time to save myself.

What fancies they had in the way of ornamenting themselves! This savage presented a strange picture as he lay decked in beads, etc., sleeping the "dreamless sleep" of death. He also carried around his neck a tiny whistle and tin trumpet.

The stolen horses, mules, and goods were divided among the soldiers, with the consent of the merchants, who could not satisfactorily identify the articles.[11] Among other things, a

[10] This was Joseph Burleson, Jr., son of Joseph and Nancy (Gage) Burleson and nephew of General Edward Burleson.

[11] The Battle of Plum Creek was fought on August 11, 1840, and was a decisive victory for the Texans. About eighty-six Indians were killed, while the Texans, who were outnumbered nearly four to one, suffered no deaths. Two thousand horses and mules were captured. Placido and his Tonkawas wore white rags on their arms so that they would not be mistaken for the enemy. They were on foot when the

Comanche mule fell to my lot, and an odd specimen he was, with red ribbons on ears and tail.

On the return march, we found a Texan dead and scalped. The explanation of his death furnished an explanation of the confusion that was observed in the Indian ranks on the advance. It happened in this way: A squad of men on the Indian trail came upon the savages' advanced guard, and thinking they could easily manage so small a force, dismounted in a live oak grove and awaited them. Seeing the full force, however, they mounted and retreated. One man, the unfortunate one whom we found scalped, was left by his horse as well as his comrades, and thus had met his terrible fate.

We also found the body of Mrs. Crosby, whom they had killed when obliged to retreat, and nearby we found Mrs. Watts, whom they had also left for dead, having shot an arrow into her breast. A thick corset board had received and impeded its force, so that though wounded, she was still alive. She was a remarkably fine looking woman, but was sunburned almost to a blister.

In 1841, the Indians made a little raid into the Burleson neighborhood and stole a number of horses. A small squad of men was raised as quickly as possible, and pursuit was made. A run of fifteen miles brought them in sight of the thieves at Fort Ridgeway on the waters of the Yegua. The warriors were eating breakfast, and as our men approached,

battle started but all thirteen were mounted when it was over. Huston cited them for bravery in his report afterward. Brown, *Indian Wars*, 78–82; Sowell, *Early Settlers*, 18–19, 312–317, 418; Sowell, *Rangers and Pioneers*, 56–57; *Telegraph and Texas Register* (Houston), September 9, 1840; Walter P. Webb, *The Texas Rangers* (1935), 56–57; Wilbarger, *Indian Depredations in Texas*, 25–33; Henderson Yoakum, *History of Texas*, II, 302–303.

made no move to retreat. As soon as we were near enough, they came forward to fight. When on the first fire we killed two and wounded one, they retreated. The whites escaped unhurt, though one horse was shot.

On their way from this skirmish, the Indians went to Brushy Creek, and coming to Kenney's Fort, pretended to be friendly, but killed Dr. Kenney and Castlebury.[12] No pursuit being made, very soon they came again into the same neighborhood on the same errand, and again they were successful. Among other horses stolen was General Burleson's celebrated horse, Scurry, a present from Richard Scurry, an intimate friend and valiant soldier, hence the horse's name. General Burleson, accompanied by eight or ten men, took their trail immediately, and having followed them to the middle Yegua, came upon them camped in the edge of a strip of timber about three-quarters of a mile distant. They had open prairie to run through, and all struck forward. Mr. Spaulding was riding a splendid horse, the fastest runner of the crowd, and he put out at full speed. The chase was exciting to all, but Burleson was almost wild in his eagerness to regain Scurry. Seeing Spaulding making the best speed, he called out, "Twenty-five dollars for Scurry, Spaulding!" Further on in a louder tone, he called, "Fifty Dollars for Scurry, Spaulding!!!" and then still further on, "One hundred dollars for Scurry!!!" Much to his joy, Scurry was regained.

Now Indian stealing became almost a constant thing. Sometimes they would make a raid in the [James] Standifer neighborhood, then on Wilbarger Creek, and then in our immediate vicinity, and along the Colorado. Indeed, their boldness and greed became not only remarkable, but alarming. A man was lying asleep in his wagon and they took his

[12] For an interesting prelude to this incident, see Smithwick, *Evolution of a State,* 187–188.

horse which he had tied to one of the wheels, without awakening him. Then they would come in daytime, and once were in the act of trying to steal a little boy, when discovered. A small company of men at length went out in pursuit. In Big Prairie on Wilbarger Creek, they saw a gang of mustangs feeding, while a solitary horse stood tied three or four hundred yards off. Their curiosity was excited; but they soon saw Indians crawling upon the Mustangs. They were so engrossed in trying to get the horses that they did not discover the whites until we rushed upon them. A running fight then commenced, the Indians retreated on foot, while we were riding. Only one man, Mike Young,* was wounded, but not fatally, while three of the Indians were killed and one old warrior crippled. It was touching to see the devotion of a young Indian, presumably a son, who lingered by him a long time, making every possible effort to reach Brushy Bottom with him. As the whites gained ground and he saw death would be the result of longer delay, he at last started off, but a few words from the old warrior recalled him. He tarried only long enough, however, to divide arrows and then left his father to his fate. The time lost in helping the old man cost him his life, for he was overtaken and killed before reaching the bottom. Three-quarters of a mile farther on, we discovered their camps, and from every sign, they had brought their families and temporarily lived there, for there was the print of a child's moccasin, as well as those of squaws. But they fled in alarm, and all was deserted.

The raids and persecutions of the Indians upon our vicinity became so frequent and constant now that it would be entirely superfluous to try to give them in detail, as well as impossible to chronicle them in regular order. After this raid occurred the killing of another of our best citizens, William Lentz,* who was waylaid and shot near where Furnash had been murdered some time before.

A little old cannon was used as a signal[13] for our men to collect at Bastrop. It was a relic of the Mexican war, having been dismounted and thrown into the San Antonio River by Filisola at the Battle of San Jacinto. Immediately upon the murder of Lentz, the cannon called together Burleson's little band which was promptly in pursuit, though as usual nothing was accomplished.

Mr. Handcock [William Hancock], one of our neighbors, brought eight or ten fine horses from Tennessee, and in two weeks all of them, together with mine and others, were stolen. A small squad of men under Captain Gillespie was soon in pursuit, and with every advantage this time. We came in sight of them on Onion Creek, at what is known as Manshack Springs. When about a half-mile off we charged upon them, whereupon they mounted. One of the warriors leading a very fine horse pretended to be leading a charge. Two came round toward us, evidently trying to draw us off. The leading Indian was cut off, and was chased about a mile up the creek by Campbell Taylor and James Patten. They hemmed him in and Patten discharged both barrels of his gun without effect. The horse fell, and the Indian left afoot and made his escape. In the meantime, Captain Gillespie with his body of men

[13] The settlers had several ways of giving warning of Indian trouble. The first was the cannon system used for the settlers in the immediate area of the city of Bastrop. Another more ingenious method was originated by General Edward Burleson. Any person who had news of Indian or Mexican uprisings was to blow a horn and fire his gun twice. Each person who heard the signal was to repeat it, thus passing it throughout the section. The settlers then collected at the nearest fort, where they awaited the bearer of the news. This method was used to gather men prior to both the Battle of Brushy Creek and the Battle of Plum Creek.
There were actually two cannons at Bastrop. One exploded in the 1850's during a Fourth of July celebration. Mr. Shepherd, a coffin maker, had charge of the other, which finally exploded also. McDowall, "Journey," 60–61; Bastrop County Scrapbook (Archives Collection, University of Texas Library).

hemmed the thieves so they were obliged to dismount and leave their horses, all of which were regained except three.

In the spring of 1842, William Perry, Henry Lentz, William Barton, and myself made arrangements for a camp hunt. We took provisions intending to stay two or three nights. We made our way toward the head of Lentz Branch intending to camp right at the Indian passway—although the Indians were still very troublesome. We were riding leisurely along in couples, about eight miles from home and near our destination. Perry was entertaining us with accounts of his numerous adventures among Indians on the Brazos, and we were all very much interested. No matter how absorbed or entertained I might be, however, I was always on the alert and wide-awake in the woods, though I would go, whatever dangers awaited me. In the midst of Perry's narrative, on looking to my left, I saw an Indian walking in the long grass, about two hundred yards off. I saw him just as a brush intervened, and rode up fast thinking to see him better, at the same time exclaiming, "Yonder's an Indian, now!" When we came past the brush, no Indian could be found. Seeing us, he had evidently crouched in the high grass, and my friends naturally argued that I was mistaken. I could have sworn if necessary that I saw an Indian and I would not go another step until we went over on the hill, and looked into the matter. We felt equal to a small force, so we planned what to do and primed our guns. We rode abreast looking cautiously around as we went.

Soon we saw dark red objects on the side of the hill, lying perfectly still in the grass. I pointed them out, at the same time declaring them to be Indians. No, they said it was a clump of red rocks. I knew the hill, however, and was certain no red rocks lay there. Then they agreed it was some red hogs belonging to Mrs. Lentz; still I was sure they were Indians. We still advanced slowly upon them and were in sixty yards of them when our dogs sniffed in that direction and barked. Still my companions were unconvinced.

Suddenly William Barton said, "Something moved!"— and almost instantly the red rocks were seen to be Indians, who fired upon us; the blaze of their guns seeming to almost touch us. The hill seemed to be fairly alive with their moving bodies, thirty or forty warriors rushed upon us. We ran for dear life, but Henry Lentz, who was carrying our provisions on a slow mule, came very near being caught. His mule ran off, or shied to one side and would not go, till the Indians were almost ready to grab him. We advised him to throw off the pack, which he did, whereupon the animal took fright, and such running as it did is seldom seen! After a run of two hundred yards, we saw that none of them were riding and felt more secure. I proposed to turn and fire upon them, and wheeled my horse to shoot. I saw them coming in a string, whooping and yelling. Mr. Perry said, "Don't shoot! They'll return the fire and cripple our horses, then we will be caught for *sure!*" I took his advice and hurrying on we went to Bastrop that night to raise men to follow the Indians.

Next morning, twenty-five men were on the ground, finding a tomahawk, a knife, and a broken bowstring—signs which the Indians had left—as well as a plain trail leading to their old passway. In four miles we found where they had cooked and eaten our provisions, and must have spent the night. It was no trouble to follow them, as they seemed to have gone without fear, taking no pains to conceal their route. We got so near them that our horses would sniff and snort, and our hound barked, which probably caused the Indians to scatter, for immediately we lost our plain trail. According to their custom of perplexing their pursuers they separated and we found it impossible to go farther, so at nightfall we turned back for home, tired and disappointed.

Their raids were constant, and in this same spring occurred

one which brought quite an interesting little adventure into my own personal experience. About midnight I was awakened by the running of our cattle and the snorting of a wild mule, which we had left out, having put our horses in the stable. It was a freezing night, but without stopping to dress, I took my gun and slipped out to the stable to guard the horses. I sat there some time, till nearly frozen. I could see no Indians, nor sign of Indians, except an occasional disturbance among the cattle. I went into the house, dressed myself, kindled a little fire, and awoke my younger brother, William,* then about fourteen years old. Taking a gun apiece, we went out together.

We started across the truck patch, taking a short cut to the fence, then remembering how well Indians could hide in the long thick grass lining the fence corners, we left the fence about fifty yards to our left all around. My dog was with us, and we kept him very near us all the time. On looking around once, I saw a dark object between us and the house, but concluded it was the mule. In an instant, however, I saw the unmistakable form of a man step toward the fence. I tried to cock my gun, but it would not stand. I then pulled the hammer back and it fired clear. Thinking the Indians would run at this, I raised a regular Indian war whoop. About six men rose from the grass in the fence corners, and with an answering yell, rushed upon us. Seeing the odds, and bidding William to follow me, I broke for the house.

My dog, "General Cos," running into the thick of the crowd, must have troubled them, for he was cut in two places. The Indians were evidently trying to cut us off from the house, which I think "General Cos" prevented.

In an instant I looked back and saw William snapping his gun at them. There was a large thicket nearby, and I told him to hide in that, while I, taking my derringer, went toward the house, and when about eighteen steps from the Indians,

I exerted by lungs to the utmost in another loud and prolonged yell, firing into their midst, whereupon they stopped,
and I ran between them and the house, at the same time
calling for William to follow. I thought of reloading, but
found I had left all my ammunition in the house when I
went in to get warm. I then snatched his gun and tried to
fire it, but no use, three snaps and no discharge. We went in,
and reloading, expected an attack upon the house every
minute. They were making every imaginable noise—crying,
whooping, and yelling.

Bob Pace, who was working at Mother's, and I got our
horses and prepared to follow the Indians and to notify our
neighbors. They were evidently carrying off their dead warrior, whom I was confident I had killed, and hearing our
horses' feet, they dropped the body in the long grass, where
he was afterward found.

Five or six men were at the scene of disturbance early the
next morning. Upon a thorough examination of the ground
there was nothing to be found except a tin cup, with its buckskin string cut by a bullet, and some wool from an Indian
blanket—not one sign of blood. The sage grass was shoulder
high and, of course, it was a matter of some difficulty to trail
or trace anything. We struck a trail of four Indians, but in
four miles came to a gravel ridge and lost the trail, then came
home once more after a fruitless search.

The next morning Mother and I went to old Comanche[14]
at the mouth of Onion Creek for a wagon, which she had
ordered made. We spent the night at Mr. Collingsworth's,
the wagonmaker. There had been so much horse stealing
that we took every precaution to secure our horses. They
were tied in the chimney corner, while Mr. Collingsworth

[14] Comanche in 1840 had fourteen eligible voters. The town was
not a success and soon went out of existence. Brown, "Annals of Travis
County," VII, 6, 68.

slept with his bed by the window, where he could see and hear any attempt that might be made to take them. I am clear of superstition, but I had a dream that night which was fully corroborated by subsequent events. About midnight I dreamed that Indians had stolen our horses. So vivid and plain did it seem that I woke Judge Smith, with whom I was sleeping, and told him about it. The old man turned, muttered something about dreams, and bade me go to sleep. In a short time Mr. Collingsworth raised the alarm—all our horses were gone. The thieves had come within four feet of his bed and cut the horses loose and taken them off. We then had to strike out afoot to borrow horses before any pursuit could be made.

Early the next morning six of us took their trail and followed them to Mr. Baker's home, where they had tried in vain to get into the stables, and then moved on. We followed the trail five or six miles up Onion Creek and here we were forced to abandon our pursuit, for a violent rain and sleet storm fell upon us and we had to come back to Mr. Collingsworth's. Here Mother and I were, twenty miles from home, and on foot. Then, too, we had left home in warm, bright weather and were unprepared for cold. I had on moccasins, pleasant and light in warm weather, but the coldest shoes on earth in cold weather. Mother bought a horse and rode home, while I walked.

Upon reaching home we saw that they had found the body of the Indian I had killed, about a half-mile from the house, lying in the grass, wrapped in a fine Mackinaw blanket. Still a half-mile farther on they found another blanket, with spots of blood and a bullet hole through it, a quirt, an Indian headdress, and the grass over a space of ten feet square was wallowed down; indeed it was plain that another Indian had been badly hurt, if not killed, and carried off. If possible they always carried their wounded or dead home with them.

This was to avoid having them scalped, it being a superstition that an Indian could never enter the Happy Hunting
Ground if he lost his scalp, or for that matter, any part of
his body. He must be whole—no limb or member missing.

After a steady walk of twenty miles, it was of some satisfaction to find that the thieves had not escaped entirely
unhurt, and although they had stolen our horses, I had killed
two of them.

There was a cowardly tribe among us, the Tonkawas, who
were at peace with the whites, but hated all other Indians of
every tribe. Only a short time before this a band of Wacoes
had killed five of them while out hunting, and of course, this
increased their hatred toward Indians. Hearing that I had
killed one of their enemies, they came in a body, thirty of
them, and insisted that I should go with them and show them
the dead warrior. As we went, their excitement and speed
increased, and every now and then they would trot on faster
than ever, while I trotted with them, determined to keep up
and see what they intended doing. When they discovered the
body, they seemed wild with delight or frenzy. They sprang
upon the body, scalped him, cut off both legs at the knees,
both hands at the wrists, pulled out his fingernails and toe-
nails, strung them around their necks, and then motioned
for me to move aside. Seeing they meant further violence to
the body, already horribly mutilated, I demanded why I must
move. They said, "We must shoot him through the head
for good luck." I tried to stop them, but they would hear
nothing, said they were *compelled* to shoot him for luck.

I moved aside and they shot, tearing the head literally in
pieces. They then went back to the house and camped,
getting me to furnish them some beef. They boiled their beef,
and the hands and feet of the dead Waco together, turning
them with the same hands. Upon inquiry, I found they
intended having a dance, and would feed their squaws on

the hands and feet of the dead Indian, believing that this would make them bring forth brave men who would hate their enemies and be able to endure hardness and face dangers. They erected a pole, to which they attached the scalp, hands, and feet of the Waco, and then with horrible yells and gestures, all danced around it, while the squaws constantly danced up to the pole and took bites from the hands and feet and then would go back and dance again. They would prolong these dances three, five, and sometimes ten days.

Very soon, probably a month, after Hancock's horses were regained, they were again stolen. A small squad of men went immediately in pursuit, trailing them about twenty miles, when striking a mustang range, the trail was lost. We concluded to try to intercept them at their old passway between Onion Creek and Blanco. Reaching Blanco a little before sundown, we camped, and the next morning went on in search of the trail, but mustang tracks again bothered us, and we had to abandon the pursuit.

Again in this spring, when the farmers were all busy plowing, John Bright took his little brother and went hunting by moonlight in Cedar Creek bottom—turkey hunting. Having killed one, he was about to start home, when right beneath him on the road, he discovered a fresh moccasin track. He then hurried in order to reach home, and give the alarm. Hearing his horse-bell, he decided to drive his horses on home before him. Hearing a noise, he looked back and saw three Indians coming right at him. Turning, he fired upon them, and saw they were trying to cut him off from the house. The little boy held on to the turkey, and they reached home in safety. Mr. Bright took a light and found an abundance of blood, which led him to suppose he had wounded an Indian. He then mounted his horse and notified the neighbors. The men who came to call me, frightened the savages away from our premises—having taken down the fence, they were going to take our horses. Frequently when they could not get a stable open, they would kill a horse with lances through the cracks.

I knew of one case where a horse was hobbled with a puzzle hobble, or a hobble that could be taken off only by those who understood it. The thieves, not being able to unfasten the hobble, killed the horse and cut off his feet in order to secure the hobbles for themselves.

About sunup the next morning, William Barton, John Bright, and myself started trailing the Indians. For three miles, at every step along the trail, a large drop of blood was found, and here under a live oak tree, from buckskin strings and other signs, we saw that they had dressed a wound. Part of the crowd evidently succeeded in getting horses, for the wounded man had been put on a horse and carried off, and all along the way blood drops marked the trail, which we followed six miles, then finding from all indications that their force was entirely too strong for us, we came back home.

CHAPTER V

Comanches, Caddoes, and Cherokees

MEN WERE "TOO BUSY," and from recent experiences, pursuit seemed worse than useless, so things went on without change, except that the raids became more common as we became more careless, until they were of almost weekly occurrence. Often the savages added murder to theft, so that there was no security to our citizens or property. When I attempt to recall even the most important of these attacks and raids, I find it absolutely impossible to give them exactly in order as to the *time* of their occurence. Suffice to say what happened, at the same time confessing my inability to give the exact date. I will try to recount some of the most interesting trials and persecutions of our citizens, which occurred along from 1839 to 1842.

The Indians seemed to be vigilant, and did not confine themselves to their raids upon our homes; surveyors and hunters seldom, if ever, escaped their attacks, and many entire parties were overpowered and slain. Early in 1839 (I think it was), a Mr. Webster, who was living in the Hornsby neighborhood, decided to move to his headright league of land lying upon the North San Gabriel. John Harvey,* the land surveyor, collected fourteen men to accompany him in surveying and laying off adjacent land. The men were to accompany Webster and board with his family while surveying. Harvey, having some business to detain him, let the company

81

of men and the family start on several days in advance of him. When they were only a few miles from their destination, they were attacked by a large band of Comanches who were, however, repulsed after a considerable fight, without loss of life to the surveying party, though one or two were wounded.

They immediately retreated to Brushy, determining to wend their way back to the settlements, after encountering a force so strong—entirely too strong for their small number. Anticipating an attack from Indians, that night before retiring they took every precaution to be ready, barricading themselves behind their wagons. Sure enough, early the next morning, a little before sunrise, the savages, reinforced and protected on all sides by timber, attacked them. The fate of the little party was, of course, sealed in the face of such odds, but from all the signs left afterwards, they made a brave and desperate fight for their lives. Arrow spikes and bullets had almost riddled the wheel spokes and tongues of the wagons, and it seemed that at last the fight was hand to hand, for guns broken and lying around had evidently been used as clubs in the terrible struggle.

It was soon over, though, and in a few days Harvey, knowing nothing of the fate of his party, went on to join them at Webster's, and came upon their skeletons lying in a circle of thirty feet around the wagons. He returned in haste and made the report. Burleson immediately raised fifty or sixty men and hurried to the scene of carnage. A strange, unreal sight of horror met our eyes. Only fleshless bones scattered around remained of a brave and courageous band of men. In absence of coffin, box, or even plank, we collected them into an *old crate,* which was found nearby, and buried them. Only one skeleton could be recognized—that of one Mr. Hicks, who had his leg broken in the Battle of Anahuac in 1835.

We supposed Mrs. Webster and her little girl had shared the terrible fate of the band, though we could find no skeletons which we could possibly suppose were theirs, and we afterward learned that the Indians had carried them off into captivity.

Having buried the bones of the slaughtered band, we followed the Indian trail some miles, and seeing nothing to encourage us in pursuit we finally came home, unsuccessful, *as usual*.[1]

The Comanches held Mrs. Webster and her child until the well-known Treaty of 1840, when they sent word into San Antonio to Captain [Henry Wax] Karnes that they wished to make peace with the whites, and proposed to come in to make or agree upon terms of reconciliation, to which the whites agreed, at the same time bidding them to bring with them all captive whites in their possession.

On the 19th of March about twelve chiefs came into town, bringing only one white captive, a Miss [Matilda] Lockhart, and a few Mexicans. They were immediately shown into the building then used as the courthouse, where commissioners, with an interpreter appointed by President Lamar, awaited them. Upon being asked why they did not bring in all of their captives, the Indians answered defiantly that these *were* all they had. In the meantime, a company of Texas Rangers were near, in readiness for any treachery or violence.

[1] The Webster massacre, as it was called, took place on August 27, 1839, near Leander, Williamson County. James Webster, his wife, son, and daughter Martha, and surveyors named John Stillwell, Wilson Flesher, Martin Watson, Milton Hicks, William Rice, Albert Silsbey, James Martin, Nicholas Baylor, Bazley, Lensher, a Mexican, and a Negro, made up the party. They were en route to what is now Burnet County. Brown, "Annals of Travis County," VI, 56; De-Shields, *Border Wars*, 280; *Monuments Erected . . . to Commemorate the Centenary of Texas Independence*, 164; *Telegraph and Texas Register* (Houston), October 16, 1839; Wilbarger, *Indian Depredations in Texas*, 19–20.

Captain [George T.] Howard was in the building noting all the proceedings. The interpreter was told to inform them that they would be held as hostages until the other prisoners were brought in. He refused to tell them, warning the commissioners that the Comanches would certainly fight. The commissioners insisted, however, and placing himself near the door, he told them and left.

The chiefs instantly drew their bows and knives, and a general fight ensued, in which the Indian women even participated.[2] Lieutenant Dunnington was killed by a squaw, who shot an arrow through his body. Seven Texans were killed and eight wounded. All the warriors, nearly, were killed, but a few were spared who agreed to return to their homes and bring more prisoners. One chief ran into a house and had to be burned out.

Mrs. Webster and her child, being still captive, heard of the proposed treaty and exchange of prisoners, and of course hoped for deliverance. But knowing finally of the departure of the chiefs with Miss Lockhart, Mrs. Webster determined to try to make her escape, and a few days after their departure left her child and fled for San Antonio. Having no knowledge

[2] The Council House Fight, as it is called, took place on March 19, 1840, in San Antonio. The fight arose during discussion of a treaty which was to be made between Comanche Chief Muguara and Texas. Lieutenant William M. Dunnington was shot with an arrow by an Indian woman. He turned, drew his pistol, and not knowing her sex because she was dressed like a man, shot her in the head. In the words of the *Texas Sentinel* of Austin: "Her brains bespattered the wall;—he turned 'round and exclaimed, 'I have killed him, but I believe he has killed me, too,' and fell and expired in twenty minutes." Others killed were Judge James W. Robinson, Judge Hood of San Antonio, Judge Thompson of Houston, Casey of Matagorda County, Privates Kaminske and Whiting, and one Mexican. This fight has been called the greatest blunder Texas made in Indian relations because it renewed and prolonged the war with the Comanche Indians. DeShields, *Border Wars*, 315; *Handbook of Texas*, I, 424; *Texas Sentinel* (Austin), April 15, 1840.

of the country, she depended entirely upon following the trail of the chiefs. As the few warriors who were spared to bring in other prisoners were going out of San Antonio, she was going in, but seeing them in time, she hid until they had passed, and then made her way to her friends. When she reached San Antonio, she met among the captive Indians an old squaw who had been most cruel to her in captivity, but who now that the fortunes were reversed, pretended to be delighted to see her and was most demonstrative in her expressions of love. Mrs. Webster could not patiently submit to her caresses and gathering a stick, made her keep at a respectful distance.

About now came what is known as the Cordova War, or the union of Mexican and Indian forces against Texas, which at one time threatened serious trouble. The Indians were very bad, and excitement rose to the greatest height, when at length a plain double-file trail through our country was found by some of our citizens. Burleson soon had a company of men ready for action. The cause or source of the trail was not an Indian army, however, as we supposed, but marked the march of Cordova from Nacogdoches with his force of Mexicans, Negroes, and Biloxi Indians on his way to Mexico. He had only one Texan in his band, who deserted and turned informer, coming to Burleson to make report.[3] General Burleson took the informer as a guide, and about sixty men made prompt and speedy pursuit.

Away up on the Guadalupe one evening we discovered from various signs that we were getting very near. Dr. [James] Fentress,* an enthusiastic Texan, instructed the in-

[3] This man's name was Robison. He arrived in General Burleson's camp on March 29, 1839, and on the same day Burleson attacked and defeated Cordova. In the battle a Negro named Raphael was captured who confirmed all the statements of Robison, but the turncoat was nevertheless closely guarded and watched during the rest of the campaign. *Telegraph and Texas Register* (Houston), April 17, 1839.

former to point out Cordova to him as they came in sight, saying that he intended to kill him first and foremost. Six miles from Seguin we overtook them, and they immediately halted and formed a line of battle. Cordova was pointed out, just as they turned for retreat. Dr. Fentress, aiming at him, fired and said he wounded him in the arm, for he saw it fall limp at his side, but some contended that he was not touched. There was a running fight for four or five miles, Cordova losing several Indians, Negroes, and a few Mexicans, but Burleson did not lose one of his force.

Cordova escaped into Mexico with a considerable little company, which he held during the Mexican invasion of 1842, commanding it with General Adrian Woll. He was killed in the Battle of Salado, and those who saw his body said that Fentress was right—his arm had been broken by a rifle ball. This was the beginning and end of all united work against the Republic of Texas by Mexicans and Indians *in league*. The Indians, however, made no pause in their stealing among and around our settlers on the Colorado.

During one raid they stole a well-known gray horse, a fine and valuable animal belonging to Bat Manlove. Their visits were now so frequent that it became a prevalent opinion that they were stopping or camping somewhere near—probably on Brushy Creek. A small squad of eight whites and three Tonkawas went out to *reconnoiter* or investigate. They camped on Wilbarger Creek, in open prairie, and early the next morning two Waco Indians rode unexpectedly in sight. The Tonkawas were considerably excited. Their rushing around for guns and weapons caused the Wacoes to turn and run—horses were saddled and just as the men were mounting to pursue them, one came riding back. Having seen the red men, they had evidently concluded that they were members of some friendly tribe. The Indian was riding Mr. Manlove's fine gray horse, so when he came near enough to see that most of our party were whites, he retreated in double-quick time. There was a terrible race for five or six miles, after which all our horses began to fall. The Indian, too, was fast losing ground from some cause, and finally dismounted and left his horse and took refuge in a little creek in the prairie. One of our Tonkawas, who was foremost in the race, jumped off his horse and mounted the fine gray horse, which had rested a little spell, and was off in hot pursuit. He soon overtook the Waco, who fought desperately. Arrows flew thick and fast and at last the Waco fell. Still he did not give up; he had his bow ready to shoot whoever would first approach him. The Tonkawa crawled cautiously up in shooting distance, then killed him, cut his throat, and scalped him. This warrior was one of the greatest natural curiosities I have ever seen. He had white specks or spots all over his skin, like a fawn.

Nothing was ever seen of the other Indian and we supposed he would notify and collect others, so our men came home, but this time brought the horse with them.

An amusing little incident occurred in this connection, though not very amusing to those most intimately involved. A man by the name of Walker Wilson lived in an upper settlement on what is called Mayhard Creek. He owned a number of very fine cows, in which his wife took special pride. Regularly, at nightfall, one could see Mrs. Wilson with her little Negro girl, "Sook," going with buckets of milk. One evening the cows were unusually late coming home, and the two women were milking for some time after dark. All had been milked but one, a favorite called Brownie. Sook was sent to find and bring her to the dairy, but she came back without success. Mrs. Wilson herself then concluded to look around for Brownie a little. Seeing a dark object moving along near her and supposing it to be the missing cow, she called out, "Why there's Brownie. Sook, I knew you never half looked!" Then stepping around, she said, "Ho, Brownie!" when to her surprise and terror she saw the supposed cow straighten up into an Indian. Almost crazy, the old lady ran for the house screaming, "Indians! Wilson! Jesus!" At the dairy another jumped out as she ran by. These evidently only wanted to steal, for they ran off without harming anyone.

In one of their raids they stole some horses belonging to a small company of Delaware Indians, who were encamped on Cedar Creek. These Delawares were friendly and honorable. They frequently camped in the settlements, hunting and trading with the whites. They even fought in the Texas army against Mexico.

Early on the morning after the theft of the horses, their chief, "Captain Bob,"[4] and two others of their tribe started with Mike Sessom,* a white man, in pursuit of the thieves. The trail was a plain one, as they had made the theft immediately after a heavy rain. The thieves, seven or eight Caddoes, were overtaken at Onion Creek, which was then very high. Having already swum the horses across, the thieves were making a raft to cross their bows, arrows, guns, and blankets. Upon seeing Captain Bob's small force, they plunged into the creek, leaving everything behind them. One of them got tangled in a vine on the opposite bank, and Sessom raised his gun to fire at him, but Captain Bob, who was more versed in such matters, stopped him, saying that he thought it possible to get the stolen horses by milder measures, whereas one shot would cause them to run. He then called to them and told them they had stolen *Indian* horses and must bring them back. Seeing he was a red man they paused and listened to him. He bade them come over, bring the horses, and get their

---

[4] Andrew Sowell speaks of an Indian called Old Delaware Bob, who was an interpreter at times for the Texas Rangers: Sowell, *Early Settlers,* 321, 372.

weapons and blankets which they had left. He assured them that in so doing they would not be hurt.

They finally consented and brought over all the stolen horses except one, which they declared was no Indian horse, for they knew they took him "right at white man's door." They would not be persuaded to restore this one. Taking a careful survey of Captain Bob's party, they looked upon Mr. Sessom with undisguised mistrust and suspicion and said, "That is a white man." The chief assured them that he was a half-breed Delaware who lived with them, and since Sessom was dressed like the Delawares, they finally accepted him as an Indian, though they never forgot to be on the alert.

They first crossed over all their luggage and then formed a circle and passed the pipe of peace around. While the smoke curled gracefully above their heads a small band of whites rode in sight. Instantly they sprang into the creek and made their escape, taking the "white man's horse" with them.

Not long after this old Colonel Gamble and L. C. [Leander Calvin] Cunningham* of Bastrop, hearing that pecan mast was very abundant, went out along the San Marcos River to investigate the matter, intending to hire hands and go into the pecan trade if the crop was sufficient to justify them in the undertaking.

On their homeward ride they were within thirty or forty steps of a bluff on the banks of the Blanco River, when a party of Indians suddenly fired upon them. Two bullets pierced the lapel of Gamble's coat and an arrow glanced across Cunningham's back, but they escaped unhurt and came on home, reporting their narrow escape—again no pursuit, and, of course, the attacks continued.

A small party of travelers who came in from San Antonio soon after this were horrified to find the body of a Mr. Robinson lying right on the roadside along Cedar Creek, about fifteen miles from Bastrop. He had evidently *just* been killed and scalped, for his blood was still flowing, warm and red, when they found him.

Besides deeds of murder and theft, many attempts were made upon the lives of our citizens which resulted only in a race for life. James Henderson formed a surveying party, which had commenced work on the Blanco River. We generally left a man to stand guard at camp while we surveyed, and it was Henderson's turn. It was a lonely, as well as dangerous post of duty. Seeing a horse raise his head as if he saw something, Henderson climbed a tree to take a good look around. Imagine his surprise and alarm when he saw about thirty Indians coming. They must have seen the smoke of the campfire. Leaning down on their horses, they evidently intended to surprise the campers. There was no time for pause or deliberation, so springing bareback on the nearest horse he broke for the surveyors with the Indians right behind him. He struck his friends exactly and after a few shots the Indians were repulsed, but the horsemen still lingered near enough to keep our attention and cause uneasiness. One of our men happened to look behind and saw an Indian in the act of firing upon us. While a few warriors had been riding around at our front, a few had slipped around to our back on foot, and in a few more minutes the surveyors and party would have perished as did the Webster party. Seeing them in time, however, a few shots dispersed them, though they robbed the camps and stole the horses as they fled. Again no pursuit.

Three men went out on Brushy from Bastrop on a bear hunt. Two of them took the dogs and went on foot into a thicket, while Claiborne Osborn,* not much more than a mere boy, was left nearby with the horses. While sitting there alone on his horse he was suddenly fired upon by Indians. No shot took effect, but they ran up, knocked him off his horse, and despite his struggles, scalped him. Then he succeeded in pulling away from them and reached his friends, who had heard the shots and were coming to his aid. *Again,* no pursuit, and they grew still bolder.

A Mr. [James] Campbell* from Bastrop took five or six men and went surveying out on the Guadalupe. In a short time William S. Wallace* raised a larger company and went to the same section for the same purpose. He struck their work and traveled on, intent upon getting above them or coming up with them, before commencing work. Only a short distance up the river, he found them all dead. They appeared to have camped a day or two, for they had cut a bee tree. Destitute of coffin, box, plank, or tool, Wallace and his men put the bodies into the stump of this bee tree, which was hollow. Not intimidated by the awful fate of these their predecessors, and having a force of about eighteen men, they went on to their work. After surveying a week or two, however, the signs of Indians became so frequent—once or twice Indians were even seen prowling around—that Wallace prudently came home with his company, warned by the horrible death of Campbell's party. Again no investigation or pursuit.

Very soon John Harvey raised a company from Bastrop and went to survey out on the San Saba. They had been at work eight or ten days and were moving from one branch of the river to another, when they saw on their way a fresh Indian foot trail. This aroused and warned them of danger, and that night guards were stationed near the horses. One of these sentinels, a Mr. Burnet, stood near a steep hollow, close by which a mule was staked. Just before daylight he noticed the mule snorting and looking over into the hollow, as if he saw something unusual. Thinking it was probably a wolf or bear he indiscreetly went to the edge of the bluff and looked down into the hollow.

Three or four Indians had crawled up and just as he was in the act of peering down they fired upon him, tearing his arm to pieces. Almost simultaneously another party, or another division of the same party, crawled up on the opposite side of the camp and fired upon the sleeping men, who returned the fire as quickly as possible.

Three of them did not tarry to fight, however, but ran with all possible speed. One was on horseback, while two, Leffingwell and Pipkin, were on foot. After running some distance these two, noticing that the guns had ceased, and thinking the Indians had been repulsed, turned and were retracing their steps toward camp when they met the Indians, who were carrying a slain warrior. At sight of the two fugitives, they dropped their burden and took out after them. Thus, headed off as it were from their companions, they struck out for home. Both were young men and entirely inexperienced as woodsmen, in a wild waste without food and unarmed except one gun for which they had only one load.

In the meantime, Harvey and his company of surveyors, after repulsing the Indians,[5] had come home and, finding the two footmen had not made their appearance, naturally conceded they had been overtaken and killed, but no investigation was made. In about ten days, however, the two men reached Bastrop almost dead from hunger and fatigue. They had traveled about one hundred and fifty miles on foot, over a rough country with no food except buds, berries, and wild

[5] Harvey's fight took place in June of 1839. There were ten men in the party. They climbed up in trees when the Indians attacked and successfully defended themselves from there. Nothing is known about Burnet or Pipkin, but the Leffingwell was probably Ira Leffingwell, born in New York in 1818. He was wounded in John H. Moore's defeat on February 12, 1839, and was living in Williamson County in 1850. *U.S. Census,* 1850, Bastrop County, 33; Wilbarger, *Indian Depredations in Texas,* 263.

edibles gathered by hand. The gun would never discharge its solitary load and they were constantly tantalized by sight of game which they could not get.

The account of their adventure was quite interesting. One evening while traveling down the Colorado River they struck a sand bar, where water was still standing on the dry sand where Indians had just watered their horses. In a short distance they found where the savages had been camped. They were now considerably alarmed and perplexed as to what course to pursue. Knowing the Indians to be very near they wished to cross the river, but neither of them could swim. They concluded to try to wade the stream and one plunged in, but soon found that the water was over his head and came out. They then slipped cautiously down the river, watching carefully and fearing an attack from Indians every instant. At length, they crawled into a steep hollow and there lay concealed for the night.

While lying in the ravine they heard the sound of approaching steps and almost gave up hope. Nearer and nearer came the regular tramp of heavy feet, even to the very edge of the bluff above them. They lay watching with bated breath, expecting to see the form of an Indian spring down upon them. Great was their surprise to see instead the black head and shining eyes of a huge bear, which after a short glance turned and retreated, leaving them in peace. Thus beset with dangers and fears, they made their way home at last, although almost dead on their arrival.

About now a Mr. Ladd and another gentleman from Bastrop went over near the San Gabriel River to camp a few days, look at the country, hunt, and enjoy themselves generally. They camped at a spring and were settled in their wild quarters, having a nice time. One morning, Ladd took his gun and went out to kill a deer, leaving the old gentleman in charge of the camp. Before he was out of sight he heard a noise back at the camp and looked back, seeing the Indians in the act of killing the old man. Knowing his time would come next, he broke to run and immediately they started in pursuit. He ran into the first thicket, which was instantly surrounded by the warriors, two of which were on horses and the rest on foot. He felt death to be inevitable, but determined to fight to the end, and taking deliberate aim at the nearest, pulled the trigger *and the cap burst!* At this the Indians ran all together on one side of the thicket, while he ran out on the other. And now his chances for life seemed indeed desperate.

He had a distance of at least four miles through open prairie before he would reach the San Gabriel, and behind him were *seven* determined Indians, two of whom were on horseback. But he attempted the run, his pursuers being immediately behind him. The two horsemen were foremost among the Indians, but whenever they would come alarmingly close, he would turn and bluff them with his gun, which he knew would not fire. When about half the way had been run they were so near that Ladd could distinctly hear them laughing, and he imagined it was in anticipation of taking his scalp. At length, they made a dash at him, at the same time firing upon him. They were so near that the report of the guns deafened him and dazed him, but he did not pause; he said that he felt as if he were fairly flying. At last the river Gabriel was in sight and he struck it at a bluff twenty feet high. Still he did not pause, for he knew a terrible death was pursuing hard behind him, so he sailed over the height, lighting on his feet unhurt, while the Indians, scared to make the leap, went around, giving him a chance to hide.

Again he concealed himself in a thicket, and no sooner did he become quiet than he was sound asleep from utter prostration. He was aroused from his profound and somewhat unseasonable nap by the voices of the Indians as they looked for him in and around the thicket. They did not find him, however, and finally left him. He lay there till night and then escaped. Coming home, he declared he would not live in such a country, where a man's life was thus in jeopardy all the time, and soon after left these parts, never to return.

Another small party of men, among whom was Taylor Smith,* had a little adventure somewhat similar to this at about the same time [1838]. They were hunting buffalo, and one day were fired upon by Indians. One man [Smith] had his arm broken, but none were killed.

All these trials and dangers of our pioneers had no effect in staying the great tide of emigration which constantly flowed into our state from everywhere.

CHAPTER VI

More Mexican Trouble

IN THE SPRING of 1842 General Vasquez invaded Texas and captured San Antonio.[1] The news created a great deal of excitement among us. The little signal cannon called us together at Bastrop, and General Burleson took a considerable force to Austin, which was by then a growing place.[2] The citizens were alive with serious apprehensions, expecting an invading army from Mexico, and as we lay in Austin awaiting recruits we could hear innumerable reports of approaching forces. Two divisions were represented as advancing upon us; one by way of Goliad, another by way of Santa Fe.

Burleson dispatched runners in every direction to test the truth of these reports and finally went with his men to San Antonio, which we found in sackcloth and ashes. The citizens, being mostly Mexicans, were not hurt; most of the American citizens had run. What a city of devastation and bloodshed has San Antonio been! Whatever trouble ever visited Texas,

[1] On March 5, 1842. *Handbook of Texas,* II, 834.

[2] Austin was practically deserted at this time. The government had been moved to Houston and most of the citizens had fled from the supposed invasion. A few of the older settlers who remained resolved to prevent President Houston's order for the removal of the archives from being carried out. Brown, "Annals of Travis County," IX, 7; Hope Yager, "Archive War in Texas" (Master's Thesis, University of Texas, 1939).

this little town seemed to be heart and center of her suffering, so that she has been well-termed as a "Slaughter Pen."

In about a month several companies were organized. I belonged to one under Captain James Gillespie.* Burleson was very anxious to make an invading attack on Mexico and spoke at length on the subject at the Alamo, but having no orders to that effect from Commander-in-Chief Sam Houston, our forces finally disbanded and came back home. While we were in San Antonio we lived by foraging on the Mexican citizens of the place. Juan N. Seguin, who had hitherto been true and loyal to Texas in all her troubles, even commanding a company against the Mexicans at the Battle of San Jacinto, now turned and became our enemy, giving as a reason for the change the fact that we destroyed many of his hogs and property while lying at San Antonio. Whatever might have been his true reasons, he went entirely over to Mexico.

In the fall General Adrian Woll came with a still stronger force and stayed longer on Texas soil. The panic and excitement became so great that some of our citizens gathered up bag and baggage and left. Once more two hundred men marched to San Antonio. Six miles this side of the city, on a little creek called Salado, they met a citizen of San Antonio and from him derived some information as to the strength of the Mexican army. Taking advantage of his familiarity with the country, they also learned from him what would be an advisable position and were led by him to the very spot, where was fought the famous Battle of Salado.

Immediately about eighty horsemen were sent into San Antonio to draw on the battle. No sooner were they in sight than the Mexican cavalry mounted and gave them a tight race back to the Salado. Forming a line they awaited the infantry, while we were making ready for fight.

Colonel Matthew Caldwell, who was one of the Santa Fe

prisoners and consequently had taken oath never to participate in the war of Texas against Mexico, had in spite of the
oath entered the Texas army and had charge of the forces on
this raid. He now gave his men a talk, explaining his position
and how little mercy he could expect if he should again fall
into the hands of the Mexicans. Then he asked them if they
would be true to him at all hazards in the coming struggle.
They swore they would stand by him to death.

The Mexicans charged several times and the skirmish
lasted over a half-day, but finally the Mexicans were repulsed.[3] In the meantime, Captain Dawson, with a company
of about fifty men from Fayette County, was on his way to
join Caldwell's forces at Salado Creek, anxious to aid in the
coming battle. His spies saw the Mexican forces and reported.
After a brief period of deliberation they decided to fight, and
proceeded to take position in a mesquite grove.

General Woll turned his attention and his forces full upon
Dawson, though he artfully hid his artillery and infantry
behind his cavalry, so that Dawson did not see the tremendous odds with which he would have to contend. His small
force of fifty-two men awaited the attack of a large Mexican
army. The cavalry marched in gunshot range, received a
volley of shots, and then moved aside and surrounded the
little company, exposing to view the artillery and infantry.

Then commenced one of the most cruel and murderous
massacres in all the annals of history. *Seeing the utter helplessness of his situation, Dawson at once raised the white flag,
as signal of surrender, but no heed was taken of the sign!*
With deliberate and vindictive cruelty, they pressed upon the
small band of Texans! First shots were high, then lower and
lower, till sweeping the ground the little force fell thick and
fast all around. With saber and lance the Mexicans fell upon

[3] The Battle of Salado took place on September 18, 1842. *Handbook of Texas,* II, 531–532.

the few who escaped death in the volleys of shot, and cut them down.

Only two out of the brave but unfortunate company escaped and lived to give details of the cruel butchery— Alsey Miller* and Gonsolvo [Henry Gonzalvo] Woods. The latter escaped by an almost miraculous combination of bravery, skill, vigilance, and fortitude. Receiving a wound in the shoulder, and several hacks over the head with sabers, he knew he could not cope with the merciless foe, who were every instant cutting down his comrades around him, so he concluded to surrender and place himself at their mercy, as vanquished. He tried to make his way with gun and ammunition to the commander, *who was none other than Juan N. Seguin, the traitor.*

The wildest disorder and confusion reigned, and only one rule was the order of the day, and that was *death to the Texans.* The snap of a Mexican gun which had been drawn upon him convinced him that surrender or escape was almost impossible, but in his desperation he broke into a run, with a Mexican horseman at his heels. Death seemed inevitable, but as "fortune sometimes favors the brave," so did it to Woods. The Mexican attempted to strike him with his lance, but missed him. With wonderful quickness he snatched the weapon with such force as to jerk the astonished soldier to the ground, whereupon he ran the lance through him and sprang upon the Mexican's horse and made his escape.

Riding full speed about two miles he saw two men, one of whom seemed to be his fellow soldier, Alsey Miller, whom he had seen make a desperate run from the scene of battle, and he turned to join them, but they were two Mexicans, who immediately rushed upon him, firing as they came. Seeing a pistol attached to the horn of the saddle, Woods snatched it to fire, but as he did so the cartridge fell to the ground, thus leaving him once more powerless to defend himself. They, however, did not know the pistol was empty, so he managed to bluff them until he reached a hollow. Dismounting, he hid himself and *finally* made his escape.

His father, an old man sixty-two years old,[4] was killed and his brother Norman was wounded on this campaign, and died a prisoner.

The next morning Woll commenced a retreat, camping that night on the Medina River, where our forces under Caldwell, John H. Moore, and James S. Mayfield came in sight of him. In the meantime, we had captured five stragglers from Woll's army and these were now tied, so that even the guards might take part in the battle which seemed impending. Our spies went out under cover of the night almost into their camps, and returned and described their position and strength. We then advanced to within a mile and a half of them and awaited daylight. We awoke the next morning to find that the enemy had retreated during the night. We marched in pursuit at once, but after following them about fifteen miles we heard shots being exchanged between our advanced guards and the rear guards of Woll's force. We were immediately ordered to halt, and our scouts returned from the firing and brought back one of our men, who was shot through the lungs.[5] Our army was composed of about five or six hundred men, and instead of advancing as a majority thought best, we were ordered to fall back three or four hundred yards into a dry creek in the prairie, near the Hondo River, where with a strong position we awaited

[4] Most accounts say Zadock Woods was around eighty years old, rather than sixty-two. After his escape, Henry Gonzalvo Woods met John C. Wilson, who washed the blood from Woods's head and poulticed the wounds with a prickly pear. They returned together to La Grange. Sowell, *Early Settlers,* 25, 316, 817.

[5] This was Samuel H. Luckie, one of Colonel Jack Hays's Rangers. He died in San Antonio in October, 1852. Brown, *History of Texas,* II, 229.

attack. After waiting a half-hour without any sign of the enemy, we were ordered to mount and advance.

A march of about a mile brought us in sight of their pickets and we could distinctly hear the yells and cheers of their forces. Now after another halt, Captain Jack Hays was ordered to take his company and make a challenging charge, while Captain William M. Eastland was to support him with one hundred of the best mounted of our force. Eastland formed a line, but was ordered back into ranks, and Hays's company charged upon the yelling Mexican guards alone.

Our delay and unaccountable wavering had given Woll every advantage to be prepared for us, and he had taken the opportunity. In the bend of the road he had planted his artillery and some infantry. Hays, coming suddenly and unexpectedly upon them, received a full volley of shot and was compelled to fall back, not being supported by the main force in time. In this charge one of the men, Kit [Christopher] Achlin,* ran around Woll's cannon, placing his foot upon it. Hays retreated and met us about one hundred and fifty yards from the scene, where again a halt was called and we were ordered to dismount.

We were now certain that a fight was at hand, and already hearts beat fast and eyes brightened in prospect of action and danger. There seemed to be a strange want of discipline or system or harmony among the officers, who could not agree as to the proper line of policy, and stood discussing and debating questions, while the soldiers were all the time growing more perplexed and impatient.

Captain Billingsley, understanding the situation, and knowing the value of prompt action called out to the soldiers, "Boys, do you want to fight?" A loud "Yes" was the instant reply. "Then, follow me!" he called, and marched on at the head of a considerable force. We were already approaching very near the Mexican infantry, and were drawn up in line of battle. In two minutes the charge would have been made and the fight commenced. But at this juncture superior authority interfered. Colonel Caldwell galloped up and called out to Billingsley, "Where are you going?"

"To fight," was the answer.

"Countermarch those men back to ranks!" Caldwell commanded, and we were forced to take our places back in the standing army, all worried and disgusted with what seemed to us a cowardly hesitation and a disgraceful and confused proceeding without motive or design. Nearly 600 men standing almost in sight of an invading army, whose guards would sometimes slip in near enough to throw bullets into our midst. There we stood till dark, suffering for water and tantalized almost to madness by the delay and want of harmony among our leaders.

We were at last ordered to mount and march up the creek above the Mexican forces. Thinking that this was done to cut off their retreat, the Mexican guard fired upon us as we got opposite their camps, but still we were ordered to march on. A half-mile farther up the creek we were ordered to halt and dismount and guards were stationed around the horses. Again we waited. In a half-hour Colonel Samuel Walker, raising fifteen or twenty men, went out to investigate. We found no Mexican army! General Woll had retracted and thus ended one of the most disgraceful campaigns of which Texas was ever guilty.

How we needed Burleson! So ready to lead, so prompt to act! But he was out on an Indian campaign when our troops left home. Hearing of fresh trouble with Mexicans, however, he came on to our help, but it was too late. We met him at the Medina, twenty or thirty miles from San Antonio.

And now we found ourselves once more at home, but not safe, for still every now and then we were troubled with Indians and occasionally we went out to bury one of our citizens who would be surprised by the skulking savages and murdered whenever they could find opportunity to do their dastardly work. It was almost a constant thing to wake and find all our horses stolen and all pursuit or effect to regain them useless.

Sometimes, however, our little runs after the thieves were interesting and exciting, although we might not catch the thieves or regain our horses. I remember one run early in the year 1843, during a very cold spell we had, that was quite amusing.

A lot of horses having been stolen, eighteen or twenty men under Jonathan Burleson went out in pursuit. We trailed them over their same old route to their same old passway. From every sign they had evidently been in a hurry and had a strong force. The first night we camped on Onion Creek very near to where they had camped on their way out only a night or two previously.

As it was severely cold, we built a large bright fire and indulged in the free and easy merrymaking life of camp life until very late. We had a fine singer in our party, James Patton, and his splendid voice entertained us through many a song as we lay basking in the genial light and warmth of the campfire. At last the silence of night pervaded the woods and we slept very soundly.

Meanwhile, we had tied our horses near and guards were stationed around them. Suddenly we were aroused by a struggling and kicking among our horses and then came a scattering and flying of fire around and over us. In an instant we had our guns in hand, thinking the Indians were upon us. The guards soon explained the cause of the disturbance. One of the horses, having been entangled in his rope, had fallen into our campfire.

One of our men was by far the most terribly frightened

man I ever saw. When the excitement first arose he rushed into a nearby thicket, leaving his gun and comrades and lay there afraid to move or speak, until the alarm had subsided. Then we heard moans and groans from the brush, and recognizing his voice, we called to him and assured him the danger and Indians were not near. He was literally scared into a shaking ague, and the next day he candidly confessed himself entirely unfit for Indian campaigning, and very truly said he did not believe he could stand the racket of such a life.

The next morning found us on the plain trail, which we followed easily, constantly finding signs of their camps every ten or fifteen miles. We began to have a strong hope of overtaking them and regaining our horses.

One night we camped with a well-laid plan to make a raid the next morning, feeling confident of speedy and certain success. Half of the company, however, surprised and disconcerted us the next morning by announcing their determination to quit and go home. A serious division and difficulty arose among the men and many "waxed warm and wrathy," feeling inclined to support their opinions with blows. As is always the case, our divided forces lost both power and design, and abandoning further pursuit we retracted, retracing our steps homeward. Arriving at the scene of our first alarm we again camped and again Mr. Patton sang for us, but just as he was in the midst of a low comic song entitled, "The Cork Leg," our guards reported a noise like that of moving Indians. The fire was immediately extinguished and we had our guns ready for action. Nothing further being heard, however, we concluded that the men were mistaken and after resting throughout the night in peace we came on home the next morning without even investigating for fresh Indian signs.

This was a piece of criminal carelessness and negligence

which we afterward regretted, for on the following day two of our men were surprised and killed while out hunting by a band of Comanches numbering about thirty, who came along on our immediate trail. Thus, we knew that our guards had doubtless been correct in thinking that they heard the muffled sound of their march somewhere near us.

The two unfortunate men seemed to have fought most desperately, for there were signs of a terrible struggle—a broken gun showing hand-to-hand fighting. They were given time to find shelter under a bluff, and thus protected they were able to prolong their lives, but against such odds they were soon killed. It is presumable that this band expected and desired us to overtake and attack them, judging from their slow march and plain trail, and returned upon our very heels. As it was, no pursuit was made and once more two of our citizens were brutally murdered and buried without one effort to avenge them or punish the murderers.

Of course, Indians grew bolder as we grew more lax and very soon our community was again shocked by their cruelty. Michael Nash,[6] a citizen, went out of town a few miles to hunt a while, and when he didn't return when expected, men went out in search of him. He was found dead and scalped about three miles from home. From all indications he had killed a deer and was cleaning it when surprised by a small party of Indians. Blood was found on their trail which led us to believe that he had at least wounded one of his murderers.

[6] Michael Nash was killed on September 1, 1840, not in 1843. Nash had come to Texas in 1830 and settled at Bastrop as a carpenter. After his death his widow married James Putnam. Brown, "Annals of Travis County," VII, 60; DeShields, *Border Wars*, 329–330; W. H. Korges, "Bastrop County, Texas: Historical and Educational Development" (Master's Thesis, University of Texas, 1933), I, 74; Sowell, *Early Settlers*, 342.

From now on these murders and raids in Bastrop County gradually abated. But the incoming Germans who settled New Braunfels and Fredericksburg still suffered a great deal from their persecutions, and along the frontier the savages never lost an opportunity of showing their cruel and vindictive hatred toward the whites.

CHAPTER VII

The Mier Expedition

WHILE IT IS HARD "to lend fresh interest to a twice-told tale," there is still attached to some of the experiences of individuals and of nations, a deep and abiding interest, which increases as the details are presented from different standpoints; indeed, there is but one way of arriving at the whole truth in any case, and that is by careful collection and examination of *all* the evidence. There are also wayside gleanings as we proceed in our searchings after truth—items of interest and even of importance, at once pleasing and instructive, robbing history of seeming harshness, at the same time impressing its thrilling facts upon mind and memory. Just as genial smiles and kind words sometimes brighten stern faces, inviting us to pleasant acquaintance, where once, by cold reserve and dignity, we were simply repulsed.

We come now to the darkest complication of affairs after 1836. Texas had for six years preserved intact her Declaration of Independence. Mexico seemed to have almost forgotten the very existence of the province which she had striven so hard to retain, at least making no serious interruption to our gradual growth and development; while on the other hand, the United States seemed to be watching or trying the strength and resources of the child republic before resuming the question of annexation.

In 1842, however, the comparative and transient calm was broken. Mexico, awakening to the fact that the prospect of annexation was assuming serious proportions, made two raids into our country—Vasquez in March and Woll in September. Then in December of the same year came the "Archives War," that bloodless battle wherein Smith, with his twenty men, authorized by President Houston, started to transport the archives of government to the city of Houston, but meeting Captain Lewis[1] with his cannon at Kenney's Fort, concluded to accompany him back to Austin.

Then came the ill-starred Mier Expedition!

There are only two men now living in Bastrop County who passed through its dangers, horrors, and suffering—William Clopton* and John Morgan—from the former of whom we have lately received the following details, and record them in full, deeming this to be one of the facts in our history which is of an intense and abiding interest—thrilling in its heroism, horrible in its cruelty, and pathetic in its suffering.

In the fall of 1842 the President ordered an invading expedition against Mexico, having probably the twofold design of retaliation and of regaining a few of our Santa Fe men[2] still held by Santa Anna. General [Alexander] Somervell, with about seven hundred men, left the Medina River on the 25th of November, and after a tiresome march over flat, boggy land, severely trying both to men and horses, reached Laredo on the 8th of December. Moving down the Rio Grande, they crossed over near the little town of Guerrero,

[1] Mark B. Lewis. *Handbook of Texas*, II, 52; for further details see Yager, "Archive War in Texas" (Master's Thesis, University of Texas, 1939).

[2] The "Santa Fe men" were the members of the Texan Santa Fe Expedition, which is recounted in the next chapter, where Jenkins in telling of John Morgan's adventures flashes back to this expedition, which was one of the causes of the Mier Expedition.

without opposition or adventure, although a force of Mexican cavalry under Canales[3] showed themselves and immediately retreated. Here they stayed one night, then recrossed and marched down the river a short distance, when, greatly to their surprise and dissatisfaction, the army was ordered home.

A determined and vindictive spirit against Mexico had been aroused to the utmost among our soldiers, and some of them were loud and earnest in their protests against disbanding. At length, without opposition from Somervell, a force of 290 men seceded from the main command, and, reorganizing, elected William S. Fisher their commander.

They marched down the Rio Grande to a point nearly opposite the little town of Mier,[4] then crossing the river went in and made a requisition upon the citizens for supplies. The Alcalde promised provisions next day, and the Texans waited for them in vain, until General Pedro Ampudia, with three thousand Mexicans, took possession of the place.

On the afternoon of Christmas Day, Fisher, leaving thirty men in charge of camp, marched with 260 across the river and on to Mier. They noted a few signs of the impending issue as they advanced, constantly running into Mexican scouts. Pressing forward, they made a straight march for the main plaza, where they were received by a heavy discharge of Mexican artillery.

Now fighting commenced in earnest. The night was dark and drizzly. Some took refuge in the stone houses, where with picks, crow-bars, and anything that could serve their pur-

[3] This was General Antonio Canales, commandant of the town of Mier. *Handbook of Texas*, I, 288.

[4] For details of the Mier Expedition see General Thomas J. Green, *Journal of the Texian Expedition Against Mier* (1845) (hereafter cited as Green, *Mier Expedition*); *Handbook of Texas*, II, 189; Houston Wade, *Notes and Fragments of the Mier Expedition* (1937) (hereafter cited as Wade, *Mier Expedition*).

pose, they cut and dug, making port holes, and fighting in
every possible way—fighting without pause for seventeen
hours! Two hundred and sixty against three thousand: Ah!
Fisher's band comprised as good material as ever marched
for battle. Some of them had fought under old [Samuel W.]
Jordan at Saltillo,[5] and all of them had proven that they
knew how to fight. "Fine marksmen, with fine rifles, fine
nerve and in a fine emergency." Rocks, rifles, and cannon
scattered fatality around, and sometimes men were fighting
hand to hand in the street. The full effect of the struggle was
a mere matter of conjecture until daylight, and then our men
could see how their old rifles "told." The cannon was silenced
until men could slip around behind houses or other refuge,
and by throwing ropes at last succeeded in dragging it out
of rifle range. The team to the artillery, and entire company
of sixty men were killed, except the captain and three
privates!

The enemy had one advantage, which was also a dis-
advantage. They could fight from the tops of their flat-roofed
houses, but as they peered over into the street below, their
heads formed excellent targets for the Texas riflemen. Very
few of the Mexican soldiers were simply wounded—the shots
nearly always taking effect in the head. The scene was one of
bloodshed and horror, which begs description. A miniature
Paris was enacted at Mier, as the sickening stream of human
blood flowed from the gutters and, curdling in the December
cold, formed great, hideous heaps, sometimes fully a foot in
height! Truly, nothing is more terrible than war!

General Ampudia sent a white flag to Fisher with fair

[5] Samuel W. Jordan and 180 Texans had fought beside the Mexican Federalists in 1839 in an attempt to set up the Republic of the
Rio Grande. Jordan defeated the Mexican Centralists in the Battle
of Alcantra on October 3, 1839, the battle of which Jenkins spoke.
Handbook of Texas, I, 25, 929.

promises and warnings, and our forces were surrendered, though many of the Texas soldiers, all scattered as they were, fought on, ignorant of the fact; most of the old soldiers whom I have heard mention it regret the surrender as entirely unnecessary and unfortunate. Our loss of life was comparatively very small, and our men as a body were still very anxious to fight bravely on. Finally, however, all surrendered.

The Battle of Mier has few parallels in our country's history. Continuous fighting for seventeen hours; 260 Texans against 3,000 Mexicans! Texas had only eleven killed and twenty-two wounded, while Mexico had about 1,200 killed, as estimated and reported by one of her own officers!

Well might she stand off and dread the fire and nerve of Texas soldiers after the Battle of Mier! No wonder that thereafter we rested two years from Mexican invasion! But despite their daring and hardihood, the brave little band of Texans soon found themselves on their way to the City of Mexico, as prisoners of war.

Meanwhile, they entered into solemn agreement among themselves that they would break at the very first opportunity, and elected Captain Ewen Cameron, one of the "bravest of the brave," as their leader. The weary, dreary marching between two lines of vigilant Mexican soldiers—a line of infantry and cavalry on either side—only served to strengthen and establish this determination, and as they trudged along on foot they watched and waited most eagerly for even a shadow of a chance to escape. It was discouraging; indeed, it was almost hopeless. Two hundred miles they marched, from Mier to Matamoros, on over a long road to Monterrey, still on to Saltillo, and then on to Salado, where they resolved to make the effort, which was brilliant and successful.

While the Mexicans were at breakfast, Cameron, throwing off his hat, gave the signal for action. "Now, boys, we go to it!" With the quickness of thought, almost, the astonished sentinels were overpowered and disarmed. The prisoners, rushing out of the enclosure, supplied themselves with whatever weapons were at hand—lances, sabers, "scopets," muskets, *anything,* and after a short, sharp conflict with the guards, they were once more free.[6]

It is said that the United States Minister to Mexico, in conversation with Santa Anna sometime before this Mier Expedition, once remarked upon the fact that in the different battles Mexico always had so many more men killed than Texas. "Oh," said Santa Anna, "that is due to the great superiority of the Texas arms." Now, these tired and defenseless Mier prisoners in their daring self-deliverance revealed wherein "the superiority" consisted much more clearly and forcibly than did the famous Mexican general, and the Minister afterward very justly inquired, "How did the Texans vanquish double their own force without arms?" Ah! Santa Anna, there are weapons more fleet and powerful than those which men can see and handle, and Texas will doubtless continue to prove her "superiority of arms" in the world's great battlefield.

But we left our prisoners free at Hacienda Salado. As they were making their departure the officer of the guards gave them a bit of timely advice, the wisdom of which was fully proved by their subsequent experience. He said, "Keep the plain, direct road. Turn neither to the right nor to the left, and there is no force this side of the Rio Grande to stop you!"

But they started for home, much divided as to what would be their safest route, though many thought that their best, and indeed last chance for freedom or life lay among the

[6] This escape took place on February 11, 1843. *Handbook of Texas,* I, 275.

mountains. Deliberation and consultation made no pause in their flight, for leaving Salado at ten o'clock, they found themselves eighty miles along the road leading to Monclova, and then all took to the mountains, thereby re-surrendering their hard-earned liberty. The mountain route was dry and rugged. The band grew tired, hungry, thirsty, and bewildered. They were forced to butcher horses in order to secure meat. Many fell in their wanderings and died. Ah! I imagine that was most trying of all! To trudge on, driven by a desperate despair, and leave comrades to a death so lonely, so ghastly, so terrible in its helpless suffering and desolation!

On the fifth day of their wretched wanderings most of the survivors were recaptured by Mexicans, who would go to the water and wait, knowing full well that the thirst would soon drive the fugitives thither.

John Tanny [Tanney],* a man from Bastrop who was a notorious whistler, was concealed in a thicket close beside the water, when a Mexican, peering in and seeing him, called out, "Ah! Mr. Whistler, how do you do? Come out, Mr. Whistler!" By the way, it was said that as the 260 Texans charged into Mier, John Tanny imitated a fife to perfection, and thus won his name of "Mr. Whistler." He was a man of whom his comrades said "fear was unknown."

On the fifth day—the day when most of them were regained—William Clopton and three or four others separated from the company, with the understanding that whoever found water would strike a fire; ascending smoke would summon the fellow sufferers together.

Wandering restlessly two days, Clopton, who was alone, lost, and almost crazy for water, saw smoke curling gracefully upward. Turning sore feet and tired body, he made painful but diligent efforts to reach the water which the signal promised. Water! Water! Water! His exhausted strength would carry him only a few steps, when he would fall, then rise and struggle onward. Water! Not a drop had he tasted in seven days!

Mexicans handed him a gourd and he drank. Then he realized that he was once more a prisoner in their hands, and around the water he recognized his fellow prisoners. Such a picture! Such a scene as presented itself in that Mexican encampment is beyond imagination or description, but not beyond sympathy or remembrance. Strong, handsome men, reduced almost to walking skeletons, confronted him, all pale, haggard, and hopeless.

Are sights and feelings such as these to be among the "half-forgotten things" of our past?

Again they found themselves prisoners of war, and were marched back toward the scene of insurrection. At Saltillo they were kept in suspense nearly half a day, and afterward learned the cause of the delay. A consultation was being held as to what disposal should be made of the prisoners. Santa Anna ordered every man shot, and the officer refusing to execute the order was cashiered. Then, by intercession of English, French, and United States Ministers, he was induced to enter into pretended terms of pardon, meanwhile sending the fatal sentence mitigated to every tenth man. As soon as the ministers learned of his treachery and cruel decree, they once more negotiated with him and once more (this time actually) he agreed to commute the sentence, but his commutation or pardon came a day too late. In the meantime, our prisoners are back at Hacienda Salado.

The "Death Lottery," as Thrall aptly terms it, has been often described, but we cannot leave our men thus. Behold the parade at Salado on the 24th of March, 1843! One hundred and seventy beans drawn from the fatal box pronounced the cruel doom of seventeen brave men, who were taken out of ranks, blindfolded, tied, and at the word, "Fire!" shot from behind.[7]

All were killed instantly except young [John Levi] Shepherd from Bastrop, who feigned death and during the night crawled off. He was taken in by a Mexican woman and cured, and then recaptured—and shot!

Was ever ingratitude, injustice, and cruelty so prominently shown as in the character of old Santa Anna, here and now and always?

A prisoner in Texas in 1836, he was shown kindness, consideration, even courtesy, and finally set free. Now, when the tables were turned, he pursued a most persistent and unrelenting course of cruelty and injustice.

The sorely tried remnant of the band of Texans were marched to Mexico City, where, under domineering officers they were placed in chains and treated worse than convicts. They were required to work hard and constantly on roads and other public enterprises.

On the 20th of September they were removed to the Castle of Perote, about halfway to Vera Cruz, and still the tyrannical life of burden and insult was imposed upon them.

In the midst of all their torture and sufferings our men always proved themselves Texas soldiers, and by that term we mean to express all of courage, fun, and fortitude that can be found in unaided human nature. Making variety in their lives by exercise of the resources within them when all around them seemed a monotonous routine of unrewarded task, hopeless bondage, and unmerited suffering. Forced to carry sacks of sand on their backs, they would manage by some means to tear them, and as they trudged along found a sly relief in the regular outpouring of a stream of sand, which

[7] The "Death Lottery," or Black Bean Episode, took place on March 25, 1843. Green, *Mier Expedition*, 169–173.

gradually lightened the heavy burdens they bore. Then there were carts for hauling rocks. Ropes were attached to the tongues and sticks tied along at intervals, to which the prisoners were required to hold, being "matched off" like horses. To one of these carts two Mexican convicts worked behind. Our Texas soldiers who pulled the sticks "in the lead" called them "the wheelers," and had great fun at their expense. Once, when on the edge of a hill, they ran away, at the same time taking care to get out of the way as the loaded cart ran off the bluff, killing one of the wheelers and injuring the other, all of which was represented to the officers as "purely accidental."

The scene now changes to one which challenges universal sympathy and indignation. One Davis,[8] a fine gunsmith from Bastrop, was required to work in the armory at Perote. He was somewhat of a genius and would furnish his fellow prisoners with little saws or files of his own construction, and with these, their chains were often cut.

One night upon the usual inspection, before locking the cells, Clopton's chain was found to be loose. The inspecting officer struck him three or four times over the head with a saber, leaving a white scar which still gleams from out his gray hairs to tell us of the outrage and indignity. With chains on both legs he was taken to a hospital, where he was confined, sick, but still in chains, for four days.

Again the scene is shifted. A high grade of typhus fever attacks them and only seven escape its ravages! Many of them die.

The authorities concluded that the damp cell floors, which were of cement, might be one cause of sickness, and so over

[8] This was William Davis, a native of Maryland. He was a member of Company C and was released on September 16, 1844. Wade, *Mier Expedition*, I, 123.

the cement they laid a plank floor on logs or "sleepers"—thus preventing contact with the damp.

John Tanny, the "Whistler," originated and engineered a plan of escape which, in its execution, serves to illustrate in a measure how capacity will sometimes assert itself despite every opposition, defying every difficulty and discouragement.

None suspected the plot, save the fifteen who occupied his cell or division and aided him in the work which was so fascinating and yet so diligently slow. A square block of the cement was carefully sawed out and removed whole, so that when replaced it would hide from superficial glance every sign of the undermining work which they cautiously carried on during the night.

Digging! Digging! Digging! Silently, eagerly, earnestly working in the nighttime, until morning. Then hiding dirt and tools between the sleepers under the plank, and resuming their chains, they would be led out to their daily labor.

Thus they dug down the wall of the fort in a slanting hole, under and then up on the outside—nearly fifty feet in all. At last fourteen of our Mier prisoners were once more free. One man refused to venture out of the cell, knowing that everything was against their escape. Great was the astonishment of officers and convicts when the cell was opened one morning and only a solitary prisoner remained where fifteen had been locked in the previous evening.

Suspicion of foul play was so strong that the officers were all arrested and sent to Vera Cruz and our prisoners worked under a new regime. Most of the "night workers" were recaptured and forced to resume the treadmill life of burden, toil and insult.[9]

Thus the ill-used band of Texans spent nearly two years,

[9] The escape occurred on July 2, 1842 [1843]. Eight of the fourteen were recaptured. Green, *Mier Expedition,* 447.

occasionally tantalized by some glowing promise of freedom in the near future. Santa Anna's birthday, the 13th of June, 1844, was celebrated as a national fete day, and this was for some time beforehand represented as the day appointed for their release. But amid the revelry and rejoicing of his subjects over his natal day, he showed no kindly feeling and sent no respite to the toilers at Perote.

· It was singular, how uniformly kind, tender, and noble our men always found the women in the land of Montezumas, while the facts of our history reveal such startling depths in the hardness and cruelty of the men.

In this same year General Santa Anna's wife died, and it was said that on her deathbed she requested her husband to liberate the Mier prisoners. Whether through her influence or not we cannot say, though we do know that the best impulses of men frequently come to them while under the shadows of sorrow; but at any rate, on the National Independence Day, the 16th of September, the Mier prisoners were set free, after all the confusion worse than death, trouble on top of trouble, pain on top of pain, sore tasks to hearts worn out with many wars, and eyes grown dim with gazing at the pilot stars. Free once more!

A man by the name of Bonnell,[10] editor, I think, of the first paper ever published in Austin, was left with the company of thirty men who kept camp when Fisher's army charged into Mier and was nevermore heard of.

His fate is among the mysteries of our past, but his name still lives in the mountain from whose summit one can take such broad survey of Austin and the surrounding country— Mount Bonnell.

Then, too, Joe Berry, one of the first gunsmiths of Bastrop, as they marched for Mier fell over a bluff and broke his thigh.

[10] George W. Bonnell was editor of the first Austin newspaper, the *Texas Sentinel. Handbook of Texas,* I, 186–187.

Six men, among whom were Bayt Berry, [Thomas] Davis, and Dr. Sinnickson, were left in charge of him at a little house in the suburbs. Next day about twelve o'clock Mexicans found them, killed the wounded Joe Berry and three others, and captured Dr. Sinnickson, while only two escaped.[11]

Some have accused Fisher and his men of remaining after Somervell left for the sole purpose of robbing Mier, furthermore saying that they disobeyed orders and deserved their suffering. Never were insinuations more unjust and untrue. If robbery was their object, why did they recross the Rio Grande and wait for the Alcalde to send supplies? And as to disobeying orders, Fisher's men received no opposition from Somerville [Somervell], or "the highest power" when they announced a determination to remain. They were "anxious to avenge the insults which the raids of Vasquez and Woll had inflicted upon Texas."

As stated in the beginning, I have lately received these details from my fellow countryman, William Clopton, and now in conclusion would like to pay fitting tribute to him as another of our brave and faithful soldiers. He came to Texas in 1837, is now past three score and ten, and has fought bravely for his adopted state all through her struggles.

He was a lieutenant in Eastland's Company on the Mier Expedition, besides taking active part in many of our principal campaigns—the Cordova, Plum Creek, John H. Moore, and others.

[11] For details see O. C. Fisher, *It Occurred in Kimble* (1937), 82–92.

CHAPTER VIII

The Texan Santa Fe Expedition

THE SANTA FE EXPEDITION has been the subject of comment and question; and while our standard histories have stated the main facts, forbearing judgment, we have found in some of the histories a few insinuations. For instance, one says, "The expedition was not only without authority of law, at the wrong season of the year without guides and provisions, but very expensive." And another says, "The wild-goose campaign to Santa Fe was an ill-judged affair," and so with other histories.

> When the die is cast
>   And the deeds are done,
> And all is past,
>   With no trophies won,

it is the rare and easy faculty of some people to make, as it were, post-mortem examinations, and sit in judgment upon the best efforts of some of our best men, generally deeming an enterprise ill-judged and wrong, if it be disastrous or unsuccessful. Views formed and expressed under such rule, however just, savor of ingratitude, and assertions should by all means be true with regard to design and effort, as well as the result. Men who were true and disinterested and ready to die for Texas suffered much and occasionally suffered defeat and persecution in lawful and laudable enterprises; this Santa Fe Expedition is a case in point.

John D. Morgan,[1] an esteemed and reliable citizen of Bastrop County for many years, my associate and friend since boyhood, is the one man of our county who now lives to recall its scenes of danger and pain. I have lately taken from his life story a full account of this interesting campaign, its design and details, and record his entire experience throughout the siege as he now recalls it.

True, we are aged and gray. The years of exposure and hardship have brought pain and suffering to us in our old age. Those same years have wrought wonderful changes in the world around us, but the facts and habits of our younger days are fixed upon our hearts and memories, so that we love to think and talk of the joys when we were boys, of all the thrilling times which are gone like boyhood's fun, and like the health and strength of young manhood.

The object of the expedition, as announced by President Lamar in his proclamation, was to get friendly intercourse with New Mexico and for protection through the intervening Indian country; it was thus deemed prudent to have military organization.

On or about the last of May, 1841, General Hugh Mc-Leod, commanding about three hundred men,[2] accompanied by one piece of artillery under Captain Lewis,[3] started from

[1] John Day Morgan was born in London, England, May 15, 1819, the son of Thomas F. and Sophia (Day) Morgan. See H. L. Morgan, "John Day Morgan," *Frontier Times,* IV, 4–8.

[2] The expedition actually started on June 19, 1841, from Kenney's Fort on Brushy Creek. Lamar's proclamation was dated April 14, 1840. There were 321 men in all. *Handbook of Texas,* II, 729.

[3] This was Captain William P. Lewis, who later turned traitor. The piece of artillery was a brass six-pounder. H. Bailey Carroll, *The Texan Santa Fe Trail* (1951), 10; George Wilkins Kendall, *Narrative of the Texan Santa Fe Expedition* (1844), I, 71.

Austin, being duly instructed to abstain from all show of hostility.

First camp was at a Waco village, located where the city of Waco now stands, and here they rested a few days without interruption or adventure. Then the men went up the Brazos to the noted hill, known as Comanche Peak, where they crossed the river and went on to the three forks of the Trinity River. Here they had another few days of quiet rest and then traveled on for the Old Santa Fe Trail. So far everything went well, and it was both interesting and unusual for our men to pass through the temporary little farms cultivated by the Indians. Corn, pumpkins, and chickens were plentiful. Their villages were all vacated, however, as the savages fled at the approach of the army.

Now their troubles commenced. At first a few stragglers were surprised and killed by the Indians, and once they faced about two hundred warriors, well-mounted and armed with bows and arrows. But the artillery and firearms kept them at a respectful distance, though our men were in constant suspense and danger. Somewhere near the Wichita River their provisions gave out, and they had to depend upon their guns to get food. This was a very trivial matter, though, for buffalo, deer, and antelope were very plentiful; nevertheless, none felt safe on account of the Indians. Men would go out in full sight of the Indians to get food, and once our men were riding side to side with a band of Indians, all chasing the same herd of buffalo. But, at length, game could no longer be found, and as they kept up their steady march for the Santa Fe Trail, men began to suffer for food, meanwhile hunting diligently for game that was now so hard to find and yet so necessary.

Morgan was making his way back to the command after a day's fruitless search for game—tired, hungry, and three or four miles from camp, when suddenly he came upon a soft-shelled turtle in the sand at his feet. Very happily he captured the reptile and carried it into camp. It was about one foot wide and made a rich supper for six of the hungry soldiers. It is a matter for curiosity to imagine how this creature came to be in that dry sand, miles from water. To the hungry men who were fast growing ravenous it seemed almost a gift direct from heaven.

At length, the jaded pack-horses were killed to satisfy the appetite of our men. About now, an intimate friend, by the name of Jones, was killed, which sad event brought a dark sorrow into camp and served to intensify the feelings of desperation that were fast taking hold of the stout hearts. Five or six dogs, which had followed their masters, were killed for meat; then came roasted terrapins, and once even a rattlesnake made supper for a starving few. Now prairie dogs became a delightful treat, as our men would occasionally find them in their eager quest for food. The pathetic look of disappointment on the face of one of the boys will ever be recalled with profound sympathy by those who saw it. Having carefully put a terrapin in the fire, he waited impatiently for it to get done. In a few minutes, coming to get his supper, lo! it had crawled off!

Three men were sent out in search of water, and on some stream in their wanderings were surprised and killed by Indians. Fifty men were detailed to find and bury their bodies, and a horrible scene greeted them, for brutal savages had cut their victims inhumanly, meanwhile using a common precaution of taking out their hearts. From all signs, the murdered men must have struggled manfully for their lives. Their horses had been killed and used as breastworks. In a few minutes the hungry men had some of this horseflesh on the fire. Alas! The men declare that in the torture of their long fast even human flesh looked tempting, and in the absence of these horses it is hard to say or imagine what might have happened at this burial of their butchered comrades!

A day or two further the command halted and after consultation agreed to separate. One hundred men under Captain Lewis, Colonel William Cook, Jose Antonio Navarro, and Dr. Richard Brenham struck out anew for Santa Fe.[4] Now was the time of "extreme extremity," for no sign of relief seemed near to the already sorely tried Texans. It is hard to place a limit upon human endurance, however, and the arduous march was prolonged ten or fifteen days longer, and they had absolutely nothing to eat during the last eight days of that period except an occasional jaded horse.

Levi Payne* and Morgan were messmates. Having drawn a pound or two of horse neck, they breakfasted on the same very economically, and put the balance into a haversack, with the agreement to separate and hunt for food individually. As it happened, Morgan carried the delicious (?) morsel of horse neck—the sole allowance of meat for two half-starved men until next morning. Dinner time found him "wearied, hungry, and almost tired of life," alone on a high hill, two or three miles from the command. Power of sense or appetite conquered every other consideration, and as he rested he picked up the neck bone and struck out for camp, which he reached about dusk. He found himself unable to wait for Payne and began to pick on the skimpy morsel of horse. Meanwhile, Levi Payne had also hunted game in vain, and came in well nigh worn out. With considerable eagerness he said, "Well, Morgan, bring out our horse neck!"

"Why, Payne, I ate it all up!" was the trying answer.

This proved too much for the starving man, and to use Morgan's own language, "He cursed me black and blue."

In vain was all pleading or apology, as Morgan tried to

[4] Colonel William G. Cook, Jose Antonio Navarro, and Dr. Richard Fox Brenham were civil commissioners for the expedition.

tell him how hard he struggled to keep the meat, how hungry he became, but the words only increased his fury, and the little morsel of horse neck proved indeed a bone of contention, because poor Payne had none.

The company of men had nothing to eat that night, but next morning another horse was sacrificed, which was soon devoured; indeed, it was gone, and they looked only upon the bones and hoop, with hunger still half-satisfied.

Once more they were on the march; soon they fell in with a few Mexicans, who afterward proved to be spies, though our men were ignorant of their true character and intention. One of these was hired to act as courier, and was sent back to McLeod with a dispatch that they were within four days' march of Santa Fe. Morgan was mounted on one of the best animals, a good mule, and this was demanded for the Mexican courier, to which he very reluctantly consented.

After a few days they struck a Mexican settlement known as Anton Chico.[5] The army presented a woebegone spectacle now, after a fast of eight days, meanwhile tugging along over rough roads and dry country. Their eyes were sunken and looked eager and cadaverous as they entered the little Mexican villa. Some sheep were immediately bought from the natives and again their long hunger was partially appeased. How the tired and starved soldiers would eat! Six men ate a sheep and a half for supper that night. Next morning they succeeded in procuring some molasses and a little meal. This was at first considered a great treat, but afterwards proved to be poisoned, or at least so it was supposed, for whoever ate of it soon grew black in the face and suffered intense agony.

Thus our men were once more freed to hunger and wait. The waiting was brief, however, for suddenly they found themselves surrounded by a mixed army of Mexicans and

[5] This village lay on the Pecos River east of Albuquerque, New Mexico.

Indians, numbering five or six hundred, who took possession of the horses and all the official papers sealed from Lamar to the government of New Mexico. At the same time Captain Lewis appeared upon the scene. He had been captured by Mexicans a few days before, and came with an order from the Governor of New Mexico to the effect that our men must give up all arms before they would be allowed to enter Santa Fe. This command produced much dissatisfaction and uneasiness, but after a little parley among the officers and privates, it was deemed prudent and best to obey.

Reinforcements from Indians and Mexicans were coming in almost hourly, and our men felt that the situation was growing more serious and desperate. As soon as the muskets were surrendered, all small arms, such as pocket pistols, bowie knives, and the like, were demanded. Again, after a vain and uneasy council, submission seemed not only best, but necessary, for the Texans were already helpless in the face of such odds. So every weapon of defense was delivered up, and now they were indeed at the mercy of the dark and motley army surrounding them, who at once proceeded to take advantage of their power.

They formed the prisoners in line in front of them. Then with guns presented, they tied eight of the men together with hands behind them. Still starving and thirsty they were marched into a house, where, through a terrible night of suspense and suffering, they were closely guarded by Mexicans.

Early next morning, without breakfast, they were led forth once more and backed against a stone wall, while Mexicans stood in double file in front of them, at a distance of about ten steps. Bill Allsbury,[6] understanding their language well, suddenly called out, "Boys, they are going to shoot us!"

[6] William W. Alsbury was official interpreter for the expedition. He was released on June 14, 1842, along with Morgan and Payne. On

The scene was one beyond the reach of language or imagination and is recalled today with a shudder by the veteran soldiers who passed through its horror. Every cry and tone of agony, all kinds of language, curses, prayers, pleadings for food and for life—all were mingled and arose in one great heart-rending wail, as the tantalized Texans heard and saw the sure approach of so terrible a doom.

Suddenly a noise from a hill on the right attracted the attention of the enemy, and in another instant they perceived a reinforcement of four or five hundred troops approaching. Allsbury, still acting as interpreter, said they had decided to await the arrival of these before executing their cruel and murderous purpose. Still, however, they stood with guns presented. After an hour's consultation they concluded to carry the prisoners to Mexico City. Still tied they were confined in the house, but a small beef was killed, upon which they were allowed a light meal. In the afternoon they marched under guard for Mexico City.

In a few days they came to what is known as "Dead Man's March," a sandy portion of the country about one hundred miles long and entirely destitute of water—a desert. Partial preparations to carry along water were made before entering upon this dry march. This supply, carried on oxcarts, in canteens, and in gourds was used with great economy, but gave out when water was still twenty miles distant.

Now suffering grew intense as the sore-footed and hungry prisoners were hurried along, every energy bent to make all possible speed to water. The Mexican guards showed no mercy toward some of the Texans who fainted by the way-

September 11, 1842, he was made prisoner by General Adrian Woll when he captured San Antonio. After being released he served as a ranger and interpreter on various expeditions against Mexicans and Indians. Brown, "Annals of Travis County," VIII, 13; *Northern Standard* (Clarksville, Texas), August 20, 1842, October 15, 1842, November 21, 1846.

side, but with a reckless cruelty shot them as they fell. Perhaps it saved the poor fellows a death of slow torture, but had they been left in peace they might have revived and struggled on to water, as did their comrades.

Nevertheless, it was not long before suffering made all equal, and the guards, impelled by the one fierce longing for water, ceased their vigilance and trudged onward, leaving behind them the weak and famished Texas boys, who labored forward until the line of march was at least a mile in length. When within a mile of water the Mexicans began to meet them with canteens and gourds full of the precious beverage. From there the Texans would get a sip—only a sip—and then it would be all gone.

Of course this was the best thing to do for men in such famished condition, but it seemed indeed tantalizing to the men, whose tongues were swollen thick and so dry that it was hard to speak. Ever and anon, though, the welcome runners would meet them with portions of cold water. At last, just ahead a beautiful sheet of water spread out before their glad eyes; here was another scene almost pathetic enough for tears, as our Texans waded into the stream and drank.

Thence they were marched to the town of Chihuahua, en route for El Paso, and there they were simply paraded without relief and housed with strict guarding; then on in a monotonous treadmill of pain to El Paso. In that town they received kindness and mercy at the hands of the natives. They ate the first bread that they had had since leaving Austin, and feasted on grapes, pears, wines, and other good things. Ah, good indeed to the half-dead soldiers, who were permitted to enjoy a few days' rest, gathering lost strength and vitality among this people who knew so well how to be kind and warm-hearted in their homes, but were always so brutal in war.

From El Paso they went on to Corretto, where they were

again well-fed but were housed in small, close quarters, almost suffocating. Then on without adventure to the City of Mexico, where they were confined and put to work on the canal surrounding the city.

At length, Santa Anna (per secretary) gave a discharge, or pass, to each of the sorely tried Santa Fe prisoners, advising them to go home and henceforth be loyal to the royal government of Mexico.

That paper Mr. Morgan still holds—an interesting relic of this unfortunate campaign. Mr. Morgan lent us the original document and we handled the old relic with a careful interest, not unmixed with curiosity. A little slip of paper, yellow and stained by time, but as we examined it our minds bridged the intervening years and in imagination we recalled the homeless, battered men, destitute of everything, in an enemy's country. How they must have rejoiced in the possession of this token of their liberty.

The Spanish reads thus:

Tejanos! La generoza nacion mejicana, a la que habeis ofendido en recompensa de un les de beneficios, os perdona. A su nombre siempre du gusto os restituyo lo libertad que perdisteis invadiendo nuestro territorio y violando nuestros hogares domesticos.

Marchad a los vuestros a publicar que el pueblo mejicano es tan generoso con los rendidos como valiente en los compos de batalla, probasties su valor probad absora su magnanimdad.

Mejico, junio 13, 1842
    Antonio Lopez de
    Santa Anna

The following is a free translation of the above:

Texans! The generous Mexican nation against which you have offended, as a reward to one of your number for benefits conferred, pardons you. In his name, which I love, I restore to you the liberty that you lost, while invading our territory, and violating our domestic firesides.

Go home and publish that the Mexican nation is as generous with the conquered, as it is valiant on the field of battle. You have proved their courage; prove now their magnanimity.

Mexico, June 13, 1842
        Antonio Lopez de
        Santa Anna

Ah, yes! Texas did bitterly prove and could in truth publish "the courage and magnanimity of Mexico" toward our soldiers. Time may in the coming years partially obliterate the memory of their persecutions; and future generations may come to regard all this as only

> An ancient tale of wrong—
> Like a tale of little meaning,
> Though the words be strong.

As long, however, as a veteran of those trying times survives he can but remember and recount the thrilling scenes of suffering and persecution—no small part of the price paid for the independence and prosperity of our Lone Star State. And though the old soldiers, retired to the quiet of their homes, may sometimes feel themselves forgotten and unknown, yet every loyal heart will grow warm in reverence, gratitude, and love at sight or mention of the faithful veterans of Texas, whose frames grow feebler with the passing months, and whose ears are now listening for "the roll of the muffled drum." God grant that when the summons comes they may have a passport from the Great Commander, which will ensure them a safe trip "through the valley of the shadow of death" into that home where they will ever more be free and happy.

The import of the pass is very characteristic of the war customs of the Mexicans in those times. See the complacent boast, "You have proved our courage!" Courage! Yes, courage or something else was required to overwhelm and imprison a small company of troops traversing their country on peaceful errand intent, and to persecute them to the limit of human endurance. And thus, no matter how brutal and ignoble a part they played in the scenes, they always publish themselves brave, victorious, and kind.

But back to our Santa Fe prisoners, who are free once more. As was ever the case, they found friends among the Mexican women. They were well-fed one day and furnished whiskey and tobacco enough to last them five or six days. And now they started out for home, passing through Puebla, Perote Jalapo, and on to Vera Cruz without adventure.

Here yellow fever caused much suffering among the already feeble men. Some died, whose names Morgan cannot now recall. From Vera Cruz on to Galveston, via schooner, and thence to Houston, which was then quite a small place. Here the little band scattered. Morgan, with two others, struck out for Bastrop County. Hatless, shoeless, and almost shirtless, they trudged homeward, finding along the road kind friends who gave them a warm and cordial welcome after their long exile. At last, footsore and tired, they found themselves at Sam Alexander's,[7] ten miles below Rutersville, where they found work. One month of rest and work at Alexander's. Ah, the luxury of good beds, wholesome fare, and healthy employment in a friendly land!

Quiet was seldom vouchsafed our people then, however, and their season of enjoyment was of short duration. Almost immediately all Texas was aroused and indignant. General Woll took San Antonio, and men rushed to the rescue.

Morgan was once again on the march. Without gun or ammunition he started afoot for the Texas army, ere long

[7] Sam Alexander lived in Fayette County. He was a justice of the peace and a captain in the Confederate Army.

overtaking and joining Eastland's company. It was hard marching on foot, but he soon got to ride some by kindly exchange, and they camped at Peach Creek, where the widow McClure lived. That kind and patriotic woman, hearing of his need, furnished him her best riding horse, having already given ten or twelve horses to the Texas soldiers. If memory is not treacherous, she afterward became the wife of General Henry McCulloch.

Pressing on they came to the scene of Dawson's massacre, which we have already described. Here Morgan recognized among the slain the body of Jerome B. Alexander,[8] son of old Sam Alexander. They soon overtook other Texas troops, among whom were Captain "Paint" Caldwell and others of the old Santa Fe sufferers. A short rest, and then all went onward in pursuit of the Mexicans, whom they overtook on the Hondo River. Here our army formed a line of battle, expecting to fight, but the Mexicans retreated. Our troops camped for the night, sending out scouts, who returned and reported the enemy still retreating. The army was jaded, and turning back, camped at San Antonio, and disbanding, the next morning found them all homeward bound.

Morgan regrets that he did not get to see Mrs. McClure and thank her for the horse, which he left on passing her home, but he has ever remembered the kindness with great gratitude. The Texas women, God bless them, were soldiers, too, in those days. In due course of time we anticipate gleaning from some of them reminiscences no less interesting than those of the old men.

Morgan left Mrs. McClure's horse at her home at Peach Creek, and plodded on foot back to Sam Alexander's, but

[8] Jerome B. Alexander came to Texas with his father in 1832. He participated in the Siege of Bexar and the Battle of San Jacinto. He was killed with Dawson's men on September 18, 1842. Dixon and Kemp, *Heroes of San Jacinto,* 181.

in a few weeks another call for men came. Captain Eastland insisted on having Morgan go with his men, although he was destitute of horse, gun, and the necessities. J. C. Calhoun,* formerly of Bastrop, agreed to furnish and equip him, and once more he marched with Eastland's men for Mexico.

In a few days the Texas army assembled at La Grange, where they received from the ladies the flag of the Lone Star. She who presented it urged them in a few fitting words to be brave and loyal to Texas. The scene impressed itself upon the memory of the soldiers. The subsequent fate of the flag may be given in brief here. At Mier it was riddled with bullets, and when the Texans found they could no longer save it they burned it, preferring anything to seeing it fall into alien hands.

From La Grange they went to San Antonio, and there, after a short time in camp, General Somervell, with his army of five hundred men, marched for Mier.

We have already followed William Clopton through the trying scenes of the Mier Expedition, and will not repeat anything concerning the movements of the main army, except as Morgan's experiences require.

They were on the Rio Grande, a few miles from Laredo, trying to crawl or creep up to the little town, expecting to find Mexican troops. As they rested a while on their horses, late one evening, Morgan, overcome with hard and continuous service, fell asleep with his bridle in his hand. He lost himself entirely, and supposes he must have slept an hour or more. Great was his surprise and dismay when he awoke and found himself alone. The army had gone! In the confusion and excitement no one of his comrades noticed or missed the worn-out soldier, who slept on, all unconscious of their movements and departure. Talk of the shifting scenes of life. Here indeed was a most bewildering change in one's surroundings. To close the eyes upon an army, and after a little nap, to open them upon solitude, vast and complete. Rip Van Winkle himself was not more surprised and startled at the work of time, during his long sleep, and seldom do men find themselves at a greater loss. Alone, at dark, in a strange country, under a cloudy sky! He knew not how to turn, and studied in blank helplessness the darkness which enveloped him, listening in vain hope to hear some echo from the advancing army, but all in vain. Every moment of delay but lengthened the distance from his comrades, and finally he concluded to let his horse take his own course.

Brute instinct, as is sometimes the case, proved more trustworthy than human intelligence. Striking a long trot and neighing all the way, the animal soon bore him safely to the army. Surrounding Laredo about daybreak they found no Mexican troops, and the women of the little village arose and went about their household affairs, never dreaming that armed soldiers watched their movements. Angry and disappointed because there was no fight, the boys turned back for camp. Morgan and a comrade stopped at a private house for breakfast, which was cheerfully given by the Mexican woman, who seemed very much alarmed and distressed on account of the presence of Texas troops in their midst. They tried to quiet her fears by assuring her that Texas soldiers were too brave and honorable to disturb women and children.

Resting in camp a while after breakfast, the two men walked up in town again, and lo, the helpless place was sacked and robbed! That, too, by some of the "Texas soldiers." Recognizing them, the women who gave them breakfast reminded them of their assurances of safety. Morgan says he turned away almost in tears to think of the exigencies of poor fallen humanity. The robbing of the town was entirely against orders.

Now on to a point near Mier. Morgan recalls the message of General Ampudia to our men: "If you want rations, come

on! I have 4,000 men who will serve you with pleasure."
Three wild cheers and the Texans voted to go over.

William Clopton has already recounted the scenes of the
struggle from his standpoint, so I will now pass on to the
interesting details of Mr. Morgan's individual experiences
after the fight. He first carried his friend and neighbor, James
Barber,[9] into the hospital, the poor fellow being wounded in
the breast. Then on his way to help others, he was arrested
by one of the guards and required to stay with the wounded.
He looked among the sufferers for Barber and hastened to his
side. The poor fellow was breathing very hard and bleeding
terribly from a bullet hole over the left nipple. Like that
"soldier of the Legion," who lay dying in Algiers, he knew he
was almost dead, and sent a message to the loved ones at
home, and gasped in death, "I die for Texas!" Surely, from
that word of the dead and dying, on through these many
years of growth and glory all Texas will thrill in memory of
that simple sentence. Bend low, oh mighty Mother State,
bend in tenderness, bend in love, bend in sorrowful pride,
and catch from the clammy lips of the dying soldiers, the
great devotion implied in, "I die for Texas!"

The next day the line was formed for Matamoros. Morgan
was once more in the hands of the Mexicans. Now came
hours of intense uneasiness for the old Santa Fe prisoners, who
knew death was inevitable should they fall into the hands of
their old persecutors and be recognized. Morgan says he
watched and prayed for some chance to escape, but all in
vain. At Matamoros, he and ten others who had charge of the
sick and wounded were allowed the privilege of the town and
suffered no great privation. In a few days, however, they
were suddenly arrested and placed in a cell about ten feet

[9] James Barber, a native of Massachusetts and resident of Bastrop,
died on March 14, 1843. Green, *Mier Expedition,* 437, 441; Wade,
Mier Expedition, I, 120.

square, with no light or anything of comfort or satisfaction. In here they contrived with a piece of an old pocket knife to get out two or three bricks and were working in patient hope to make their way out.

Late one evening the door was suddenly thrown open and the ten prisoners were rushed into the street to find themselves suddenly and completely surrounded. With a company of infantry on each side, cavalry on the outside, artillery before and behind, they were marched to Victoria. Later on they received an explanation of the sudden and strange proceedings, which was the story of the Texas prisoners rising on the guards at Saltillo. A march of eleven leagues that day after their close confinement left them very tired and low-spirited at night, with no possible chance for escape. From Victoria to Tampico suspense and despair filled their minds, for they felt that certain death awaited them at Mexico City.

Driven onward toward a cruel death, suffering meanwhile severe mental anguish and physical misery! Toil with hope may give one pleasure, but toil without hope or recompense must indeed be hard, especially when the physical powers have been taxed and tortured almost beyond endurance. Thus the little squad of ten Texans were driven along. At Tampico the natives were very kind and they were allowed some little liberty, but no possible escape. Thence, en route for the City of Mexico, they came to a little town, "Un Riel de Monte," where there was a large silver mine worked by Englishmen. These offered to assist them if possible, but no opportunity was given and on they marched to the city of doom. Arriving there, however, Morgan was much relieved to find himself unrecognized as one of the old Santa Fe band. In a few days they were sent to a small town, Reno de Melone, and put to work on the roads, etc. Here he was recognized and much disturbed in mind by one Mexican, who was disagreeably inquisitive and showed himself by no means

INDIANS. *From Homer S. Thrall,* A Pictorial History of Texas, *1879*

STORMING OF THE ALAMO. *From Homer S. Thrall,* A Pictorial History of Texas, *1879*

INDIAN HORSEMEN. *From Homer S. Thrall, A Pictorial History of Texas, 1879*

SANTA ANNA[1]

FELIX HUSTON[2]

EDWARD BURLESON[1]

BEN McCULLOCH[2]

[1] From Homer S. Thrall, *A Pictorial History of Texas,* 1879
[2] From Dudley G. Wooten (ed.), *A Comprehensive History of Texas, 1685–1897,* 1898

SAM HIGHSMITH[2]
in Santa Anna's uniform

R. M. WILLIAMSON[1]

JACK HAYS[2]

JOHN B. JONES[2]

[1] From Homer S. Thrall, *A Pictorial History of Texas,* 1879
[2] From Dudley G. Wooten (ed.), *A Comprehensive History of Texas,*
1685–1897, 1898

CADDO CHIEF

PLACIDO, CHIEF OF THE TONKAWAS

KIOWA CHIEF

From Homer S. Thrall, *A Pictorial History of Texas*, 1879

THE BATTLE OF PLUM CREEK. *From J. W. Wilbarger, Indian Depredations in Texas, 1889*

INDIAN WAR DANCE. *From Homer S. Thrall,* A Pictorial History of Texas, *1879*

COMANCHE WARRIOR. *From Homer S. Thrall,* A Pictorial History of Texas, *1879*

TRADING WITH THE INDIANS. *From Homer S. Thrall,* A Pictorial
History of Texas, *1879*

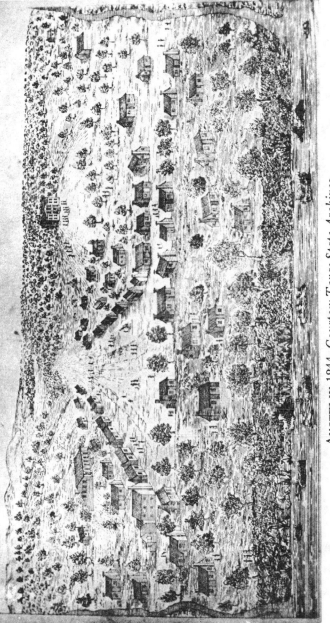

AUSTIN IN 1844. *Courtesy Texas State Archives*

TEXAS RANGERS, COMPANY D, *at Realitas, Texas, in 1887*

Back row from left: Jim King; Bass Outlaw; Riley Boston; Charles Fusselman; Mr. Durbin; Ernest Rogers; Chas. Barton; Walter Jones. *Sitting:* Bob Bell; Cal Aten; Capt. Frank Jones; Walter Durbin; Jim Robinson; Frank Schmidt. (Title and photo copyrighted by H. N. Rose.) Courtesy Ed Bartholomew, Frontier Pix, Houston, Texas

HOME OF A. WILEY HILL *built on part of the old Jenkins league in 1854*

THE FRENCH EMBASSY IN AUSTIN *built by Saligny*

HOME OF CAMPBELL TAYLOR *built on the Old San Antonio Road in Bastrop about 1840*

HOME OF COL. WASHINGTON JONES *in Bastrop built about 1840*

HOME OF JOHN HOLLAND JENKINS *in Bastrop*

JOHN TWOHIG RESIDENCE *in San Antonio before the Civil War.*
Courtesy Ed Bartholomew, Frontier Pix, Houston, Texas

satisfied when Morgan evaded his questions, assuring him he was mistaken.

And now being recognized he felt that his worst fears were about to be realized and determined to make a last desperate effort for his freedom. He found a friend who promised to hide him if he could manage to get away. Morgan and three [?] others made the effort.[10] They found two houses close together, not more than two feet apart and about ten feet high. Climbing this alley they found another height of ten feet confronted them and no way to climb—no foothold—nothing. They felt that "standing still is childish folly—going backward is a crime," and soon proved that extreme difficulties vanish before undaunted and determined effort.

See the three men pause in the face of the new obstacle! See them look up at the height that must be reached, then around in vain effort to find some means to climb, and down into the street whence they have fled! What if the guards are already upon their heels! A happy thought comes to their aid. One of the number is tall, over six feet high, and a comrade is helped to his shoulder, on which he stands. From there he can reach the battlements of the roof, then up onto the roof. Here he fastens a rope up which they all climb. And now they are close to an aqueduct. Letting themselves into this they travel down it until they find a low place. Lowering themselves they are soon out. In eager haste they strike out as nearly as they can toward the friend who has promised to hide them.

The three fugitives soon came to a paper mill, where they were invited to take refreshments, after which they were guided two leagues further, where there was another paper mill belonging to an English company. There they were hid-

[10] Apparently only two others, George C. Hatch and Neal, escaped with Morgan on April 10, 1843. Green, *Mier Expedition,* 448; Wade, *Mier Expedition,* I, 130.

den for about three weeks, thus allowing time for the excitement to subside before again exposing themselves to the danger of arrest. Under cover of darkness they were taken in a carriage to the residence of the English minister, who knew all, but received them by asking, "Where were you shipwrecked?" The Texans stood in silent and puzzled confusion. Then laughing, he said with an oath, "I guess you were shipwrecked on high and dry land, were you not?" He was so generous and kind to the homeless men, that they felt for a little time almost safe, as they were "feasted and wined" under his protection two days, gathering lost strength and courage for their dangerous homeward trip. Then he "capped all" by presenting them with twenty dollars apiece, and had them driven in a carriage out of the City of Mexico after dark. Borne three leagues from this city of terror, they were put out on the road and directed to an English silver mine, still three leagues further on. And now farewell to safety and friends. They are again left to the suspense and danger of their trying situation.

They occasionally meet patrol-guards who question them with evident suspicion, but allow them to pass on when they claim that they are miners—as instructed by the English minister. Near daylight they grew very hungry, and ate at a wayside house, then on to the little mining town. Here they were hidden for three days, when they were appointed to guard a freight of silver destined for Vera Cruz. On to Perote, and here came the greatest trial of all, for here their comrades, the remnant of the Mier prisoners, were in bondage, and the three men were in constant danger of exposing themselves. Morgan, walking along with one of the guards, was strangely startled to hear him observe in passing, "We have a good many Texans confined here!" Of course, he had to ask why and wherefore, but it was somewhat akin to torture for him to quietly listen to a disinterested, cold account of the battle of Mier and its subsequent results. He says he waxed warm at the guard's expressions of anger and condemnation toward the Texans, trying thereby to conceal the excitement and alarm of his situation. The guard wound up the history with, "Poor fellows! They fought manfully at Mier, and after all had to be brought here and put to work!"

"That is mild punishment," Mr. Morgan remarked in reply. "They ought to be taken out and shot!"

Meanwhile, their fellow soldiers—that larger body of Mier prisoners—were toiling under insult and persecution almost in a stone's-throw, and these three must hear unfeeling, barren facts, without the simple freedom of being honest and frank. Strange, to think of the power of circumstances! Soldiers with brave hearts, beating in wild, tumultuous rebellion at thought of the outrages upon their comrades— and yet they must seem only English miners, guarding their freight of silver.

They had been instructed to apply to the commander at Vera Cruz to secure his signature for their passport, and with much fear they went before him—two of them. They were kindly received, however, and their papers were fixed and they were soon in search of a conveyance. They were at supper, feeling relieved and to a certain extent safe, when a foreigner, coming in, made a special inquiry concerning "some Texans." All were mum and busily engaged eating, as the landlord scanned the crowd about the table, and knew nothing about any Texans. As soon as possible, Morgan shoved his plate back, and retreated to the street, followed by the foreigner, who seemed never to dream that Morgan was one of the objects of his search. Morgan cooly inquired of him why he was seeking Texans. "I heard there were some in there, and I wanted to hire them," he answered, but his manner was noncommunicative and evasive. He was doubtless in search of the three guards from the silver mine, our three escaped Texans, and did not know that he talked with one of them. Getting together after supper they "concluded to get out of there," and were soon on board a schooner for New Orleans.

The Yankee skipper, who was commander, "found out their little pile" and charged the very last cent for passage, twenty-one dollars apiece! Few seem as anxious to let live as they are to live, and he was doubtless as happy in the possession of his sixty-three dollars as if our men had been well-supplied. Some souls are too narrow to separate, or to distinguish between the power and the right to do a thing. But we imagine life was not half so sweet to the captain of the schooner, as it was to three Texans, enjoying the rich delights of freedom for the first time in so long. Morgan is eloquent in memory of "the fair weather and pleasant trip," and how they enjoyed it. At New Orleans, moneyless, friendless, and without clothes, they separated. The mate kindly gave Morgan supper at night, and now he found himself again alone, but this time "alone in a crowd." After a day's search on the wharf he found one schooner for Galveston, and proceeded to state his case to the captain, asking to be allowed to work his way. "No sail for two or three days, and my crew all made up," was the discouraging answer. Now came a blank search for work.

In the midst of a busy crowd an idle man is uncomfortable enough, but a suffering, needy man, is most miserable. Like Tantalus of old, who needed most, watched the flow of water as it laughingly eddied past him, almost touching his dry lips, then receding, to leave him dying of thirst. At length, while a steamboat was being loaded, the captain turned and asked Morgan if he "didn't want to work."

"Yes, and I will be glad."

"To work then."

The work was too heavy for the taxed prisoner, and in

three hours he was perfectly exhausted. Receiving three bits (12½ cents an hour) for his work, he wandered forth once more, now only hoping to find somewhere a friend, for his strength had failed him.

Wandering up and down the streets he met a Texas agent and once again submitted his forlorn condition. The man said it was utterly impossible for him to furnish the distressed man any relief, but said, "Meet me at the schooner in a few days and I'll try."

Arriving at the schooner according to appointment, he did try, and after some parley with the captain received for answer, "I am tired of taking loafers to Galveston, but go to the foremast and stay; we'll see."

Out in mid-river he was set to work "belaying"—untying and tightening ropes, and work of that sort. It was very trying to stand and work all night in his condition. In three days he landed at Galveston and again wandered out, a friendless stranger, alone and needy. At last he struck an old Santa Fe comrade keeping bar, who said he was "broke" and was working simply for his "grub," but "Come around at lunch time and I'll give you something to eat, anyhow." After two days' waiting and wandering and watching, a steamboat landed from Houston. He immediately went on board in hope of securing passage up the river. Luckily, the watchman of the boat was another old Santa Fe comrade, who kindly took him in his berth and as soon as they were under headway brought him a good supper. Ah! indeed, "A fellow feeling makes us wondrous kind." The old Santa Fe and Mier soldiers learned the value of sympathy and kindness in their hard life among the Mexicans, and could not refuse help, when they thus met, after all the trials and outrages.

At daylight the boat landed at Houston and Morgan set out in search of friends, several of whom he found, all money-less and friendless like himself. Resting one day, he started afoot for Bastrop County. He was nursed tenderly as a sick child along the road, indeed nothing of interest now came except kindness, but to be treated with consideration and confidence seemed the crowning glory of his regained liberty.

Once more Morgan stopped at his home with Sam Alexander, among old friends. After a short rest he decided to come still further, and resting again a little while at "Aunt Lookie Barton's," he came on to Wylie Hill's. Thence after another short rest he went to "Mother Barton's." She knew him afar off and came to meet him, her face aglow with all a mother's love and fear as she asked eagerly, "John, where is Jim?"

He found it hard to tell her the sad truth and the scene of the dying soldier in the hospital at Mier seemed all to harrowing for the poor woman who had been watching so anxiously for her boy to come home.

And now we quote Morgan's closing word, "so ends a trying experience through which I have been safely brought by a kind Providence."

CHAPTER IX

People of Note

THE EARLY CIRCUMSTANCES and opportunities
of a man's life naturally constitute most important and
powerful agents in shaping his future character, forming
generally a groove or channel down which his life and habits
will unconsciously, if not inevitably, drift. Not only is this
true with regard to their power in the formation of human
character, but the scenes and condition of boyhood and early
manhood form an ideal world that abides in an old man's
heart forever, growing nearer, clearer, and dearer. Whatever
changes may be wrought upon our country by enterprise and
progress, in their might and energy, there are no times like
the old times to us, and we linger fondly and constantly amid
the scenes and struggles of a past that was full of interest and
activity, as well as danger, to the old settlers. Alas! The
friends and fellow soldiers of my youth and mature manhood
are passing rapidly from earth, and it is truly said that the
company of Texas veterans grows smaller day by day.

Amid the struggles and dangers through which the old
settlers in Texas passed, no family bore a more heroic part
than did the Hornsbys. I often think what an interesting and
valuable record would be contained in a detailed account of
their thrilling experiences here, but the silence of death and
time is fast pushing the old scenes off, till some of the names
we should revere and cherish as part of our state's life and

history fall on the ear like an echo of an echo, and too often one might search in vain for grateful mention of them anywhere in the annals of our current histories.

A few words of what I know of this brave family may prove interesting to those who love our large and growing state, and who still find solid food for thought and gratitude in the thrilling scenes of her past history. All the old veterans and all the true young Texans must forever be interested in these things so closely connected with our country's present greatness. Of course, I cannot begin to wander away back into the times of strife and bloodshed and give in detail the many trying scenes through which this brave pioneer family passed.

Coming to Texas at an early day they at once identified themselves with her in all her struggles for independence and freedom, always being among the first to strike for her defense and preservation. A large family, consisting of five boys and two girls, they came and took hold of the rough wild life as true men and women, having the courage and the good sense to adapt themselves to all its circumstances. And as the years rolled on, they mastered the many difficulties and trials of the situation, rising above its discouragements.

The new era of peace and prosperity found them all alive and prosperous, and now comes the tragedy all untimely and terrible as such things always are. It was after 1845. A time of peace was here. Men had almost forgotten the old days, when savages lurked in cruel malice, waiting for the unwary and the helpless. The youngest boy, Daniel, and a Mr. Adkinson went out fishing on the river. Mike Hornsby, who told me this incident, says he remembers very distinctly the morning they left home. He was a very small child, but begged and cried to accompany his Uncle Daniel on the fatal excursion. His request was refused, but the desire and grief with the added horrors resulting fixed the facts upon the child's mind.

144

The two young men went unarmed, without fear or suspicion, and soon settled down to fish under a high bluff on the river's bank. No note of warning mingled with the liquid flow of the winding waves; no whisper of treachery or murder came in the south wind's kiss—no shadow dimmed the spring sunshine. But from behind, a cruel death came suddenly and surely. A band of Comanches slipped up and announced their deadly purpose by sending a shower of arrows down upon their unarmed and helpless victims. Hemmed in as they were on the river's brink, the water was their only refuge and into its depths they sprang, and made vigorous strokes for the opposite bank. Immediately at their heels came the band and into the river they also plunged. The lifeless bodies of the unfortunate young men bore terrible evidence of the ending of that dark day's deeds.

It seemed that they would come in reach of young Adkinson and strike or cut him with their sharp arrows and spikes, as his body was badly gashed, and finally coming to shallow water they overtook, killed, scalped, and as a crowning outrage, disemboweled him. His body was quickly and easily found. It was a harder matter to learn anything of the fate of young Daniel Hornsby, however. From all signs he escaped the ruthless touch of their barbarity, and they never caught him at all. Mercifully the cooling waters had closed over him, giving him peaceful escape from so violent a death. After considerable difficulty, delay, and agonizing suspense, the poor dead boy was drawn from his watery grave and thus came the highest sacrifice borne by this heroic family![1]

Texas history holds the name of Colonel Jack Hays prominently among those of her brave soldiers. Coming from Tennessee to Texas before her annexation to the United

[1] One of the last Indian murders in the Travis–Bastrop County

States, he was commissioned by President Houston to raise a ranging company for the protection of the western frontier. This is said to be the first regularly organized company of rangers in the service of this western country. John Wilbarger, in his recent *Indian Depredations in Texas,* says, "With this small company, for it never numbered more than three score men, Colonel Hays effectually protected a vast scope of frontier country, reaching from Corpus Christi, on the gulf, to the head waters of the Frio and Nueces Rivers."[2]

From a number of his brave adventures and raids I have procured the following account from my old fellow soldier, [Cicero] Rufus Perry,* who participated in the scenes herein described. The old soldiers call it "Hays's Fight on the Pinta Trail," which took place near the head of Salado Creek. In the summer of 1844 a company of only thirteen men under Colonel Hays started from camp at Hackey Madea in search of Indians. After traveling for some time, they discovered five Indians some distance off, close to a thicket. Instead of attacking these five, Hays came right on through the brush and charged the main band, which was forming line behind the others. The Indians charged, too, and ran right through our lines two or three times. Three or four warriors would come together. Here Colt's five-shooter was first used — two cylinders and both loaded. The Indians were astonished and terrified at the white men shooting their "butcher knives" at them, and soon retreated in confusion and dismay. One of the boys killed their chief and this added to their consternation. However, they fought as they retreated, the running fight continuing for about ten miles. Sam Walker and Ad Gillespie determined to kill one Indian apiece and started

---

area, this event occurred on June 7, 1845, at Blue Bluff, eight miles down the Colorado from Austin. Brown, "Annals of Travis County," V, 16; Wilbarger, *Indian Depredations in Texas,* 260.

[2] Wilbarger, *Indian Depredations in Texas,* 72.

146

RECOLLECTIONS OF EARLY TEXAS

after them. The Indians, resorting to an old trick, fell in behind them and speared the both severely, but both got well, and lived to give faithful service for Texas afterward. Finally both of them were killed in the Mexican War.

In the fight two horses and saddles were taken, but not one Indian. On the next day two of the men, Peter Fohr[3] and Andrew Erskine,[4] who were left at camp during the fight, saw five Indians coming toward the camp and killed all of them. Peter Fohr was killed and Andrew Erskine wounded. See what odds here! Eleven white men against sixty Indians out in the open prairie, and back at camp two white men against five Indians!—and this was only one adventure of the many through which they passed.

In 1847 General Winfield Scott called for volunteers. Colonel Hays took half the force and made a raid into Mexico while [Col. Peter H.] Bell held the other half on the frontier for protection. The first fight of any note made by Hays in Mexico occurred then, and the whole campaign or raid was full of interest. At Vera Cruz they took line of march for Mexico City, and being the first soldiers after Scott they naturally anticipated an attack all the time. Their fears were, however, unfounded and from Puebla they were ordered one hundred miles south.

The object of this raid was the capture of Mexican robbers. At this time the guerrilla band might have been termed an organized army, working systematically and with telling effect upon the peace and prosperity of Texas. Traveling thus far without sign of danger or trouble of any kind, the officers grew very lenient—even lax—and our men enjoyed every privilege.

[3] Peter Fohr, a Texas Ranger, was a resident of Bexar County.
[4] Andrew Nelson Erskine was born in West Virginia in 1826. He moved to Seguin, Texas, in 1840 with his parents. See Blucher Erskine, "Andrew N. Erskine," *Frontier Times,* IV, 40.

At Matamoros they found abundant quantities of whiskey and various Mexican drinks, as well as government stores and fine horses stolen and held by the guerrillas. The bowl went merrily around, and next morning they marched back for Puebla, thoroughly out of fighting trim in every respect, and seldom did soldiers ever march in greater confusion and disorder.

Captain [Jacob] Roberts' company was in advance, and the "lively" little squad suddenly received a charge from a guerrilla band, numbering about eight hundred! They retreated in double-quick time back to the main army. General Walter P. Lane ordered the discharge of artillery, and the men who manned the cannon were too drunk for action! There was no time for deliberation or delay. The need of the hour was action, prompt and voluntary. Hays and two or three others, dismounting, fired the cannon and then charged with about one hundred men right into the enemy's ranks. Meanwhile, excitement and danger had in a measure sobered the men. As the fight continued up a long slant or hill, Lieutenant Ridgeby, a brave soldier and an officer from the United States Army, called out, "Boys, I am shot all to pieces!" Upon being urged to go back and find a doctor, he answered, "No, I will fight till I die," which he did.

At the top of the hill they received a fresh charge from another band, and Hays ordered a retreat. Now they fought between two guerrilla forces, and soon it was a hand-to-hand fight, in which the Texans and Mexicans were all mixed and commingled, going and coming. Captain Roberts had his horse shot from under him just as the retreat commenced, and several of our men were killed, but another discharge of artillery finally dispersed the Mexicans.

At Matamoros a good many oxcarts had been "pressed" and loaded with government arms, and now on the homeward march the teams began to fail, until at night orders were received to burn the carts, break the sabers, and destroy all the confiscated property, which had become only an impediment to the progress of the army. It was very dark and a slow, miserable drizzle made the surrounding night seem indeed "a darkness to be felt," as the blaze of the burning carts flared and flashed in the gloom. Just as the fire was getting under good headway a fresh charge from an unknown enemy came, and men stood in doubt while bullets whistled up and down. The volley was quickly over, however, and upon investigation loaded muskets were found to have been burned with the carts, causing the "fresh charge." Marvelous to say, nobody was hurt.

From Puebla on to Mexico City, where Scott held headquarters, they traveled slowly but surely. At dusk one evening they marched for Toulon Singo. Traveling in a gallop across a mountain it was wonderful to note the variations of temperature or climate, even in a single night. At dark they left tender young orange shrubs, with leaves just "wooed from out the bud" by the balmy air and dewy freshness of springtime. On they galloped, and at midnight they found themselves in an icy winter clime on the summit of the mountain, the weather literally freezing cold. Still forward and daylight revealed to them a glorious summer land, where they could gather ripe oranges in passing.

Finding no guerrillas at Toulon Singo, they kept an unbroken march on to Secqualtapan, about one hundred miles distant, and there they found a very large guerrilla band, quartered or stationed over the town. By thorough and cautious reconnoiter of the place they soon learned the whereabouts of the different guerrilla quarters, and the command scattered, different companies going to different localities.

Colonel Ford was adjutant. Captain Roberts being sick, his company was commanded by Lieutenant Dan Grady,* my neighbor, who is another loyal and devoted Texan, the greater part of whose life has been spent in active service for our state. His company charged upon one of the guerrilla quarters, and one man was instantly killed and several were wounded. The Mexicans had every advantage, being safely housed, and Grady soon ordered Private Swope to fire their quarters. Climbing from the tremendous gate to the stone wall, thence the shingles were easily fired, as the roofs were very low. No sooner did the shingles blaze than a white flag was shoved out in token of surrender. The bodies of the dead, with the quarters, were burned by the time the prisoners and wounded could be taken out. This occurred in one of those long dry spells so common in that section, and timber burned like powder. Sheets of burning shingles were raised by heat and flame and borne to adjacent roofs, which in turn would blaze and burn like a flash. Destruction of the town was so rapid that the army had to tear down buildings in order to save quarters for the night. Upon leaving the next morning, another touch of the match, another blaze, and the army of Texans looked back as they marched out to see only a mass of smoke and ashes, where yesterday stood a town.

Our entire body of men were cavalry, while the captured guerrilla forces were on foot, but commanded by their own officers, who quirted them along as if they had been beasts of burden, keeping them in a trot along with the cavalrymen, meanwhile bearing the wounded men on litters. Four men were thus hurried forward with a litter until broken down, then four fresh ones would pass under and take the burden, while the tired ones would trot on without a halt in ranks! And thus the march was continued to headquarters in Mexico City.

While there one of our men, an old gray-haired Dutchman, was found in one of the hardest, roughest portions of the city, murdered—terribly cut and mutilated. Our soldiers avenged his death by killing a few in the immediate locality. This in turn aroused others, until about forty Mexicans were killed as a result of the death of the old Dutchman.

Five or six hundred soldiers collected and were eager to rob the whole place and kill its inmates, and only firm interference of the officers subdued the spirit of insubordination until they reached Texas soil again.

Now came one of the last, as well as most effectual raids ever made against the Indians. It occurred in 1847. Captain Samuel Highsmith[5] had commanded a company under Hays during the Mexican War. It was detached to protect the frontier, which was still often and severely troubled by Indian invasion. The company was stationed near what is known as the "Enchanted Rock," fourteen miles from Fredericksburg, on Crabapple Creek. This rock, by the way, is a very remarkable freak of nature, being solid granite and covering an area of six hundred and forty acres of land, it is studded here and there with a kind of glittering material that resembles diamonds.

All through this vicinity the Indians had found easy victims among the German settlers. Captain Highsmith, camping on Crabapple Creek, sent out a small scouting party, consisting of white men and one Delaware Indian. Returning in a short time they reported a large Indian trail coming from the Fredericksburg vicinity.

Highsmith started out immediately with his company, following the trail with all possible speed. They soon came upon about forty Waco Indians encamped on the Llano

[5] Samuel Highsmith was born in Boone County, Kentucky, in 1804. See *Handbook of Texas*, I, 809; Ray, *Austin Colony Pioneers*, 307–308; *Telegraph and Texas Register* (Houston), April 17, 1839; Thrall, *A Pictorial History of Texas*, 552; Maude Wallis Traylor, "Captain Samuel Highsmith, Ranger," *Frontier Times*, XVII.

River. The warriors were at dinner and did not perceive the whites until they were right on them and in gunshot distance. Highsmith, however, thought it best to parley, wishing to discover the character and intentions of the band before any attack was made upon them. So John Connor, the Delaware scout,[6] was appointed spokesman and interpreter. He first called for the chief of the Wacoes. Upon appearance of the old chief a few questions were asked, which the chief answered in a surly, defiant manner. Connor, seeing that they were hostile, warned Highsmith to open fire upon them.

Noting the words of the Delaware, the Waco chief, helpless to give other aid to his men save that of warning, placed his hand behind his back and motioned for his men to run. Seeing the preparations among the whites for battle, he himself turned to run, but was killed instantly by Highsmith as he turned. When this happened the Indians retreated in disorder and confusion with the whites at their heels, firing as they ran. Without thought of anything but their great and imminent danger, the Indians ran to the river, which was one hundred yards wide at that point, and plunged wildly into its depths.

The whites stood on the bank and shot at them as they swam for the opposite side, killing all forty of them, except some four or five who escaped. Some of the warriors would try to turn and shoot from the water with their bows, but this did not work.

---

[6] John Connor was also interpreter when a peace treaty was signed on October 9, 1844. He was a guide on the Chihuahua–El Paso Expedition under Jack Hays in 1848. On February 7, 1853, he was granted a league of land by a special act of the Texas Legislature and was required to pay no dues or office fees. H. P. N. Gammel, *The Laws of Texas, 1822–1897* (1898), III, 1402–1403; J. E. Haley, *Fort Concho and the Texas Frontier* (1952), 18; Harry M. Henderson, *Colonel Jack Hays, Texas Ranger* (1954), 93; *Texas National Register* (Washington-on-the-Brazos), 1845.

This band of Indians was supposed to have been the same party that attacked Captain Bartlett Sims* while he was out surveying and killed two of his men.[7]

This raid seemed to have been exactly what was needed, and did much toward securing peace and safety along the frontier. A bare record of this and similar raids, where the Indians were the sufferers, would arouse some sympathy for the savages, perhaps, in the minds of those unacquainted with the terrible outrages and murders perpetrated by them upon our early settlers. We, however, who have lived amid the horrors of their cruelty and have gone out to find and bury the maimed and disfigured bodies of our friends who were victims of their hatred, can understand and recall the indignant and burning desire to pursue the savages and rid our country of such persecution and death.

It seems but justice to insert a few words by way of tribute to Judge N. W. Eastland,* now a resident of Bastrop County, who has given and suffered much for Texas. He is now eighty-two years old, having served under Andrew Jackson in the Seminole War. He came to Texas in 1833, and has been a devoted and active participant in all of her struggles and triumphs since then. A gentleman of fine military education, of varied experience, and rare conversational powers, he is even now, despite his extremely advanced age, agreeable and entertaining, giving in detail and from personal experience, many important incidents connected with our past history.

Two sons and a brother went out from the old man's

[7] The fight mentioned by Jenkins took place in October of 1846. There were four men in the party: Sims, his nephew, Grant, and Clark. Sims was the only man to escape. Wilbarger, *Indian Depredations in Texas,* 286.

house to battle for Texas, and were killed. His oldest son, Robert M. Eastland, a man of sterling qualities, was killed in the Dawson Massacre, but made a brave and heroic struggle for his life. Nat [Nathaniel W.] Faison,* who is still living, saw him fall. He says Robert Eastland was first struck by a grapeshot, which broke his leg just above the ankle. In this condition he leaned against a mesquite tree for support and fought on, loading and shooting several times, until the Mexicans crowded on him and killed him.

By the way, Judge Eastland had quite an interesting experience about the time of Fannin's massacre in 1836, which is worthy of note. He joined Fannin's body of men near Goliad, just as the officers were about to hold a council as to what measures of action to adopt. Having been an old friend and roommate of Fannin at West Point, he was invited to be present at this council of officers, by Fannin, whose tent served as council chamber. The discussion was hot and earnest. At last a vote was taken as to whether they should take immediate action—that is, go on that night, evacuate Goliad, and attack the Mexican force of cavalrymen, then about six miles off, or wait until daylight for further action. The latter motion prevailed, although a number of the officers, together with Eastland, were in favor of the former plan. Alas! If they had pursued that plan, Fannin's unfortunate band might have been spared their terrible fate, for the Mexican forces would have been surprised; besides, during the night they received heavy reinforcements under General Urrea, thus increasing the fearful odds that awaited the brave band of Texans, whose names will be cherished among the many martyrs to Texas' liberty.

They waited for daylight, and after evacuating Goliad started east to attack the army. Judge Eastland belonged to the advanced guard, a company of cavalrymen under Albert C. Horton, whose name is not unknown to Texas history, and whose conduct some have criticized, though unjustly, for he acted as he was compelled by circumstances.[8] Truly, "a small incident brings wonderful results," and Eastland's experience, then, is a case in point. His horse having foundered, his company left him, and he thought he would have to remain with the main army. An old soldier seeing his trouble, however, informed him that nothing was better medicine for a foundered horse than running, and advised him to try it, saying he might thereby not only cure the animal but also overtake his company. So putting out at full speed he did accomplish both results, and was once more at his proper post in Horton's company.

As they left Goliad, they came first to the fresh trail showing the march of a larger reinforcement of Mexicans, and very soon could see Mexican spies going to and fro. Everything indicated not only the close proximity of the enemy, but eager interest and action. The company of scouts halted at a fire they found in their march, when suddenly a loud and terrible roaring was heard. Some said it was the noise of an approaching storm from the north, but it proved to be the tread of the Mexican army bearing upon Fannin's doomed band. This was indeed a critical situation. Horton's small company of men found themselves separated from the main army of Texans by a force of three or four thousand Mexicans. They stood helpless, but unhurt, until two or three charges had been made. They could see some sign of the brave fight made by Fannin's men, as ever and anon from the din and smoke of battle a Mexican horse would come charging back without a rider, but they knew the terrible

[8] This company of cavalry arrived at Goliad on March 16, 1836, but after a skirmish with the Mexicans on the next day it was sent to examine a route for retreat, thus missing the horrible Fannin Massacre. Horton was criticized for not trying to return to the main army, but this would probably have resulted in the loss of his entire company. See *Handbook of Texas*, I, 840.

odds of the struggle, and felt that the fate of their fellow soldiers was sealed.

Meanwhile, they soon realized that lingering there would endanger their own lives, so they retreated. In the course of their retreat they met Carra Bahalle, a notorious and wealthy Mexican, who questioned them with interest concerning the cannonading, which he had heard. Fearing betrayal, they prudently withheld from him the true state of affairs, informing him that they supposed it to be a little fight at sea between Texas and Mexico. At the same time they repeated to him a current rumor that Houston was on his way with an immense army to attack Mexico. This company of scouts escaped almost miraculously, as it were, for after the war Eastland met Bahalle and learned that a Mexican force came to his ranch immediately after their departure, but made no pursuit, as Carra Bahalle, knowing nothing of the truth, simply repeated to them the report concerning Houston's coming.

Another family who ranked among the bravest and best of our Texas soldiers and pioneers was that of the Neills. Colonel James Neill, already spoken of, came to Texas in a time of war, but he already bore the scars of wounds received in service under General Jackson in 1812—he was wounded in the Battle of Horseshoe Bend, again in the taking of San Antonio, and also in the Battle of San Jacinto.

It is not recorded, but is nevertheless a fact that Colonel Neill fired the first gun for Texas at the beginning of the revolution—the famous little brass cannon at Gonzales.

A visit from his son, George Neill,[9] a man every whit

[9.]George Neill participated in many of the early Indian fights of the Texans. He was in the Battle of Plum Creek and a Texas Ranger in Hays's company, in which he participated in the Battle of Bandera suited to the scenes of his early manhood, possessing by nature the faculty not only to endure, but even to enjoy the struggles of frontier life, brought up many old times and faces.

Talking with George Neill made me think of "mustanging." I expect there are very few of the readers of my reminiscences who know the plan we used to pursue in taking the herds of wild horses that were wont to graze through these parts, and I imagine a few words in description thereof will not be uninteresting, at least to the young men and boys of Texas.

The first item was a mustang pen, or stronghold, which was built on some one of their regular passways, cautiously avoiding cutting timber, for at any sign of civilization a mustang is "off." The pen was of very large, heavy logs, generally enclosing a small circle—small because it was important that the frantic herd should have little room for play—a very short run would give them striking force enough to knock down almost any wall, however strong. The wall was ten or fifteen feet high and raised from the ground all around, so that when the heavy bars were closed on the herd and a horse was to be taken out, men tied and dragged it out underneath the wall. Then attached to the sides were the "wings" which extended a mile or two in both directions, generally embracing the entire range.

The common little partridge net furnishes a very good illustration of the pen, plan, etc. Horses well-fed and fast were kept and trained for that special purpose, and the herdsmen going around "afar off" would ride in behind the herd, which would break for their lives, and then, "Away to the chase!" Sometimes the run was for miles and miles over hill and valley, going at full speed and crowding considerably as we neared the bars.

Once a few of the boys had a whipping race back to their mustang pen, which is rather more amusing to us now than it was then to the runners.

In July of 1842 four men—George Neill, James Curtis,* and two Mexicans, went out on Plum Creek Prairie to herd and drive in mustangs, having first prepared a pen. As usual, they went on fine horses and without arms or any encumbrance, so that the run might be unhindered. When about fifteen miles from home they were surprised by a large band of Comanches. Nothing but the superior fleetness and endurance of their horses saved them from falling into the hands of the Indians, whose horses failed when about one and a half miles from the pen. All of the men except James Curtis were wounded, and arrows were sticking in all the horses when the race was done.

These races for life were not uncommon, however, along in those times, and many men were not even allowed to run for their lives, but surprised and overpowered, fell without warning or help. Ah! "The voice of many a brother's blood called from the ground," as it were, to us who knew them, seeming to plead for at least the simple boon of remembrance. Hard lives were suddenly cut short, and the manner of their deaths was hardest of all. There is a queer but strong sympathy which sometime forces my mind to dwell upon, work out, and try to record the details of these sad tragedies of my early days, and it seems to me the names of men who thus fell, innocent, brave, and defenseless, should at least be enrolled among the great ones of the earth.

CHAPTER X

Recollections at Random

IN THE REMAINDER of my personal reminiscences of Texas history, I will say that I do not henceforth confine myself to Bastrop County, but will speak of men and circumstances as they came into my life, were connected with my experience, and now come into my memory. Perhaps they may come with irregularity and confusion, but they are none the less vivid and true, and this record is given with the double desire of casting a mite into the *Treasury of Truth* and rescuing from threatened oblivion incidents of interest connected with the history of Texas.

I will first tell of the Karankawa Indians,[1] whom I have never mentioned, and whose career among us was not without interest. They might well have been termed giants, for they were most magnificent men in size and strength, seldom below six feet in height. They lived for the most part along the coast and were most remarkable in their skill as fishermen.

When on the warpath their costume and general appear-

---

[1] The name Karankawa comes from the Coahuiltecanian word "comecrudo," meaning "dog lover." This could mean either liking for the dog as a pet or enjoyment of the dog as a food. They were known to be cannibals. Pioneers recount that their abominable body odor caused horses and cattle to run away from them. The tribe fled to Mexico prior to Texas statehood. Roy Bedichek, *Karankaway Country,* (1950), 8–11; *Handbook of Texas,* I, 938.

ance were quite peculiar and striking. Each warrior painted one-half of his face black and the other red. Then he was entirely naked except for a breechclout or apron, with its long sash, bordered with tassels and fringes, almost touching the ground behind.

He carried a bow as long as he was tall, with arrows of proportional length, with which he could kill game a hundred yards distant. I knew an instance of the terrible force of these arrows which is worthy of note. Aimed at a bear, three years old, that had taken refuge in the top of a tree, it went through the brute's body and was propelled forty or fifty yards beyond.

It was said by early settlers that they were cannibals, and I remember the experience of one man which corroborated the truth of this report. He was a large, fleshy Scotchman, John Lawrence by name, who worked on Mother's place, and I have often heard an account of this adventure from his own lips. A band of Karankawas having captured him, they immediately began preparations to eat him, declaring, with evident sincerity, that he was, "A nice fat man—good." The fire, which was to roast or broil him, was beginning to burn and, being securely tied, Lawrence was already anticipating the excitement and novelty of such a death, when he was rescued by a party of white men. He always believed that they would certainly have feasted on his huge form, and felt, as it were, that he was snatched from their jaws.

They frequently came to Matagorda and other interior points, and generally assumed a friendly attitude toward the Americans, but were always bitter in their hostility against Mexico. This was not without cause, for in the early settlement of Matagorda many of them were murdered and cruelly treated by the Mexicans, and it is a well-known fact that an Indian seldom forgets or forgives an injury.

A company of Mexicans came into Matagorda for the

purpose of trading, without fear or any evil design. They barely escaped with their lives, for a band of these Karankawas, under their old chief, Hosea Marea, all painted and armed for battle, appeared upon the scene and would have killed the entire company of traders without delay or mercy, but for the timely intercession of the Texans.

At length, they began to show a spirit of hostility toward Texas. I cannot now give details of all the murders and invasions of which I knew them guilty, but two of them are especially fresh in my mind, and will serve to mark the cause of their defeat and subjugation.

Five men had brought a boatload of supplies for immigrants, and were lying near the mouth of the Colorado, when they were surprised by a band of the Karankawas and all killed except one, a Mr. Clark,[2] whose escape seems almost a miracle. Receiving a shot which broke his thigh, he crawled out of the boat into a canebrake, and lay there alone and defenseless, bleeding terribly. In this condition he was striving to stop the fearful flow of blood from his wound, when hearing a slight noise, he looked out and saw two dogs coming upon his trail. His chance for escape seemed indeed a desperate one now, for he felt confident that the Indians had put the dogs upon his tracks, but his relief may be imagined as time passed and no pursuers came. He was in a short time picked up by Americans, and lived to engage in many of the after-struggles of our country, being alive at the close of the Confederate War, when last heard from.

Again, Indians fell upon a white family by the name of Cavina[3] and massacred the entire household except the

[2] This fight with the Karankawas took place in 1823. Two of the men killed were Loy and Alley. Clark received seven wounds. See Brown, *History of Texas*, I, 114n.; *Handbook of Texas*, I, 355–356; Wilbarger, *Indian Depredations in Texas*, 200.

[3] This was the family of Charles Cavina, who was one of Austin's

father, who made his escape unhurt, and a little daughter five or six years old, whom they left for dead, having first shot her through the body with one of their tremendous arrows. She recovered, however, lived to womanhood, and as far as I know is still living.

The citizens took prompt measures to avenge and subdue this spirit of cruelty and hostility. Captain Aylett C. Buckner raised as large a force of men as possible and went out in pursuit of them. He attacked them on Battle Island, four or five miles from where Matagorda now stands, and, after a considerable fight, defeated them, forcing them into a treaty. Williams, a participator in this battle, gave me the particulars. He said that after the struggle a squaw with a baby on her back sprang up from some drift where she had been concealed. The women were very large, and he mistook this one for a warrior, so without pausing, shot. Great was his surprise and regret to find he had killed a mother and her child—the bullet having passed through both. The treaty made on Battle Island was religiously kept by the remnant of this giant tribe, which, I believe, is now almost extinct.

I have seen the defeat and subjugation of three tribes here in Texas— Lipans, Karankawas, and Tonkawas. The first named, I believe, are now totally extinct. They possessed finer, more regular features and were the most intelligent and ambitious Indians I ever knew; they were second only to the Karankawas in physical size and strength. The Tonkawas were small and comparatively insignificant, though

Old Three Hundred. The family lived near Live Oak Bayou on "Old Caney Creek," but it is not known which of the thirty Texas streams known as Caney Creek it was. About seventy Karankawa Indians attacked Cavina's household and killed Mrs. Cavina and three daughters. A Mrs. Flowers was killed nearby. Captain Buckher and his company attacked the Indians and killed between forty and fifty of the band. The Cavina Massacre and Buckner's fight took place in 1831. Wilbarger, *Indian Depredations in Texas*, 209–210.

stronger in number, and living among the white settlers more than other tribes.

In the foregoing description and account of the Karankawas, my memory has lately been somewhat refreshed and aided by conversation with Judge N. W. Eastland, who in an early day lived near this giant tribe, and was thereby familiar with their peculiarities of form and custom.

In the interim between 1839 and 1846, the section of country in and around Austin was the scene of many deeds like this, and nearly always the perpetrators would go unmolested, for never could thieves and murderers find safer refuge than the mountains and cedar brakes about Austin.

There was a man by the name of Schriff killed near Barton Springs in 1837 or 1838.[4] He went riding out one evening and did not come home, so immediate search was made for him. From signs, they found where his horse had run, and could trail the animal all through the country, but for some time were unable to discover sign of the missing man. At last, coming back to the place where the horse had first taken fright, they made more thorough search and found him dead and scalped in a hollow on the roadside. He had evidently been going up a steep hill when shot, and, had fallen and rolled into the hollow, and therefore all effort to find the body was, for a time, in vain.

The county judge, by the name of Smith, was another victim. Taking his little son behind him, he rode a short distance out of town to see about stock or something and was killed in a little mot of timber by Indians, who carried off the child.[5]

[4] This may have been Thomas Shuff, who was killed on Barton Creek in the spring of 1842. Wilbarger, *Indian Depredations in Texas*, 274.

[5] This Judge James Smith, not to be confused with Judge James Smith of Bastrop County, lived one-half mile north of the Colorado River at the north end of Montopolis, now part of Austin. At the

Again, an old man by the name of White, who once lived in Bastrop County, was forced to abandon his home out on Shoal Creek and move his family into town through fear of Indians. He continued work, however, on his land out there, and with two other men went out one morning to work. He was somewhat used to the tricks and dangers of the times, cautious and nearly always prepared. In the evening, taking his rifle, he walked out to look around for game and to see that the coast was clear. In a few minutes the two men heard a report which they recognized as the crack of his rifle—a very fine, large-bored gun, and immediately another firing followed. His two friends hastened into town, reported, and soon a crowd was upon the scene, finding signs of a considerable fight, but another man lay dead and scalped.

A Mr. Joynes, living in Austin, was standing out in his front yard, holding his little child in his arms, when a band of Indians came riding up to the house and introduced themselves as Tonkawas, "friendly Indians." He stood till one of the warriors made a grab at the little child and tried with all his might to pull him out of the old man's arms. The father held to his child, however, and at length succeeded in wrenching him from the Indian, and ran for the house, whereupon they shot, killing him at his own door.[6] I received the particulars of this from Colonel Joe Lee, who was the first

time of his death, in January of 1842, Smith was Chief Justice of Travis County. He might have escaped the Indians pursuing them, had not his horse run under a low limb and thrown them off. The son was captured and a year later ransomed by John Roland for $60. He was still living in 1900. *Austin City Gazette,* January 27, 1841; Hardy, "A History of Travis County, 1832–1865" (Master's Thesis, University of Texas, 1938), 44, 85; Wilbarger, *Indian Depredations in Texas,* 140–141.

[6] This took place on July 10, 1842. Judge Joynes, or Jaynes, lived where the Austin State Hospital for the Insane now stands. Brown, "Annals of Travis County," IX, 35, 64; Wilbarger, *Indian Depredations in Texas,* 141–142.

man to reach the scene of the tragedy. He says he found the mother trying in vain to pull an arrow out of her child's arm, while her husband lay dead at the door.

A widow, Mrs. Simpson,[7] who lived at the edge of Austin, suffered greatly. Her little son and daughter were out at play not far from the house and were captured and carried off by a band of Comanches. This occurred only a day or two after Hays's fight on the Guadalupe, and the Indians of course had vengeance and wrath in their hearts, so that people naturally expected that little mercy would be shown the children. As quickly as possible, however, a body of men went out from Austin to overtake the Indians, and, if possible, regain the captives. On the trail as they went up the river through the mountains, they occasionally found pieces of the girl's dress, which had been torn off by thorns and branches in the flight. These shreds of calico were all, however, and finally the trail was lost, so the men were compelled to return to the bereaved mother with no tidings of her little ones.

Some time afterward the boy was regained. He gave a touching account of what he saw and felt while in the hands of the savages. He said his sister seemed to be crazed from terror, and would persist in fighting the Indians most furiously all the time, despite his repeated warning and begging her not to provoke them, assuring her that they would certainly kill her if she did not become calm and less troublesome. Still the poor child fought and struggled, till, when five or six miles above Austin, two Indians dragged her off over a mountain. They returned to the band bearing a fresh scalp to tell the tale of horror concerning the fate of his sister.

[7] Mrs. Simpson lived on West Pecan Street, three blocks west of Congress Avenue. The children were Emma, aged 14, and Thomas, aged 12. Thomas was ransomed at Taos, New Mexico, in 1844. The kidnaping took place in the summer of 1842. Brown, "Annals of Travis County," IX, 30; Brown, *Indian Wars*, 101–102; Wilbarger, *Indian Depredations in Texas*, 139–140.

Guided by his description of the locality, the neighbors once again took a search for her body, and found a skeleton which was supposed to have been that of the little Simpson girl.

Sometimes the citizens would arouse themselves and make extra effort to secure peace to their homes and security to their lives.

In 1840 or 1841 the Indians made a raid of unusual atrocity and a squad of men went out in pursuit. They followed a plain trail all day, and could note signs of gaining upon the savages as they advanced. At dusk they found the water still muddy and unsettled in a branch which the Indians had evidently just crossed. It was too dark to discern the trail further, so they decided to wait and watch for the gleam of a campfire.

After a while a ray of light flashed down on them from the top of a bluff close to the river. The men waited a little longer, so that the savages might be asleep and at their mercy. Finally, the time for action being at hand, they slipped cautiously around and almost had the entire band in their power when one of the horses neighed and betrayed them, so the Indians fired the first shot, severely wounding a Mr. Black, though none of our men were killed. Nearly all the Indians were soon killed, and in the excitement one of the warriors spurred his horse off the bluff, down a height of fifty or sixty feet, and the mangled body of the horse was afterward found below, but no sign of the desperate rider was ever discovered.

Then in August of 1842 a company of about thirty men attempted to procure provisions and ammunition for an extended Indian campaign. We camped at Shoal Creek, about three miles above Austin, awaiting recruits and supplies, and sent to the arsenal for ammunition, but the man in charge refused to open, declaring that the store of ammunition was very small. Upon this some of our men threatened to enter the arsenal by force. He said that such a move would be made at the risk of their lives, as he had muskets so arranged that at the slightest touch of violence they would fire into a keg of powder. After a good deal of talk he told us that, having no authority from Houston, it was impossible for him to take the responsibility of admitting them, at the same time assuring us that if we took the key out of his pocket by force, unlocked the door, and went in, he would be clear and no harm done. We found only a few pounds of old musket balls and very little powder. See the store of ammunition at the capital in 1842! Our enterprise had to be abandoned, but we lingered through there till next day.

In the previous spring, while on the Vasquez campaign, the Texas army had camped there, and in priming their guns the soldiers had fired a great many shots into the trees around, and now some of us walked about cutting the bullets out of the trees, where we had lodged them in the spring. The day following our departure for home, the Mr. Black who was wounded in the fight on the bluff, was riding through there with a friend, and both were killed on the very ground where, twenty-four hours sooner, William Barton and I had wandered cutting out rifle balls.[8]

In 1843 two young men, Coleman and Bell by name, were riding in a buggy just below Waller's Creek, and suddenly found themselves surrounded by a band of Indians. The horse became frightened and upset the buggy, and the savages killed Bell and captured Coleman. Several men, among

[8] John R. Black and George M. Dolson were killed on August 1, 1842, on their way to swim at Barton Springs. The two were buried in the same grave. Dolson was twenty-nine years old and Black was thirty. A year later Captain Jack Hays captured three Mexicans under a notorious brigand, Rubio, who said that they, not Indians, had killed and scalped Dolson and Black. Brown, "Annals of Travis County," VIII, 11, IX, 33–34, X, 17; Alexander W. Terrell, "The City of Austin from 1839 to 1865," *Quarterly of the Texas State Historical Association,* XIV, 123.

whom were Joe Hornsby, James Edmondson,* and a Mr. Johnson, were just starting out of Austin for home when they came upon the Indians driving young Coleman along, who was almost naked, and bleeding from a lance wound in the back. They immediately made a dash and rescued him, at the same time giving the Indians a considerable chase. Several shots were exchanged, but nobody else was hurt.[9]

Joe Hornsby was riding a fine horse belonging to Anderson Harrell,* which was shot through the nose just below the eyes and died from the wound. At dark the chase ended; the little squad of men returned and found two horses saddled and tied, which they carried with them into Austin. Their owners were never discovered, so they were both given to Anderson Harrell to somewhat pay him for the loss of his fine animal.

All these tales of wayside murder and desolated homes may seem out of harmony and far removed from the scenes and people of the present. Yes, many who looked upon the grand parade and ceremony attendant upon the laying of the cornerstone of our capitol (March 2, 1885) may fail to

* This attack took place on New Year's Day, 1843. The two men were Captain Alexander Coleman and William Bell. Hornsby and Edmondson were unarmed except for one single-shot pistol, but nevertheless determined to try to stampede the Indians and save Coleman. Coleman, although nearly naked, ran back to town and gave the alarm, while Edmondson and Hornsby chased the Indians, putting forth what later became famous as the Rebel Yell and shooting the little pistol as quickly as it could be reloaded. The citizens of Austin soon caught up with the two heroes and fought a little battle with the Indians, killing three and capturing all their accouterments. A Mrs. Whipple saw the fight from the top of the hill where St. Mary's Academy stood in Austin and counted forty Indians. The people of the town learned the next day that the Indians had, previous to killing Bell, captured one child of Judge Nolan M. Luckett and killed another. Brown, "Annals of Travis County," X, 46, 49; Sowell, *Rangers and Pioneers,* 58–59; Wilbarger, *Indian Depredations in Texas,* 143–144.

168

RECOLLECTIONS OF EARLY TEXAS

see the connection and may deem this record of old-time
tragedy and suffering simply "a tale that is told."

There are a few of us, however, who can never forget how
much it has all cost—this prosperity and development in our
land. Of course, Wealth, Enterprise, Intellect, and indomi-
table Energy, have contributed their part.

There were noble men, who lived to lead in the great work,
and justly "achieved unto themselves an undying glory."

But we knew of others. Aye, we knew them well, whose
blood helped pay for all these advantages. Theirs was no
unimportant part in changing the little Waterloo into the
prosperous capital city of Austin.

There were brave men who dared the dangers all in vain
and fell in all the vigor of hope and courage, leaving helpless
women and children amid the wild lawlessness of an unsettled country. Ah! To my mind they served most faithfully,
and paid by far the highest price for the glory of Texas.

I myself commenced in my fourteenth year and served
through the siege of 1874, during Coke's administration.[10]
At that time I was captain of Company D of Jones's Battalion.[11] We encamped about a mile below Menardville on
the San Saba River. My wife was with me. Our tent was
about two hundred yards from the main encampment. One
night a considerable force of Indians came along right at us,
even riding over my hack tongue. My wife woke me with the
information that she heard Indians crossing the river. I had

[10] Richard Coke was Governor from 1873 to 1877, and his administration ended Reconstruction in Texas. *Handbook of Texas*, I,
370.

[11] John B. Jones was commissioned major of the Frontier Battalion,
which consisted of six companies of Texas Rangers of seventy-five
men each. Organized in 1874 to protect the frontier and clear it of
hostile Indians, this battalion was largely responsible for the tradition
associated with the term, "Texas Ranger." *Handbook of Texas*, I,
651, 924.

some scouts out and thought they were coming in. I listened for the song or laugh or whistling which usually accompanied the march of American parties. The silence of the force was evidence enough they were Indians. A number of Dutch wagons with bells some distance off had attracted their attention and they positively failed to see us as they moved steadily, almost noiselessly forward with their shields glittering like diamonds in the moonlight. I took my gun and stood guard while my wife and boy went to alarm the main campers. Next morning we started in pursuit, running about twenty-five miles, but we never could overtake them. Evidently something must have aroused their suspicion for they were wide-awake and in a hurry. They turned back without committing any depredations, leaving the Dutch campers with their jingling bells to go on in peace.

That night we moved camp to Elm, a small stream running into the San Saba River. Scott Early and William Fravick were sent after beef. They soon came upon a party of Indians and returned, reporting at once. Lieutenant Dan Roberts[12] with a squad of men was immediately sent out in pursuit. They struck the Indians' trail, pursued it about ten miles, and came up with them; then a running fight ensued. Results: five Indians killed and one captured, the celebrated Little Bull. He ran on foot and hung on to the horses' tails until he was almost exhausted. Finding both flight and fight impossible he threw up his hands and turning, ran to meet Lieutenant Roberts. Not one of our men was hurt. Roberts and another man had horses shot from under them. Major Jones's escort came up just as the fight was over and we chased the Indians into a cave. Insufficient guard gave them

[12] Dan W. Roberts joined Jones's Battalion of Texas Rangers as a lieutenant and later rose to the rank of captain, which he held until he resigned in 1878. He soon returned to the Rangers and served until 1882. *Handbook of Texas,* II, 483.

opportunity and they made good their escape. A moccasin was found shot through and a great deal of blood all around proved that one had received a serious wound. From all attending circumstances we were satisfied that not one Indian ever reached his destination.

In about one month another party of nine Indians made a raid in between the San Saba and the Llano. We chased them out, killing three of the little band. I was sixty-seven years old in August [1889] and the very thought of those stirring old times makes me feel a degree of excitement even now.

During the administration of Lamar and Burnet the situation of our Republic was one of intense and almost unabated excitement. Early in 1839 Canales succeeded Filisola in command at Matamoros, and strove in all possible ways to incite the hostility of the Indians against Texas. In March came the Cordova Rebellion, which has already been described. Then came the attempt to establish the *Republic of the Rio Grande,* in which not a few of our Texas soldiers took part, and which resulted in the famous betrayal and triumph of Colonel S. W. Jordan and his 260 men at Saltillo, on the 23rd of October.[13]

President Lamar was not only opposed to annexation, but also to all conciliatory treatment of the Indians, and changed the policy of kindness as advocated by Houston into one of hostility and exclusion, proposing to "mark the boundary of the Republic with the sword" if necessary. Of course, this tended to increase the complications and arouse the hostility of the savages, whose hunting grounds were so rapidly passing from their possession.

In 1840 came the treaty with the Comanches at San An-

[13] For an account of the effort by border Mexican Federalists to break away from the Centralist government of Mexico, see *Handbook of Texas,* II, 460.

tonio, resulting in the killing of the warriors, which has also been described. Then in August came the atrocious raid resulting in the Battle of Plum Creek. And now, in October, Colonel John H. Moore* made his second raid[14] against the Comanches, more telling in its effects than his previous one, wherein nothing was accomplished. An advantage at one time secure and promising was ignored, and like all neglected opportunities, brought disaster, defeat, or nothing. It is not only by the mistakes of others, but also by their own past blunders that wise men rectify and improve their lives. So Colonel Moore had some light from the raid of the previous year to guide him now.

He commanded between eighty and ninety Texans, and was accompanied by a small band of Lipans under their celebrated chief, Castro.[15] All necessary preparations for an extensive campaign had been made, the army carrying along about sixty beeves. Going up the Colorado and on to the Red Fork, they noted frequent signs of Indians in the curious pictures and hieroglyphics on the rocks. Even a rude, uncultured savage toys with art, and unconsciously pays tribute to various branches of science, proving it to be one of the natural instincts of humanity to find pleasure in mental exercise.

Noting their grotesque drawings and further on finding pecan hulls just lately scattered, indeed, the signs became so abundant and fresh that the command, concluding that the Indian encampment was very near, stopped in ambush under a mountain, while Castro sent out a few of his warriors to reconnoiter. The little detachment started early in the morning and was gone nearly all day. Our men grew restless and

[14] Moore commanded three volunteer companies against the Comanche Indians in January of 1839 and again in the battle in October, 1840, recounted here by Jenkins. *Handbook of Texas,* II, 230.

[15] Castro lived at Estacas below Laredo. He and his band served as scouts for John H. Moore and Edward Burleson. *Handbook of Texas,* I, 308.

impatient as the hours dragged along without alarm or adventure. The old Lipan chief gave special signs of uneasiness, and when evening came with no sign of his scouts, he went out on the mountain top and stationed himself "like the watchman on the tower," eagerly waiting and watching.

At length, he called to the men below, and pointing westward, said his scouts were coming, and moreover, he said they had discovered an Indian village. Afar off, two or three miles, he had seen and understood their shield signal, and thus knew with what success their efforts had been crowned long before they reached the army. Sure enough, they came, ready to lead the way to the enemy, and the army immediately took up line of march, reaching the Comanche village in time to make the attack by daylight next morning.

The charge was made on horseback this time, taking one item from past experience—i.e., never to leave horses behind without guards. The savages were completely surprised, but made some resistance as they were driven into the river, falling as they fled before the determined Texans. Some were shot in the water and were drowned, while others lived to reach the other side of the river, where pursuit and search were still continued, for the Indians hid themselves with their characteristic cunning and quickness.

Judge Eastland and Charles Shuff of Fayette County had quite an amusing little adventure in this battle. They came upon an Indian lad about fourteen years old, who instead of surrender or flight made bold and persistent efforts to defend himself. Their first impulse was to shoot him, but seeing that he was a mere boy, they concluded to take him alive if possible. But even when they had closed in around him, snatching up a mesquite limb he kept them at a respectful distance, flailing right and left as they endeavored to catch him. Another gun was raised to shoot him, but Judge Eastland interposed and knocked it up, claiming that the boy deserved to be spared for his bravery and pluck. So, after some time, he was captured, together with thirty or forty others, while a great many were killed. Indeed, it was impossible to estimate the number they lost, many being killed in the village, in the river, and in the prairie across the river. It was said that the water was red with human blood, but the waters of the Red Fork of the Colorado are always clay-dyed. However that might be, the slaughter was terrible, and this raid was a considerable blow to the Comanches, the most deadly and most persistent of all our savage foes.[16]

A great deal of the plunder found in this Indian village was recognized as that taken from Linnville the previous summer, and this was doubtless the identical band which had made that raid.

A curious relic of civilized government and times was also found here upon one of the slain warriors. A silver medal, anchor-shaped, bearing date and seal of the United States to an Indian, but hardly to a Comanche, for that tribe cherished eternal hatred and hostility toward the white man, and it is a subject for curiosity to think how came this memorial from the highest power in our land to be treasured by one of our most bitter foes. Strange, with their cruelty and inhumanity, they possessed a rude idea of beauty, and were fond of displaying their taste for trinkets and trumpery.

The wounded Indians were left in one large wigwam in care of a few squaws, and our men, after destroying the rest of the village, struck out for home. All the way back to

---

[16] In this raid 130 Indians were killed, among them the Indian chief Machochochomochouch, and 34 squaws and children were captured. It took place between the Concho and Colorado rivers near Colorado City. Colonel Moore carved his name on the ruins of the old San Saba Presidio nearby. There were 12 Lipans under Castro and his son Flacco. Brown, *Indian Wars*, 83–84; *Texas Sentinel* (Austin), November 14, 1840; *Telegraph and Texas Register* (Houston), November 14, 1840.

Austin they were troubled by small bands of Indians, who dogged them incessantly, but skillfully escaped being caught. The Indians strove in every way to get some revenge or satisfaction, and when on the Pedernales even dared to crawl in through the guards, stealing four horses, including the fine saddle mule of Colonel Moore.

As soon as they had gone out of line of danger, they gave a keen and triumphant yell, which aroused our men, but being unable to find any Indians, all retired again, resting under the impression that they had acted under a false alarm. In the morning, though, the missing horses revealed the theft of the night, but it was too late for pursuit, so they came on, arriving at Austin with plunder, horses, and prisoners—and no loss of life in the fight.

One of our soldiers, however, died on this campaign, being seized with sore throat. This man, Garrett Harrell[17] by name, developed a choking "quinaz" [quinsy?], something very similar to, if not identical with, diphtheria.

The citizens of the now thriving young capital city were exultant over this successful campaign and gave a splendid ball in honor of the returning soldiers, nearly all of whom attended. A ditched field below Waller's Creek was selected for penning the horses, and as they were at home, guards were stationed only at the gate. While the ball went merrily on and the sentinels at the gate stood at their post, feeling secure in their vigilance, the persistent savages slipped around, filled up the ditch, and stole thirty or forty horses! So our men were partially foiled at last, and once again quite a number were compelled to walk home.

The French Minister, M. de Saligny,[18] who lived on the

[17] Garrett Harrell, a son of Jacob Harrell, died on October 16, 1840. Colonel Moore himself read the burial service over Harrell. *Texas Sentinel* (Austin), November 14, 1840.

[18] Jean Peter Isidore Alphonse Dubois de Saligny, chargé d'affaires

edge of Austin, taking a great fancy to the young Indian lad who had wielded the mesquite brush so vigorously, received him as a present from the Texas soldiers. His subsequent history furnishes a somewhat amusing instance of the cunning and daring of the Indian, even in childhood. The residence of the minister was on a hill commanding a good view of the surrounding country. Gradually the young Comanche grew into his new life, until he seemed to feel at home and satisfied, so that he was allowed many privileges. His apparent content and good conduct won confidence, until he was trusted almost anywhere. In the evening he would ride the fine saddle horse of De Saligny all around, while the French consul would sit on his gallery and watch him without thought of fear or suspicion. Thus for a considerable time he would ride gaily around day after day, coming in every time.

One evening, however, he rode his usual round, then enlarging his circle, he went round again, and still enlarging the circle further and further, until he circled out of sight, and was never more heard of.

Judge Eastland brought home from this raid another bright, fine-looking Indian boy, eight or ten years old, whom he named Sam Houston. His succeeding history was not without interest.

Arriving at home all very dirty and very tired, Judge Eastland and Captain Dawson went immediately to the creek for a bath, taking the captive boy with them, who watched them with evident distrust at every turn, but not knowing English he could neither understand nor be understood. The weather was very cold, and they put some water in a pot on the fire to be heated; meanwhile the boy evinced greater alarm and uneasiness all the time, as he watched with increasing excitement their every movement. Months after-

---

to Texas from France, built the so-called French Embassy in Austin, which has recently been restored. *Handbook of Texas*, II, 533.

ward, when he had learned to speak our language, he gave an account of his fear and its cause. He said he felt absolutely certain that they intended boiling him in that pot. They cut off his hair and then dressed him in shirt and breeches, and it was indeed comical to notice how awkward he seemed in his new garb.

He was very apt, soon learning to speak English with perfect ease, and became much attached to the family, calling the judge "father," as did his own children. After he had been here for years and was quite a large boy, he was demanded by his tribe after a treaty and exchange of prisoners. He seemed very much distressed, even weeping bitterly, and when finally forced to go, he declared that he would not live among Indians; he said he would stay with them a while, then steal some fine horses and come back to "father."

Years afterward Colonel [John R.] Baylor, who was government agent among the Indians, saw a Comanche warrior whom he recognized as Sam. The Comanche at first feigned not to know him, but at length acknowledged his identity with the little captive boy. Now he was grown and married to one of his own tribe, with neither the intention nor the desire of ever returning to civilization.

Some time later, Colonel Baylor heard a great sound of wailing and lamentation among the Indians. Upon inquiry he learned that Sam Houston with his entire family had gone out on a thieving expedition, and all had been killed except one who escaped to tell the news, and hence this loud distress.

The oldest man I ever saw, at least judging from appearances and every available sign, went out under Castro with this command, and I think often of the poor old Lipan warrior, known as "Pole Cat." He seemed completely dried up; he was bald-headed except for a few scattering hairs, which were long and as white as snow. He scarcely seemed like a living man, entirely within himself. He went along unarmed and took no part or parcel in the questions and pleasures which agitated his comrades. At length, one of our men asked him why he came on that campaign, so old, so feeble, and without arms.

The broken-down old Lipan, pointing long, bony fingers to the mountains and valleys around him, answered slowly and with effort, "I came to take a last look at my old hunting grounds!"

Ah! Old warrior, you felt that your dim eyes would soon close forever! You thought of the wonderful changes you had known and would know as you gazed upon the wild scenes, amid which you had reveled when your heart was young and strong! But these mighty changes were not confined to your own waning life and strength. You are gone to your "happy hunting grounds" and so, too, that prairie and wildwood are among the things of a dead past, hewn down and buried by civilization and progress! Many of us cannot repress a sigh of something like regret or sadness as we watch new worlds of action and of life rise above them, while the resources of our land are being developed, and we are justly proud of Texas, yet we can understand something of the feeling which impelled that warrior to toil along that dreary march of near three hundred miles "to take a last look at the old hunting grounds!"

CHAPTER XI

In All Fairness...

BOWIE'S CELEBRATED FIGHT on the San Saba in 1831 has been often told and commented upon, and very justly, for no body of men ever displayed greater courage and heroism than was displayed by the Bowie brothers and their companions in this fight.[1] Whenever I see an account of this desperate struggle or hear allusions made to it, however, I can but recall a few other encounters of equal desperation and courage of which I have seldom seen the slightest mention.

For instance, Captain Bird's fight with the Comanches a few years later—in 1837 or 1838. This occurred at a time when all the Indian tribes were very bitter in their hostility against the whites, and tragedies most cruel and horrible were quite common. Due to this prevalence of danger and bloodshed, several minute companies protected the frontier, one of which was commanded by Captain Bird,[2] who lived

[1] On November 21, 1831, James Bowie, Rezin P. Bowie, eight other men, and a boy were attacked by a large body of hostile Indians in a battle which lasted all day. One Texan was killed and three wounded, while at least twenty-one Indians were killed and an unknown number wounded. "Report of James Bowie," in Brown, *History of Texas*, I, 170–175.

[2] John Bird was born in Tennessee in 1795. He brought his family to Texas in 1829 and received title to a league of land in Burleson County on October 14, 1831. He was killed in the fight recounted by

179

in Washington County. In the fall, I think it was, this company, comprising not more than fifteen men, went out on a raid against the Indians.

On a little creek running into the Leon River five or six miles east of Belton, since then known as Bird's Creek, they came upon five or six Indians—merely a decoy squad. Bird's men pursued them and were led over a hill into a band of nearly one hundred Comanches, who received them with a heavy shower of arrows. Seeing the fearful odds against them our men retreated and took shelter in a hollow, one of our small number already being wounded. The affray commenced early in the morning. All through the day the Comanches charged upon the little band, who held their ground amid a shower of deadly arrows and bullets. Yes, they held their ground, while a dreadful destruction went on around them. Captain Bird was killed and several of our men fell bleeding to the ground, and still the fight went on—fiercely and almost uninterrupted all day long. Finally, in the evening, the chief of the Comanches was killed and they retreated in dismay and confusion, thus closing the terrible conflict.

Like Bowie's fight, this was a struggle which once commenced could neither be postponed nor avoided. Our men were compelled to fight or be butchered by the blood-thirsty band, who had lured them into their very clutches—hemmed in with no shadow of a chance to escape or retreat. Captain Bird's rallying cry embodied the terrible truth

Jenkins on May 26, 1839, in which he and a force of thirty-four men fought about three hundred Caddo, Kickapoo, and Comanche Indians near Temple. Buffalo Hump was killed in this fight by Lieutenant James Robinett. Five Texans were killed or died from wounds and the number of Indian casualties has been estimated at between thirty and one hundred. *Handbook of Texas,* I, 163; George W. Tyler (edited by Charles W. Ramsdell), *The History of Bell County* (1936), 61–72; Wilbarger, *Indian Depredations in Texas,* 367–371.

of their situation, and he bade them, "Stand and fight like men, or die like dogs!" Nearly every one of the small company was wounded and a few died from their wounds, after reaching home.

One of our men proved himself a hero indeed, through this memorable day of daring and danger and suffering. I wish I could remember his name and record it, but I cannot. We can cherish his memory, however, as one of those sleeping in unmarked graves, who, in life, erected to themselves monuments more enduring than brass or marble, by a fortitude and bravery unsurpassed by the most hardy of Spartan warriors. Early in the morning he received a deadly wound— a poisonous arrow sinking a message of death throughout his strong frame, but, pausing not for pain, faltering not from fear, he stood with his comrades, loading and firing upon the savages. All through the heat and fervor of the day he fought, and, at last, as the battle was ending, the soldier's life struggle ended, too. The Night of Death brought its strange peace to the life thus given for Texas. How many in the world's broad field of battle thus fell—the results of their mightiest efforts unknown to them.

> Calmly rest in peaceful triumph,
> Soldier brave, *the day was won.*
> And we know your single valor,
> Aided in the work these have done;
> Thus it is in all our life work,
> We must strike with might and main,
> And full oft we leave the issue,
> Knowing not its loss or gain.
> But, 'tis written, He will crown us,
> And up there we will know no pain.
> Conflicts over; blessed triumph;
> Of that rest that doth remain.

The battered, bleeding remnant of men made their way

back to the settlements, leaving their dead and carrying their wounded who could not go without help. Then, collecting as many men as possible, they went back, buried their dead, and taking the trail of the Comanches pursued it a short distance, finding the body of the dead Indian chief, which they had carefully borne away and concealed. This was in accordance with one of their most sacred superstitions. Indeed they would risk life itself in order to preserve their dead from scalping and mutilation. Should a warrior suffer any such desecration at the hands of an enemy, his body was left to the mercy of the wolves and buzzards, for they held that the Great Spirit would not allow a scalped warrior to enter the Happy Hunting Grounds.

Again, in 1839 or 1840, Burleson was returning from an unsuccessful Indian campaign when one of his men proposed leading the way to a village of Tejas Indians, a hostile tribe that covered their tents or wigwams with grass. Burleson with the main army paid no special attention to the information and came on home, but twelve or thirteen men volunteered to accompany the self-appointed guide, anxious for the excitement and adventure as well as the plunder they might secure. I do not recall the captain of the little squad, but I remember a few of the volunteers Christian, Buckman, and others. All their arrangements were made and their plans were well-laid. They struck off to burn the village with its roofs of dry grass. On their way, however, while they were cutting a bee tree, they were surprised and attacked by a large band of Indians.

Taking refuge in a hollow, they fought faithfully and kept the Indians off. But, as in the Bowie fight, the savages finally set fire to the grass surrounding them and they were compelled to retreat. Nearly all of them were killed, but the dense smoke concealed a few, who escaped, among whom was Buckman, from whom I received the details.

RECOLLECTIONS OF EARLY TEXAS

Among the standing mysteries of those terrible times is how the families lived through some of the sieges and horrors. Women and children sustained themselves bravely and acted nobly in many a fearful extremity, which would try the nerve and soul of the bravest men. Somewhere about 1834 or 1835 the Taylor family[3] had their almost miraculous escape from a most horrible fate. Mr. Taylor was living on Little River, where he had lately built a new cabin and settled there with his family. The Caddo Indians came in and out, pretending to be friendly, but in reality very bitter in their hostility.

One day a band of twenty-five or thirty surrounded the house of the isolated settlers, yelling "Burleson killed Caddoes!" as they came. Mr. Taylor barely had time to bar the doors when they began a persistent assault upon the house. The father, mother, and a son of about fourteen years composed the force that had to stand up against this savage band. Through portholes they fired out upon them and as both father and son were good riflemen the contest waxed warm and interesting. Charging the little cabin they tried to break down the doors, but Taylor sprang on the table, which had been drawn up against the door, and shot down, killing the leading warrior instantly. While he was reloading his gun, the boy leaped to the table and shot down a second warrior, who was trying to move the body of the one just killed. Meanwhile, Mrs. Taylor was not shivering or screaming or faint-

[3] The Taylor family were attacked on November 12, 1835, by eleven Indians at their home in Bell County, three and one-half miles southeast of Belton. After the fight the family went to the home of Gouldsby Childress. Soon after they left, Captain George W. Chapman and a company of rangers passed by, saw the dead Indians which were being eaten by wild hogs, and concluded that they were the Taylor family. They soon found their mistake, however, when they arrived at the Childress house. The family moved to the settlement at Nashville-on-the-Brazos, where there was more protection. DeShields, *Border Wars*, 136–143.

ing under the bed or in a corner. Hers was a most important part of the terrible ordeal. In the din of the fight an Indian had crept around and succeeded in setting fire to the house. This she promptly extinguished, and it is said she punched a green pecan board through a hole, giving the savage such a sudden blow that he abandoned the post. The Indians soon gave up the fight, thereafter leaving the Taylors alone.

There was an Indian campaign under John H. Moore in 1839, before his more famous one in 1840. "First come first serve," is a very good rule, I know, but in my reminiscences I wander here and there, as memory wafts me a fact from her exhaustless store, and this expedition seems somewhat worthy of relation, even though I have been past that period in my memoirs several times.

One who has never tried to recollect and record past events of his life in proper order and as to time, etc., may deem it an easy task, and will doubtless find abundant food for criticism in the "cart-before-the-horse" style, and the jumbled dates of an old man's tales. Those, however, who have given time and labor to like enterprises, understand the difficulties so well that they are prepared for what I promised in resuming this record of facts, given perhaps in irregularity and confusion but none the less vivid and true.

Fayette and Bastrop counties uniting, formed a company of about sixty white men and twenty-five or thirty Lipan Indians. Under John H. Moore they started on an Indian campaign without preparation, except salt, coffee, and a little bacon. By the way, this bacon cost twenty-five cents a pound. A man living in a very exposed section sold them meat "cheap," because they were going to fight Indians.

Marching up the river, they were at length forced by a heavy snowstorm to camp at the head of the Lampasas River, where they bided their time as best they could, suffering intensely from cold. While quartered here two men, Joe Anderson and Felix McClusky,[4] went out hunting. Anderson, who was a short distance ahead of McClusky, saw a large band of Indians, and McClusky, coming along, heard the noise of their marching down the country toward home. Coming into camp they reported this to John Moore, but no attention was paid to the alarm. From subsequent events, this band was supposed to have been the one engaged in the Brushy Creek battle and in the killing of Mrs. Coleman.

As soon as possible the small army made its way back through the mountains and cedar brakes to the rye bottoms along the Colorado for the purpose of recruiting horses, men, and supplies before resuming the invading expedition against the Comanches. While encamped there, quite a tragic accident occurred, which cast a gloom over the entire band.

It was about the middle of January and the weather was most excessively cold, so that campfires needed frequent attention. One of the Lipan Indians was bringing wood and struck it against a loaded gun, which went off, mortally wounding one of the soldiers. Prompt effort was made to save him. A skiff was constructed of buffalo hides, and two of his comrades were detailed to carry him down the river to Austin for medical attention. But he died on the way, and rowing to the river's bank, his comrades dug his grave with the blade bone of a buffalo and buried him.

There is an intense pathos and solemnity in the scene suggested here, as we in imagination follow the little skiff down the Colorado. See the two soldiers exerting every power to make all possible speed, at the same time noting with anxious suspense the fluttering pulse, failing strength, and at last

---

[4] Joe Anderson and Felix McClusky were members of the ranger force stationed at Coleman's Fort in 1836 and 1837. McClusky, a wild and somewhat crazy Irishman, was later killed in a drunken brawl. Nothing is known of Joe Anderson. Smithwick, *Evolution of a State*, 164, 201, 202, 273.

pausing to catch dying words! See how wind and wave and
oar are unheeded as the holy hush of death falls upon the
trio—the living and the dying! See strong men bend in
sadness over a suffering friend, powerless to aid or cheer in
that mysterious struggle, wherein "a solitary soul must need
go forth alone," at least from all human standpoint.

Then, when that is over, see rough hands tenderly close
the eyes! And then see the mournful sublimity of the simple
burial on the river bank!

But we will return to John H. Moore and his men, whom
we left with their horses in the rye bottoms, trying to re-
cuperate after the terrible siege of cold and snow. As soon as
practicable, they marched out and up the river once more,
sending on four scouts—Mike Hornsby,[5] Joe Martin, and
two Lipans—who by cautious reconnoiter found a large
Indian encampment on the San Saba. The company immediately turned in across the river about twelve miles below
the mouth of the San Saba, where, arriving at a point near
the Comanche village in the night, they waited for dawn.
This winter campaign had so far been exceedingly severe,
and our men had suffered intensely for so long that everything which in the least brought to mind home and comfort
was welcome, even though tantalizing. Their Comanche foes
seemed to have established for themselves all manner of
home pleasures, for as they lay in the darkness our men could
hear chickens crowing, dogs barking, horses neighing; indeed, all of the many sounds with which farm life is vocal.

The encampment was situated on a horseshoe prairie
lying in the forks of the San Saba and a little creek, and our
men lay on the timbered side under the bank, ready for

[5] "Mike" Hornsby was Malcolm M. Hornsby, a son of Reuben
Hornsby.

action. At length, when it was light enough, the order came to charge. Our men ran nearly through the village, driving the Indians before them—and, by the way, the warriors were all at home this time, about 500 in number, against 90! John H. Moore ordered his men back to the timber, whereupon the Indians, rallying, charged, but were repulsed immediately, as the killing of their warchief, Quenisaik, confused, distressed, and completely routed them for a time. Fighting was continued, nevertheless, until two o'clock in the afternoon.

A somewhat ludicrous incident occurred as our men lay in the timber between the charges. When Pat Moore, a little Irishman, crawled cautiously up to the edge of the bluff and presented a cocked gun, some of the boys said, "What are you doing, Pat? Your gun is not loaded!"

"Hush!" he answered in a loud stage whisper, "Bejabers, they don't know it!"

During the first charge De Witt Lyons called ever and anon for his brother Warren, who was at that time a captive among the Comanches, but received no answer. Later, when the fight was hottest, he called out, seemingly in great distress, "Run here, boys! Run here!" Several of his comrades rushed to him, expecting to find him in great peril, when he exclaimed, "Here is a dog without one bit of hair on him!" Some laughed, while others cursed, at this untimely joke, which was somewhat characteristic of the man, to be cool in excitement or danger.

Our men left their horses without guards about two miles back, a very singular proceeding for which they paid dearly, as the Indians, slipping around, stole them, together with all the baggage of the soldiers. Much to the vexation of a majority of the men, Moore ordered a retreat, and the band marched back home on foot, bearing their wounded on litters. We had none killed instantly, but seven or eight were wounded, and one Martin, from Bastrop, died in a few days from his wound.[6]

During the Republic our frontier was protected by regular militia, which was often reinforced by companies of volunteers from interior portions of the country, and many an interesting campaign lives now only in the recollection of a few old soldiers.

One, in particular, comes to my mind, which occurred in 1840, and will serve as an illustration of others of similar character, in which wholesale waste and destruction of life and property were perpetrated.

Major George T Howard, in command of not more than two hundred men, comprising regular soldiers and volunteers, left San Antonio on a raid against the Comanches, who had lately been a source of constant annoyance and loss to the young Republic.[7]

The army was fully equipped for travel or for battle, while every precaution was taken to preserve quiet, and, if possible, surprise the savages in their stronghold, wherever that might be. For a time the march was without success, but finally on Turkey Creek, beyond Uvalde, they found signs revealing the recent march of a band of Comanches.

Following a plain trail to the head of the Los Moros, where Fort Clark now stands, they surrounded a large Comanche town or encampment, and charging into it, found but little trouble in its evacuation, as the warriors were nearly all

[6] Moore's Defeat, as this battle was called, took place on February 12, 1839. Colonel Moore had fifty-five Texans and forty-two Lipans under his command. The wounded were William M. Eastland, Ira Leffingwell, James Manor, Rufus Perry, Felix Taylor, and Joe Martin. Martin died of his wounds. Brown, *Indian Wars,* 74–75; Smithwick, *Evolution of a State,* 217–219; Wilbarger, *Indian Depredations in Texas,* 144–146.

[7] This expedition occurred in November and December of 1840. Wilbarger, *Indian Depredations in Texas,* 374–375.

188

absent on a raid into Mexico, and the village was taken entirely by surprise. There was some resistance, however, and our men killed four or five Indians in a running fight and regained a few Mexican children who had been held captive by the savages. An amusing incident occurred in this run. As the Indians retreated, fighting their pursuers, an Irishman by the name of Donnelly, who at home kept "Bachelor's Hall" with a Mr. Perry, was chasing a young squaw and seemed to have "nor eye, nor ear, nor mind" for anything else. At length, he caught her and tied her securely despite the most violent fighting and struggling, and with a triumphant air exclaimed, "Bejabers, and I'll carry you home for our housekeeper!"

Having thus secured her, he continued the chase, leaving her till his return, but in the meantime some stragglers, supposed to have been Mexican soldiers, found and killed her, so he was deprived of his prospective "housekeeper." The scene, combined with the droll tone and manner of earnest Pat Donnelly, afforded considerable amusement to the soldiers, some of whom still laughingly recall the circumstances.

The chase was continued some distance, and they did not reach the Comanche village on their return until next evening. They were tired and hungry, having neither halted nor eaten for more than a day, and we may imagine how they enjoyed finding immense quantities of food all ready for them —Indian bread, made of pecans, honey, and mesquite beans, a kind of fruit cake, and what seemed to be fine, fat buffalo meat. Our men ate heartily, almost ravenously, asking no questions, and were considerably refreshed after their long run and fast. Imagine their feelings, when around the camp they found heads, tails, and hides, abundant proof of the fact that they had feasted not upon buffalo, but mule meat!

"A thing of beauty is a joy forever," and a rest of twenty-four hours in this Indian village fixed its locality and the lovely picture it afforded upon the minds of many of the soldiers. A beautiful valley of prairie land, extending toward the Rio Grande, sometimes shooting into little peaks or mountains, and dotted with the snow-white wigwams made of dressed buffalo hides. The village was comprised of at least three hundred of these wigwams, and the horses and mules, which had been stolen and herded there by the Comanches, were estimated by the officers to number about six hundred head. These were, however, nearly all regained, as the Indians could run in all during the night and cut them off unhindered. This our men were powerless to prevent, because their horses were broken down and change was impossible—the stolen horses being all wild and unbroken.

Ever and anon, throughout the day and night the Comanche squaws would ride into their village bearing burdens of pecans, mesquite beans, and wild berries, not dreaming of the tragedy which had taken place there, as they had searched the forest intent upon collecting ingredients for their wild bread. When they would perceive the army of white men, their fright and dismay may be imagined, and peals of hearty laughter would follow them, as, "without pausing for reflection," they would throw themselves from their mules and make for the bottom land, leaving their hard day's gleaning behind.

The campaign not being ended, it was an item of paramount importance to save the horses, so it was strictly against all orders for our men to try to carry off anything, no matter how valuable. Some of the boys, however, did pack as many buffalo robes as they could on a mule, and then on top of the heap they securely fastened a huge brass kettle, whereupon the mule stampeded and cut off and frightened a large herd of horses. The race which followed formed a queer and comical scene. As far as the eye could reach the panic-stricken horses fled in wild terror and confusion, followed by the mule with its brazen burden.

Before leaving the encampment everything was burned, and it really seemed hard to sacrifice so much that was valuable—about ten thousand dollars' worth of property besides the horses.

On return march they changed direction where Uvalde is now situated, and going up through Sabinal Valley crossed the mountains to the head of the Llano, down that stream to the Pedernales, on Pinta Trail leading into San Antonio. Homeward bound now and yet no Indians. Meanwhile, the soldiers were required to preserve all possible quiet, and it may be imagined that they were severely tantalized as they rode along and saw deer in gunshot all the time, and yet no shooting allowed. Finally the temptation was too strong for some. Nine men, among whom were Dan Grady, Creed Taylor,[8] and William H. Kelly, concluded to "slip off" from the command and enjoy a little hunting and a bite of venison despite orders.

Time went merrily with them for a while, as they amused themselves killing deer and securing the choice bits, until toward night they selected a strong position for camp and fared sumptuously on the spoils of the day. Supper over, they made ready for a nice, quiet time of smoking and resting about the campfire, when suddenly about fifty Indians charged upon them, blowing their war whistles, yelling and making every conceivable noise, in order to stampede the horses. The camp was in the edge of a thicket, situated in

[8] Creed Taylor was born in Tennessee on April 10, 1820, and came to Texas in 1834 or 1835. His reminiscences of the Texas Revolution are given in James T. DeShields, *Tall Men with Long Rifles* (1935); see also Fisher, *It Occurred in Kimble,* 138–150; Sowell, *Early Settlers,* 804–810; Sowell, *Rangers and Pioneers,* 225.

the bend of a creek, and the main body of Indians charged upon the rear, the thicket intervening, while two warriors rode around in front to cut off the horses.

Dan Grady and Creed Taylor ran around and drove all but three of the horses back into camp, at the same time firing upon the two warriors, one of whom was killed by Taylor. Immediately the entire band collected about the warrior who was shot, and then commenced a fight that continued until midnight. Nine against fifty and no loss of life on our side! Thus powder and ball outsped and kept at bay the fleet and ofttimes fatal arrow, though the savages lingered near a long time, filling the air and forest with the sound of yell, war whoop, and whistle, which could be heard for three miles, as at last they went slowly off.

Never did men hold more earnest council than was held in the little clump of bushes by our nine hunters as the Indians departed. Behold how quickly change the scenes and circumstances of life, even in a single day! We imagine the sport of the day, the fine supper paled into insignificance and aroused but feeble emotions compared to the sensations of the nine as they stood in the darkness deliberating. By burning their packs and riding the mules they were all mounted once again, despite the loss of their three horses, and at last they ventured forth with guard before and behind, changing at intervals, till at daylight they regained their command.

Their escapade had given them somewhat more serious fun than they had anticipated, besides the loss of their packs, and a severe reprimand from the commander.

Many of the raids and adventures of our early days here in Texas are thrice-told tales and yet when we old settlers read the accounts, especially if they be attempted record of our personal experience, or those of some intimate friend, we

192

miss little incidents here and there. These touches of reality
are necessities in historical narration, just as salt, pepper, and
sauce are essential to the right flavoring of soup, roast, and
vegetables. Without these, history seems an endless maze of
dates and figures—a long series of monotonous details which
for sake of brevity and convenience might well be cut even
shorter and abridged at every turn, until all the revolutions
of the world's history, all the struggles and changes might be
told in a brief chapter, with the little incidents all left out.
Then San Jacinto and the Alamo and the thousand thrilling
events in Texas history all would be concised into few words.
We would read how Texas had some trials and came out all
right, while many a hero whose heart's blood stained her
virgin soil will sleep on in death, forgotten as a dream. Not
so fast, dear friends! Wait till the old Texas veterans are all
gone, then come with your dissecting knife and hash up the
truth, taking just a little here and there. As long as memory
lives in us, we will be always trying to fill up these vacuums
so detrimental to a real conception of the true greatness of
Texas, and so fatal to all genuine interest which in justice
belongs to her history.

That Captain W. W. Hill commanded a company of Texas
Rangers along in 1836 is well-known, and doubtless many
have read brief sketches of some one of his campaigns, or
perhaps all of them. Having often heard a full account of this
campaign on the San Gabriel and always finding it interesting, I have obtained all its details from a member of the company, my old friend and comrade Rufus Perry, and submit
it to our readers as worthy of attention. In the beginning I
would, if possible, place before your eye two pictures or pen
portraits of one man. One represents a young man—tall,
muscular, erect—a perfect specimen of the strong and brave
in young manhood. Dark eyes, bright with the fires of intelligence and enthusiasm gleam forth underneath the black

brows and lashes, while the waving masses of black hair fall
in careless grace upon a smooth, broad forehead. This was
young Rufus Perry. Now, after the lapse of forty years, we
behold his handsome face all drawn and scarred, his eye
distorted, and twitching while he walks with the aid of a
cane—all the result of Comanche arrows back in the early
days of Texas history.

But why mention these little items? Well, I believe every
true and loyal Texan loves the brave old Texas soldiers
wherever found—and here is one who suffered the next thing
to death for the Lone Star. I give the narrative as nearly as
possible in his own language:

Captain William Hill organized a company of between fifty
and sixty men at Asa Mitchell's in July, 1836. We came along
the Gotier Trace to Bastrop, thence to John Caldwell's ranch,[9]
where we found plenty of corn to feed our horses. From this
point we proceeded to the San Gabriel, finding bee trees and lots
of fish, then down a stream some distance we came to a high
bluff where we struck an Indian trail making towards Cole's
settlements, where the town of Independence now stands. We
followed the comparatively fresh trail nearly two days and
nights and overtook the Indians in thick post oak country.

About sundown we discovered the smoke of their campfire
not very far off. Dismounting, we prepared to attack them in
camp, but a straggling warrior hastened the issue by coming out
and meeting us accidentally and unexpectedly. Of course, we
killed him immediately but not before he had raised a war
whoop, rousing his comrades to action.

We continued to advance, notwithstanding the fact of their
being aroused and ready to meet us. We killed three and

---

[9] John Caldwell lived on the west side of the Colorado River several
miles north of Bastrop along the Bastrop–Travis County line. Caldwell
was senator from Bastrop and adjoining counties for many years in
the Congress of the Republic and the legislature of the state. Ray,
Austin Colony Pioneers, 346.

194

wounded several whom we did not get. Andy Houston[10] was the only man in our company who was wounded, he being struck in the wrist with an unspiked arrow. This occurred on a prong of the Yegua, twelve miles from the settlements.

We were somewhat surprised and puzzled just after the fight to see a member of our company, an old backwoodsman named Dave Lawrence, step up and cut off the thigh of one of the slain Indians. I asked him what he intended to do with it.

"Why," he answered, "I am going to take it along to eat. If you don't get some game before noon tomorrow we'll need it!"

At sundown we camped about a mile below the battleground on a little creek. I doubt if any of the neighbors in Burleson County know how that little creek got its name of "Cannon Snap." Thus it occurred on this very night in the summer of 1836 that a Portuguese, a dark, very dark man, so black that we called him "Nigger Biddy," was placed on guard.

During the night he rushed in on our crowd exclaiming, "Oh! I heard a cannon snap!" Poor fellow, he was so much frightened that he magnified a twig's snapping or an owl's laughing into threatened danger. Then and there the little creek received its present name of "Cannon Snap."

Next morning we marched to Yellow Prairie on the waters of the Brazos to old man Thompson's.[11] The hospitable old gentleman furnished us beef and corn, a sumptuous dinner, so old Dave Lawrence did not have to eat his Indian meat. Turning up Little River we scouted about two months longer but found no more Indians.

In 1844 four of our fellow soldiers passed through an ordeal of suffering and danger that well deserves to be recorded among the sacrifices made for Texas in those

[10] A man named A. Houston, who was killed in the Surveyor's Fight in Navarro County in October of 1838, may have been Andy Houston. Brown, *Indian Wars*, 50.

[11] Jesse Thompson, an Old Three Hundred Colonist, lived in Fort Bend County, on the east bank of the Brazos River, where he ran a ferry. *Handbook of Texas*, II, 774.

critical times. Jack Hays commanded a company of rangers, and having received news that Mexicans were trying to get some horses between the Nueces and the Rio Grande on Turkey Creek he detached Rufus Perry, Kit Achlin, John Carlin, and James Dunn to go out and investigate and stampede them.

They reached the Nueces and began to scout along its banks, Perry riding slowly along and taking note of the trails and woods, while the others he sent on ahead, advising them to select a high place for camp so that they could have a good view of the surrounding country and thus guard against surprise from Indians or Mexicans. Riding along alone he struck a horse trail, which he followed until he discovered that he himself was being followed. He then went on as if all was natural and joined his comrades in camp, which contrary to his advice they had pitched in a low brushy spot. He felt much dissatisfied and uneasy on account of their selection of camp and took his gun and went over on top of a hill to look around, but could see nothing.

After dinner Dunn and Carlin took the horses for water and went in bathing in the waters of the Nueces. Just as they had undressed for bathing, twenty-five or thirty Indians attacked Perry and Achlin back at camp. The first thing they knew the Comanches came upon them with a whoop. Achlin fired and then ran off afoot, leaving the horses. Just as Perry was in the act of firing he received an arrow in the shoulder, which forced him to drop his gun. He then drew a five-shooter and retreated for his horse, firing as they advanced upon him. A second arrow struck him in the temple, severing an artery, and a third struck his hip, going clear through his body. This he pulled out of his back. Just as he was firing his fourth shot he fainted from loss of blood.

When he regained his consciousness his first thought was to commit suicide to escape death from the savages. He cocked his pistol and put it to his head, but paused, then discovered that he could get up. He made his way to the two men who were bathing. They had crossed the river, but came back when they saw Perry. In a second Achlin joined them, and pulled the arrow out of Perry's shoulder. They then began to make ready to run from a second attack, which they felt sure the Indians would make. Achlin tried to persuade them to take Perry behind on a horse, but they would not, probably thinking from his weak and suffering condition that he would die anyway—then, too, they were anxious to ensure their own escape and knew a wounded man could but impede their ride. He caught hold of the tail of one of their horses and was thus helped across the stream, when he again fainted. They must have supposed him dead, for they robbed him of his gun and pistol, and all left him to his fate.[12]

He became conscious again just as the Indians were making a second charge. He struggled to his feet, and ran with all his little remaining strength for a thicket, at the same time trying to stanch the blood from his wounded temple by

[12] Dunn and Carlin rode 120 miles to San Antonio completely naked. They arrived in bad condition, horribly burned by the fierce August sun. They were censured by Captain Hays and others for deserting their two comrades. This amazing experience took place in August of 1844, twelve miles up the Nueces River from Uvalde. All four men fully recovered after the careful nursing of the San Antonio women, but Achlin and Perry carried permanent scars.

James "Red" Dunn was wounded in the Battle of Bandera Pass, and participated in the fight at Laredo on April 7, 1841. He and Mike Chevallie were captured by Vasquez in 1842, but released soon afterward. Dunn also took part in the Nueces Canyon battle in July of 1844. Later he became a captain in the Confederate Army and was killed at Brownsville in 1863.

Nothing is known about John Carlin except that he was in many of the battles in which Hays's company participated. Ilma M. Benavides, "General Woll's Invasion of San Antonio in 1842" (Master's Thesis, University of Texas, 1952), 11; Henderson, *Colonel Jack Hays, Texas Ranger*, 9, 21, 22, 26, 59–60; Sowell, *Early Settlers*, 22–23, 132, 148–154.

holding his overshirt closely against the wound as he ran. He crawled into the depths of a dense thicket and lay on the bare ground, securely hidden from the savages; at the same time the dust and sticks on the ground stopped the bleeding in his wounded side. The Indians surrounded his hiding place, knocked around in the brush, but for some reason did not enter the thicket, probably thinking Perry was armed and feared to risk one of their own to kill an already seriously wounded man.

He waited until dark and then started toward the roaring of water which he could hear, but every time he would get up and start he would faint from pain and weakness, so that he did not reach water till daybreak—all night going about two hundred yards! Then he washed the blood and dirt from his face, drank, crossed the stream, and crawled into a hole at the root of a large tree that had been blown down.

That night he started for San Antonio, a distance of 120 miles, wounded, unarmed, and without provisions. In spite of weakness and pain he persevered the first day until he was three miles on his way, then being utterly prostrated had to lie and rest. When able to proceed he went on at intervals, getting only two or three miles at a stretch till he reached San Antonio. On the seventh night just at dark he reached the city, more dead than alive, having traveled all seven days with no food except three prickly pear apples and a handful of mesquite beans.

With every attention his recovery was a very slow and painful one, keeping him in bed about three months. His clothes were pierced by twenty-one arrow holes when he reached home.

Rufus Perry is an intimate friend and acquaintance, an associate veteran, and for more than twenty years was a citizen of Bastrop. I have gathered this account from his own lips, and can vouch for its truth. In giving the details of this adventure, he always mentioned the kind and untiring attention he received from two women of San Antonio, one a German, the other a Mexican. The former often shed tears over his crippled and wounded condition. Perry prior to this was a good looking man, but now after the lapse of forty years, still bears a drawn and scarred face, a twitching eye, and walks with the aid of a cane—all the result of the Comanche arrows.

Achlin reached San Antonio on the morning of the eighth day, having fared like Perry on prickly pear apples and mesquite beans. He was, however, not so mutilated and battered up as his comrade. He was almost well in two weeks.

CHAPTER XII

Hunting and Social Life

I HAVE OFTEN REALIZED that the early circumstances of my life, together with an instinctive fondness for nature and her wildest, most secluded spots, have made me closely akin to Indians or Arabs in taste and habits of life. Looking back to early times in Texas, I recall with a thrill of sympathy, not unmixed with envy, the evident pleasure my father found amid the wild scenes of our young republic. Even now, though time has dimmed my eyes, frosted my head, racked and somewhat enfeebled my frame, my heart remains unchanged in this respect, so that in the midst of business cares and family responsibilities there comes to me at times a restless longing for the wildwood, which nothing can satisfy except a few days' camping amid scenes as much like those early ones as I can reach. Of course, I would not, if I could, stay the hand of the progress which is doing such mighty work for Texas, yet I must in honesty confess to a pang of regret and sadness when I realize that the good old bear-hunting days are but things of a dead and buried past.

We enjoyed life then. But perhaps our joys were not derived simply from those grand old Texas hunting grounds. There and then we were rich in the possession of youth, strength, and hope, with the "wide, wide world" of life before us! Now as we stand on the shady side and look back, we see not only vanished forests and pleasures, but also time and opportunities that can come but once in a lifetime. Still we can but remember what a country this Colorado Valley was then, and even now when in Austin I can almost for a time forget the sights of the city by becoming absorbed in recalling how I have chased mule-eared rabbits along where main street now lies.

I remember just how I felt as I stood amid these wilds, as tough as a bear's cub, young and strong and armed with bowie knife, tomahawk, and derringer pistol, besides my rifle, which was a very fine one. By the way, I gave 300 acres of land for that gun, and it was generally pronounced a good bargain. The land now lies in Lee County and could not now (1886) be bought for $20 an acre. I had from earliest childhood quickly and eagerly caught at every scrap of woodcraft, and under the teaching of old "Indian Phillip," was an adept sleuth in the science of bee hunting. I never saw a man who could beat me coursing bees.

While riding along on the prairie, I have seen a bee soaring past me heavily loaded, and have chased it a full half-mile. Even on foot I have kept in sight of them as their course would be impeded by a strong south wind, and they flew with seeming labor close to the ground, occasionally lighting as if to rest. Association, surroundings—every circumstance of my boyhood combined to feed and foster my passion for hunting and I reveled in the rich field which was open to me, free and full of game.

I believe I could imitate every sound one ever hears upon the broad plains or in the dense forest. I have by howling summoned packs of hungry wolves, which would come as if called by one of their own species. I could gobble like a turkey, cause owls to answer and come in gunshot, and reproduce the squall of a young bear.

Along in June or early July a few of us were always ready

to start. With only a few simple preparations, bread and coffee enough to last us several days, we went out determined to have venison, honey, and "fun," and it was seldom, if ever, that we failed. We were always careful to camp near good water, generally took an ax to cut our bee trees, but never carried vessels of any kind for the honey; this we saved in a "cased" deer hide. This is doubtless a thing unknown among our modern hunters, so I will describe how we constructed our honey vessel.

Of course, we first killed the deer and hung it by the head to the limb of a tree, then taking a knife we would cut through the skin around his neck just above his shoulders. Two of us would now take hold of the skin and gradually pull or strip it down to his heels, stopping at the bullet holes to tie them up tightly with buckskin strings, putting tiny little pegs to keep the strings from coming off. Then when off and turned wrong side out with all the holes tied up, we would blow it up, inflate it till it would be perfectly tight, and lay it thus stretched in the hot sunshine to dry.

This required only a short time, when it would be clean and dry and ready to hold the wild honey which we were sure to find. And in the meantime we would have our scaffold ready for barbecuing our venison. Ah, what meat we would have on these excursions, fat and tender and juicy and browned!

With these preliminary preparations, the most scientific bee hunters would then strike out for a bee course, with or without bait. Soon we would find and cut the bee tree and fill our deerskin case, which would hold from fifteen to twenty gallons and weighed nearly two hundred pounds. Then bearing our sweet wild burden into camp, we would hang the case up by the neck to a tree and whenever we wished to draw therefrom, we would simply untie a leg and the pure stream would flow at our will.

Then and there we had feasting and pleasure better than that of kings, as we rested and chatted, surrounded by everything wild and picturesque and free, relishing as only a hunter can relish, the venison, wild honey, bread, and coffee.

The American Field,[1] dated April 17, 1886, contains an interesting "Texas Pecan Hunt," by "Foxhorn," now of New Orleans, formerly of Austin. He begins by stating a fact I well remember, "Regularly every fall the settlers would organize what was called 'a pecan hunt,' the object of which was to gather pecans and 'lay in' as much buffalo, bear, and deer meat as would last their families during the winter. The hospitality of these frontiersmen was unbounded, and as immigration was pouring in constantly, it was rarely that any one had a surplus of supplies remaining over."

Foxhorn's pecan hunt occurred in the 1840's, headed by John C. Duval, one of the Mier men and one of Fannin's band, who when he was led out to be shot was unhurt at the first fire, but falling down feigned death until he saw an opportunity to escape.

It is pleasant for us who have been all along there, to follow Foxhorn's hunting party from Swisher's Tavern, across the Colorado near the mouth of Shoal Creek—on over the rolling prairies that extended from the Colorado to Onion Creek. Not only are all the scenes and localities familiar to us, but Foxhorn was accompanied on this hunt by some of our oldest and earliest acquaintances—Bob Pace, Captain Grumbles and his son Perry, Tom Collins, and others.[2]

[1] The full title of this magazine is *American Field; The Sportsman's Journal.*

[2] Captain John J. Grumbles was a ranger captain in the 1840's and 1850's. He lived first at Webber's Prairie and then bought the William Barton home and mill. Grumbles died in 1859.

Tom C. Collins, born in South Carolina in 1817, lived in Bastrop, then in Austin. He died in the early 1870's. Brown, "Annals of Travis

He speaks of the "would-be typical Texan" of today and shows how different he is in appearance from that of the pioneer settler of our state. He justly says,

The broad Mexican sombrero covering long shaggy locks, short jackets, a pistol belt and an arsenal of sixshooters attached, long topped boots, jingling spurs—all are inventions of a later day. In that age no one thought of his personal appearance, as it was not a time for stage get-up, marrying, or giving in marriage. I doubt if there is now living—and there are many of them yet to be found in and around Austin—a man who can exactly describe the appearance and makeup of such men as John Duval, Bob Pace, Tom Collins, [James] Monroe Swisher,* "Old Rip" Ford, and other Indian fighters of those days.

But I must come back to my own personal recollections of early Texas hunting days. I now propose to give a few items and incidents connected with buffalo hunting in my young manhood. One of the hardest, most pleasant, and most exciting hunts I ever had occurred along in 1843 or 1844, after immigration and adventure had driven Indians and game further west, and when buffalo were very wild and scarce in our vicinity. Indeed, the object of our present excursion was the finding of pleasure, honey, and venison, and we had no hope of finding buffalo in the locality to which we went.

A few words here as to what I have seen and do know of this animal may not be uninteresting. No meat is more palatable and better than good fat buffalo meat, and it was a matter of considerable importance in those times to kill and cure the year's supply in season. They are very easily killed, but the head of the buffalo is the very last place at which to aim in shooting, for the mane or "mop" often be-

County," V, 14; *Handbook of Texas,* I, 742; Ray, *Austin Colony Pioneers,* 307–308; *U.S. Census,* 1850, Travis County, 38.

comes so clotted or matted with sand and mud that it serves as a kind of armor or shield—indeed, an ordinary rifle ball could not penetrate through this mop and the *double skull to the brain.* If we could "get the wind of them" we could sometimes kill four or five at a time, and when they were bayed by a pack of dogs, they would circle around in wild, aimless terror or fury, never noticing our gun reports, until we would perhaps kill the whole herd. They were guided principally by the sense of smell, and therefore nearly always fed toward or against the wind.

Where ground is smooth and firm and the herd is large one can on almost any horse run upon and catch a buffalo, but in rough, uneven country it is almost an impossibility for one on horseback to catch up. Headlong the great body plunges forward, without turn or pause no matter what obstruction or difficulty presents itself—over bluffs, hollows, saplings, caloes [callows?]—everything! And there is no earthly chance to break down a buffalo which is in medium order and fresh at starting. It is wonderful how long and how fast they can run. As they go in a *one-sided* gallop, they seem to use only the strength of one side at a time, thereby saving the resources of the other side for prolonged speed and danger.

He sheds his heavy coat of wool every spring, and in summer walks forth a veritable specimen of naked and ugly hugeness. Then in winter he takes on a warm new coat— always seeming uglier with each successive change. The wool made knitting thread; the mop made ropes, girths, bridle-reins; the hide was sometimes dressed and used for "lariats" and moccasin soles; and the meat was delicious. I have often been impressed with the fact that nature holds and dispenses some of her richest treasures and rarest delicacies for those who throw themselves dependent upon her bounty, ignoring luxuries and the provisions of art.

But we will return to these ugly wild cattle which once dotted our broad prairies. They were so ugly, yet they were never dangerous, except when wounded. Then they became furious with pain and terror and nothing was more terrible. Even now some of us get together and laughingly recall a somewhat serious experience of two of our acquaintances— James Manor* and Ham [Hamilton] White,* out on a buffalo hunt just below Austin.

They had wounded a young buffalo very badly and were trailing or hunting for him among the dogwood swamps and thickets. As they went around one of these thickets they suddenly came upon the wounded buffalo lying down near them. It arose and took after them at such speed that they could take time for nothing but flight. White ran fastest and succeeded in taking refuge behind one of the thickets whence he could in safety watch the race. The mad beast kept after Jim Manor, the nearest man, who was now in extreme danger as he could almost feel the breath of the furious animal hard behind him. Finally he dropped his gun, and as a last resort concluded to spring for the limb of a tree ahead of him. Just as he succeeded in grasping it, the buffalo struck the limb and jarred him loose. The huge animal rushed forward in its wild fury and could not turn very fast, so that Manor succeeded in putting the body of the tree between himself and his mad pursuer. There he dodged around and around, evading by the main strength and awkwardness of the formidable plunges and thrusts of the buffalo, as it hooked first on one side and then on the other. Off a few steps in security, White was laughing violently at the terrible predicament of his fellow hunter. At length, he called out, "Shall I shoot him, Jim?" Speaking in a loud whisper, Manor gasped, "Yes!" So the buffalo was shot and Manor rescued from his perilous situation, but he could never appreciate the ridiculous part of the scene that aroused White's laughter, and in considerable anger assured White that he felt very much inclined to shoot him for indulging in laughing at so unreasonable a time.

But I will go back to our hunt here. After all buffalo were out of these parts, as we thought, Bill Barton, John and Tom Bright, and I concluded to make a deer and bee hunt over on Peach Creek, about twenty-five miles away. We camped at what is known as Steward's Prairie, on the old Gonzales road—a very wild and rough country. This section of the country is still unsettled—constituting the largest uncultivated portion of Bastrop County.

Striking out we easily secured nice fat venison and plenty of honey. In the evening, after feasting on nature's good things, seasoned by camp yarns, while taking another round for game, we were greatly surprised and pleased to find signs of where a herd of about thirty buffalo had been feeding. We took their trail at once and followed them into the sand hills around Iron Mountain. After a run of six miles we came upon them as they traveled slowly but steadily along. We tried to get around them near enough for a shot but they suddenly "got whiff" of us and broke into a run.

Bill Barton and I were riding good horses and concluded to run them. The cloud of dust was terrible and so dense we could hardly see the herd of frightened animals, which seemed like a great rolling body as they plunged along. Our horses soon were left behind and gave out in the unequal race. They were so hot and tired that we were compelled to stop, unsaddle, and stake them a while to rest and cool. Sitting there, talking over the excitement of our race, we suddenly saw two bear cubs running toward us from the herd of buffalo. Seeing us, they whirled. Springing on our horses bareback, with stake ropes for bridles, we took after them and a merry little race we had. Both cubs took a tree, and we shot them, bringing back to camp fine bear meat in addition to our store of venison and wild honey. Now we had enjoyed a good time—a surprising time and had plenty of game, but I could not be satisfied as I thought of that herd of buffalo leaving us behind. So I challenged my friends to stay with me—to declare that we would never under any consideration give up until we brought in buffalo meat. All agreed. Early the next morning we went out and soon struck the trail of our herd. Another run of six miles brought us to their beds, where they had evidently rested and fed a little. Then the trail led us on into even rougher regions between Peach and Tinney Creeks on Iron Mountain.

Soon we came in sight of the herd which was still moving steadily onward. Being close to them we dismounted, tied our horses, and followed them about a half-mile. As we entered a sandy glade, about eighty yards off from the herd, we fired upon them as they walked along. After that we found blood on the trail, and soon a fine buffalo fell dead on the march. We took a supply of the meat, taking pains to secure the marrowbones—always considered a rare delicacy. With these additions to our feast of good things, another night ended our surprising hunt.

Ah, I was young and full of fun then, and that was indeed one of the gala weeks of my hunting days.

Sometimes in the midst of my reminiscences I am troubled with a restless feeling of uneasiness as to the construction which may be placed upon this record of my younger days. Some may accuse me of egotism and bragging, or of ignoring others and placing myself to the front. It would probably seem more fitting that other tongues than mine should tell of my battles and triumphs, but there are only a very few survivors of those scenes now—besides, my children want *my* life and *my* experiences in early Texas times, and hence the personal nature of my reminiscences. Of course, I know many men whose services were given to Texas, and whose lives would form a volume more interesting and exciting than these chapters of mine, but history will do its duty by them. For my children I have consented and striven to give the truths of *my own personal experiences,* while at the same time I have introduced other incidents of which I was thoroughly cognizant.

Those old times were practical as well as dangerous, and there was little room for poetry, sentiment, and all that among the early settlers. We were generally poor and honest, and necessarily compelled to stand by each other, but life was not too serious for us to have a good deal of fun sometimes; young people are almost the same in heart and practice the world over, and today it is not unusual to catch gleams of life and merriment among our boys and girls which enlivened the social gatherings a half-century ago, when Mary Jane[3] and I first began to look at each other—and it does not seem so long ago now although our hairs are so white, our eyes dim, and our frames growing feeble and full of pains.

Even in my very young boyhood, before Mary Jane came to Texas, I remember a little group of young people who threw a little love-making and teasing and marrying into the wild prose of the early days here. The star of the circle was Miss Parthenia Barton,[4] a fine girl—nice and quite pretty, with a winning way for old and young. Her two uncles were young men, and the wooing of Miss Barton was a matter of considerable interest and amusement to them. One young gentleman, Levi K——, was among her suitors and my recollection paints him quite a "character" in his way. He

---

[3] Mary Jane Foster was born in Missouri, September 29, 1826. She married John Jenkins in 1845, and they had eight children. She died in 1907.

[4] Parthenia Barton, one of the four daughters of William Barton, later married Richard J. Lloyd. Probate Papers, Travis County.

was very conceited and very green, a combination of elements which nearly always produces something rich and rare if not ridiculous and absurd. He loved the girl and thought he could get her, but was ignorant as to how he should proceed; she meanwhile was rather shy, very dignified, and disliked him as thoroughly as she could dislike anybody. So he walked around and looked at the fair maid and studied the vexing question, until he determined to settle it at once, and consulted one or two of the boys on the subject. They advised him "to ask the old lady first," assuring him that was the only way here in Texas. And they watched the poor fellow throughout the whole ordeal. Mrs. Barton said Parthenia could use her own mind in the matter, but Parthenia gave his asking no hearing and his dreams vanished like a bubble into thin air. This heart was, wonderful to say, elastic, however, and in a short time he was corresponding with another girl in San Felipe and more infatuated than ever, showing the same confidence in his comrades as before.

How interested they made themselves in every letter that came and how they listened to all his plans, founded, as usual, on his self-confidence and conceit! Finally, I remember seeing them forge a love letter to Levi, and then I remember Levi bringing the letter to the wicked young forger, who read it aloud, pausing and studying portions of it just as if he had not been its author. It was a letter full of the brightest fruition to all of Levi's hopes crowning his marriage with an immense fortune inherited from a rich uncle of his ladylove. And I recall him as he reveled in his air castles, walking the floor and talking of how suspense and poverty and hard work were all at an end for him. It was all cruel, but such things still happen. And I remember when the real truth came to poor Levi, and the girl refused him. He left the country a victim of disappointed love. I wonder whatever did become of him.

And so life went on! Soft eyes looked love to eyes that answered love again. There was a marriage occasionally, by bond before a justice of the peace, and then ratified at the coming of the priest, this under Mexican law. After Texas Independence, in case one of a couple had died, the bond marriages were declared valid under the constitution. I think right often of our boys and girls who made society here in West Texas then. The girls were so strong and fine and healthy-looking and they seemed so wide-awake and earnest. Their waists were not so waspish nor their bustles so large as they are today. Their cheeks were as fresh and rosy, but they were painted by Nature's touch in God's own sunshine. They were raised on bear and buffalo meat and venison and wild honey with plenty of good pure fresh air and work to do.

Women and men are like the plants and trees—they require air and sunshine for strength and growth. And our girls knew how to weave and spin and churn and do anything that came along there. They did not stop and primp up to entertain company in those days; our boys "who would a-wooing go" did not send a note beforehand and await an answer, as is today's custom. No, arrayed in coonskin cap and moccasins with a hunting suit in harmony, carrying a gun for game or savages, the young Texas beau would have to march up to loom or cowpen or garden and there make known his fondest hopes, while the work went on. But "all work and no play makes Jack a dull boy," and we had a party now and then—not often, but when the occasion came we made it count sure enough, generally running the thing all night long. Ah, then we had fun! There were no cotillions, no round dancing, nothing quiet or modern. We danced the regular old reels to the most stirring old tunes ever played by fiddle or banjo, harder work than plowing or hoeing cotton. It was like our lives—all full of earnestness and energy—vim was an element in everything here then.

Fashion meant common sense and economy and comfort. A lady made a splendid-looking and fitting costume out of seven yards of cloth. To my mind, she looked just nice enough for anything in the world, but I suppose in an average ballroom now she would be regarded as a relic of anteflood times. I believe the women here now are as pretty and fair as can be found, but they do not look so healthy and comfortable and happy, and I do not see many who look like they could pass through what Mary Jane and others of our veteran ladies of Bastrop County have endured.

CHAPTER XIII

From the Sublime to the Ridiculous

THERE IS BUT A STEP from the sublime to the ridiculous, and we are often forced to take that step all along through life. I am driven into this extremity at the present writing by the importunity of certain friends who beset me on sight with gentle reminders of some of the "jokes" at my own expense, which they hold treasured up against me, and as my reminiscences proceed, they grow more and more uneasy lest I should fail to recollect and record these important (?) facts.

Hence, from the toils, sufferings, fatigue, and dangers of army and prison life, I would bring my friends to the quiet and comfort of my boyhood home, and proceed to relieve my mind by satisfying theirs, assuring them that I have no intention of shrinking from the facts in my life, even though they may expose laughable blunders. After all, what is better than a good hearty laugh?

First, there is that everlasting old story of "The Buttons." It is not only queer, but exceedingly vexatious, how these downright good jokes, no matter how we try to crush them to the earth, will rise again and continually confront us, demanding recognition and acknowledgment at all times and seasons. We can neither outgrow nor kill the recollection of these absurd mistakes and blunders of other days, and whether we choose or not, will have to "face the music" throughout.

Now, there are practical jokes—capital jokes, so called—whose perpetrators almost deserve capital punishment, and whose victims often suffer untold horrors of agony and pain. Of all such "crimes" I would wash my hands, but where a man originates and perpetrates the fun, and is the butt of his own joke, whether intentionally or unconsciously, why all men everywhere can afford the luxury of a good laugh.

This "button" incident occurred back in our young days, when the only store in Bastrop was a little old elm log house, kept by Dr. [Thomas Jefferson] Gazley, and the entire stock of goods might have been carried on one horse. Though little, it nevertheless did quite a thriving business. Butter, chickens, eggs, indeed all home produce, was taken in trade; and while our men were on duty abroad, our good women could carry on this exchange in their own peculiar province. My experience in the field and forest had been rather more extensive than in trade and commerce, and even now I am somewhat more comfortable on a camp hunt than in shopping, a fact of which I think my friends are right well aware.

I was a mere boy, and Bastrop was comparatively an infant. Mother sent me one morning with butter to Dr. Gazley's, at the same time telling me that I must bring her back some buttons. Catching my horse, I asked just as I rode off, "How many buttons?"

Misunderstanding my question, she answered, "Four pounds."

It never entered my head once to be surprised or puzzled at the immense quantity of buttons she demanded, but going on to Bastrop and delivering my butter, I informed Dr. Gazley that my mother wanted four pounds of buttons.

I will never forget his look of amusement and surprise as

he protested, "Surely, you are mistaken! Your mother cannot want four pounds of buttons!"

I stood my ground firmly and vehemently; indeed, I grew downright mad when I found myself unable to convince him that she really wanted the specified quantity of buttons.

And finally he became more serious and somewhat puzzled as he remarked, "Probably your mother is trying to make fun of my small store and still smaller stock of goods!"

At length he prevailed on me to carry home two dozen buttons, and I left feeling almost furious as he said, "Why, John, there's not a store in New York containing four pounds of buttons!" How my mother laughed when I went in with my little card of buttons and very indignantly informed her that, "I tried to get the four pounds of buttons, but Dr. Gazley would not let me have them!"

This is the true story, now, friends, and the obvious reason was that I simply thought she said four pounds of buttons when its was four pounds of butter. From boyhood until now in my old age, the memory of those buttons has abided with us, and at this late day one may occasionally hear in our household the caution, "Now, don't go and get four pounds of buttons!"

Secondly and lastly, long after my marriage, when Billy [William Edward Jenkins*], my son, was quite a good-sized boy, I committed the absurd blunder from which arose the standing joke of "The Auger Handle," which has been and is still repeated with endless preludes, interludes, and variations. Nearly every time I ride into town some one of my interested (?) friends asks a question, or makes a remark, which seems to insinuate that I will take care not to record that incident among my reminiscences of the past.

But I will record it freely and fully here and now. Behold, these are the plain facts in the case:

I bought an auger—a fine auger without a handle, and

procuring the good solid heart of a post oak, proceeded to make a stout handle, a splendid handle. By the way, it was a considerable job, requiring some little time, labor, and patience, "quartering out" the timber, fitting it to the auger, etc., but after a while it was finished, and I was very complacent at the idea of having it ready for the first emergency. Near time for plowing I needed a rake, which with the help of my new auger I soon made, and proceeded to try it immediately. A worrisome round with unruly steers, and lo! I had put only half enough teeth in my rake, needing just as many more, a tooth between all the other teeth.

I was very tired, very warm, and very mad when I sent Billy in a run for my new auger and waited impatiently, taking no inventory of plan for the necessary work until he came.

Then throwing the rake over on its back and placing the auger, I tried to bore a hole. It would not turn all the way around because it would strike the teeth. The brilliant conclusion that the handle was too long exasperated me, and snatching an ax I cut it off short enough to revolve between the teeth. Then I finished my rake and worked on the stubble field until noon. After eating dinner, while resting, I remarked to my wife, "I ruined my new auger handle after all my work!"

"Why and how?" she asked. I explained how it was too long to turn between the teeth, and I had to cut it off.

"Why, John," she said, "Why didn't you turn the rake over and bore from the topside?"

Springing to my feet I poured forth unbounded abuse upon my head, making an oft-repeated statement, which she always hears with an appreciative smile, "I never did have one particle of sense anyhow!"

Well, there is some shadow of consolation and allowance to be found in the remarkable fact that many famous men of genius and power struggled hard and in vain to conquer that "abstraction or distraction known as absence of mind," which is not only an affliction to its possessor, but often an infliction to his friends. It is said that the famous Ben Jonson once failed to recollect even his own name.

By previous appointment and arrangement I lately spent a day gleaning some facts from the memories of a few of my dear old veteran friends, and desire to chronicle informally the pleasant and interesting data and items gathered as they talked in free and familiar terms of the olden times, when they were young and Texas was in danger and they stood ready to dare even death for her welfare and safety. It is like an interesting dream to thus drop out of the present and let the mind fall back into a forgotten state of affairs which existed a half-century ago. Last Tuesday at Captain Grady's home in Bastrop, we were found wandering away back fifty or sixty years as two old soldiers talked it all over, with occasional comment and suggestion from Sarah, which added no little to the value and interest of their recollections.

"Time brings many changes, John!" It was a trite remark but its full force came home to me as I tried to imagine what they were thinking. From the white hairs, somewhat enfeebled frames, and the scenes of hardship and danger and fun through which they had passed, I caught a faint glimpse of them as they stood in the wilds of young Texas, revealing the strength and hope and life of a vigorous youth and a broad field of adventure around and before them. Troubles and trials, like all of life, die and yet come to be only a memory and after fifty years men bring into an hour's conversation the most terrible suffering and the most comical situations.

First came a hearty laugh over a false alarm, and exclamations upon how a man can run when he realizes that death is hard behind him. It occurred along in 1841 when previous depredations had been frequent and daring, so that the settlers were constantly on the outlook for the Indians. Captain Grady and a friend were traveling between Gonzales and La Grange, and stopped for the night at young Vanham's house, which was only a short distance from his father's home. After supper they suddenly noticed a bright light, evidently a large fire, seemingly upon the identical locality of the old home. All grew much excited and the son cried out in alarm that he knew the Indians had killed his mother and father and were burning up the place. They made all possible speed in reaching the scene, but the mail rider who formed one of the party, went a nearer route. He soon discovered that the flames were simply from burning brush and started back to quiet the fears of the boys behind. Riding along, while yet out of sight of the excited trio, he suddenly launched forth with all the power of powerful lungs into a curious kind of French or Dutch song, filling the night air with a most unearthly yell or chant. Thinking it was the triumphant war song of the savages coming on to finish or continue their work of destruction—all turned, and then came a merry race for life. Captain Grady being unable to keep up, hid at the roadside and watched the "fun." He declares that no man ever turned more quickly or ran faster than young Vanham when the strange song burst upon their ears. He actually leaped over bushes as high as a man and seemed almost to fly.

Then the chat drifted backward to 1834 or 1835 and they told of an interesting adventure or event of that period, all regretting their inability to recall names. Two men with their families were traveling on Little River, in the bottom lands, when they were stopped by a band of twenty or thirty Waco Indians, who made every sign of friendly conciliation, begging for tobacco, provisions, etc. The two travelers were not inexperienced in Indian warfare and kept a strict watch on every movement. At length, one of the warriors, waxing over-

218

impudent and bold, climbed into the wagon, whereupon the white man knocked him out. It was rather an imprudent act, but the Indians went their way showing no sign of resentment or anger. On a little further, however, they shot from behind trees upon our travelers, giving one of them a severe wound through the body. They fought on and kept the cowardly savages at bay, though their chief did manage to slip around and steal a lead horse from one of the wagons. Mounting this he beat a hasty retreat, lying down on one side of the horse to evade or escape the flying bullets which pursued him. Reaching the river he plunged in, and was nearly across when curiosity or a sense of security got the better of his prudence, and he raised his head, just a little in order to look back, when a ball struck him exactly in the center of his forehead, and he sank under the dark waves, and as usual his followers fled, panic-stricken at the loss of their chief.

On the old folks talked, soon bringing up a tragedy of later date, occurring in 1860 or 1861, probably. Wofford Johnson was well-known all through here, having lived in this country for a number of years. He had with his wife and children been spending the day with a friend and was on his way home in the evening. He was entirely unprepared for danger, unarmed and unsuspecting. Suddenly a band of Comanches came upon them, killing the wife, husband, and one child, throwing the other into a thicket near the road. Next day neighbors and friends went to bury the dead and were puzzled to find no sign of one of the children. Hoping it might possibly have been spared they sought and called eagerly and constantly but could get no answer. The fate of the missing child was a mystery. Finally, Mina, the Negro boy who played with and watched over the little ones called aloud and alone. The familiar voice roused the child and quieted his fears so that he answered from his brushy hiding place, where he lay more dead than alive, from fear and the exposure of the night.

Then Mrs. Grady gave an interesting account of some troubles and adventures of which she was thoroughly cognizant at the time and which I think are worthy of mention in this irregular chronicle of early times. Mrs. Wheat, wife of one of our old fellow countrymen, moved from these parts and settled about seventy miles above Uvalde County where these thrilling scenes were enacted. It was about 1850. Her father was killed by Indians and her life was surrounded by fears and tragedies. Some of her nearest neighbors, the entire family again, had been visiting, and in the evening were quietly wending their way home. Coming to a point where the road diverged, the wife with the little ones took the nearest way home, while the husband went the other in order to find and drive home the cows. Upon reaching home, he was filled with surprise and dismay to find no wife and little ones awaiting him. Hurrying back along the road they were to come, he soon came upon them dead, cruelly murdered by the Indians, who, "thus upon the spots most wild and lone and fair, when peace seemed resting in the very air, would gorge their battle-ax with blood," and slay "e'en wailing babes and shrieking maids, and matrons brave and calm."

A rare bit of local history came up as the talk went on and I learned all about the first grave ever dug in Fairview Cemetery, at Bastrop. A child of old Marty Wells was buried first on that hill which now bears record to so many sad hearts and still homes around. The little grave was dug by Bill Duty and Bob Pace.

Then Captain Grady went over the time when our men were called to San Antonio in view of Mexican invasion. He told how Vasquez captured all our spies except Ben Mc-Culloch, who escaped, and sent in proposals of a cessation of hostility till four o'clock—how before that hour orders were issued for all ammunition to be destroyed and preparations be made to evacuate the place. All was chaos and confusion. Kegs of powder were thrown into the river. Liquors and cigars were plentiful and very soon many of the soldiers were dead drunk, while nearly all were in a mild (?) state of intoxication. Jim Kincannon gave rise to an amusing excitement which might have resulted seriously for some. Mounted on his horse, he seized a powder keg under his arm and rode along pouring out the gunpowder in a stream behind him. Jack Bibb, with reckless and grim humor, sang or said in a loud and distinct tone, "Hark from the tomb!" and at the same time touching the lighted end of his cigar to the stream of gunpowder. A wild scene of panic, confusion, and laughter followed, but no damage was done. Then came some wrangling and division as to how to dispose of the artillery, but finally they decided to remove them with ox teams. When ready to take up the line of march, lo, some of our men were too drunk to move and were lashed to the cannons and thus borne out of San Antonio.[1]

Marching to Seguin and finding no sign of invasion they returned to San Antonio to find it literally sacked and in a terrible state of desolation. It was then that the banker, John Twohig, burned up his splendid storehouse and valuable stock of goods rather than see it fall into the hands of the Mexicans.[2]

[1] This evacuation took place on March 5, 1842. When Vasquez ordered the Texans to surrender, a council of war was held with Captain Jack Hays presiding. Lieutenant James P. Kincannon, mentioned by Jenkins, was one of the officers present. It was decided to take a vote among the men and when the votes were counted, fifty-four were in favor of retreating and fifty-three voted to stay and fight. The men threw 327 kegs of powder into the river. Brown, *History of Texas*, II, 213; Henderson, *Colonel Jack Hays, Texas Ranger*, 33.

[2] As soon as the Texans retired from the town, about one hundred

I have promised Jack[3] a chapter on panther hunting, but since there is little of interest or excitement in such sport, I will just add what I know about them to this chapter. My experience in connection with this timid animal will doubtless seem very tame to the children, for all of us can remember how our early years were haunted with terrible tales of terror —cruel, horrible fears as we in imagination could hear the strange wild cry which was said to be very much like the wail of a child or the scream of a woman in distress. Yes, we all used to hear how they would by their weird wailing decoy people and destroy them. A great deal of experience with them in later years taught me the fallacy of such tales, for I always found them very wild and timid and easily killed.

Once on the trail of a panther the work of hunting and killing was about as simple and exciting as squirrel hunting, and I never knew one under any circumstances to show fight —always running a very short distance and taking to a tree, whence one could easily shoot and kill. As to the weird wail like the cry of human distress, I recall only a loud, hoarse

Mexicans ran into Twohig's building for plunder. Twohig had made a trail of powder from the storehouse and lit it as the Texans retreated. The powder set off the ammunition stored in the building and killed a large number of the Mexicans.

John Twohig was wounded and made prisoner on September 11, 1842, when Adrian Woll captured San Antonio. He was taken to Mexico where he escaped from Perote Prison with some of the Mier prisoners. Twohig became a successful banker in San Antonio and lived there until his death in October, 1891. Benavides, "General Woll's Invasion of San Antonio in 1842" (Master's Thesis, University of Texas, 1952), 12–13, 25; Brown, *History of Texas,* II, 211–212; Chabot, *Perote Prisoners,* 47, 96, 216–218; *Handbook of Texas,* II, 813; John J. Linn, *Reminiscences of Fifty Years in Texas* (1883), 326–327; *Telegraph and Texas Register* (Houston), November 2, 1842.

[3] This was Jenkins' grandson. He was about ten years old while Jenkins was writing his reminiscences. Jack Jenkins was county attorney of Bastrop County from 1904 to 1913.

mewing like the me-ow-w-w of some tremendous cat—a doleful sound, however, and rather terrible to young and inexperienced minds. This was quite a familiar sound among our woodland echoes years ago, and was considered no sign of danger except to hogs, colts, and other small animals.

I have known only a very few instances of men being hurt by them—I remember one Tonkawa whose body bore scars from wounds caused by a panther. An animal of the same species used to haunt our woods—the "Marsh Tiger," so called—a large bobbed-tail wildcat which was justly considered much more dangerous, but it would be a rare accident for any of these to straggle in here now, so our children will not likely ever see one. The young panthers, like a fawn or leopard, are spotted, but as they grow older the spots disappear, leaving them of a light, brownish-red color—very much like the color of a deer in the "red season." They rarely ever were lean or poor, for being skillful and incorrigible hunters, they feasted upon the fat of the land. They were very powerful, as well as active and quick, and would often kill horses, hogs, chickens; even a full-grown buck was killed as quickly and easily by a panther as a mouse is dispatched by a cat. I never saw one being weighed, but a full-grown panther would measure at least nine feet from end of nose to tip of tail—the tail alone measuring from three to four feet in length. In appearance, they are simply a specimen of huge house cat.

Our earliest settlers were much troubled with their raids upon our small animals. Col. Wylie [Abraham Wiley] Hill* and I lived near together and owned good dogs, and we used to have frequent occasion to meet and go panther hunting. I remember an incident which occurred on one of these little hunts, which was indeed a hairbreadth escape to me. One of his finest hogs had been killed by a panther. He sent for me.

From all signs there had evidently been two of them—an old one and one just grown. We soon treed and killed the old one and then the dogs started and treed the young one. As we galloped up to the tree I proposed that we dismount and shoot at one and the same time. He agreed. As we struck the ground his gun hung on his saddle and in some way went off —the ball passing through my shirt sleeve and the powder burning my arm. The shock to us both was considerable, and Colonel Hill was much excited and relieved to find the accident had not produced serious results. I waited until he reloaded and we took our simultaneous shot, killing the panther instantly. The old pecan tree still stands on the banks of Sandy Creek and reminds me of how narrowly I escaped being killed by a good friend.

So many interesting things used to happen, that even in this connection I could spin out incidents *ad infinitum*. About forty years ago now, Wylie Hill was at his gin, which stood near the big springs, and hearing something catch one of his hogs, he called his dogs. Setting them on the trail they treed something immediately, whereupon he holloed for me to bring my gun. By this time it was dark and I could barely see the outlines of a large panther as it crouched in the darkness and leaves of a post oak. I shot and the animal fell as if dead, but in an instant it rallied and we heard signs of a fresh and furious fight, as the dogs would bark and howl and yelp in the gloom. The night was a very dark one, and that hollow in that cedar brake could come nearer illustrating "a darkness to be felt" than any place I ever saw. True to the native fearlessness of his character, Colonel Hill went into the thick of the fight, in the thick darkness of the cedar brake, and killed the panther with his knife.

Another instance in his life was equally unusual. He happened to be in the pine hills across the river accompanied by his dogs, but without a gun. They jumped a large bear and treed it. He pelted it out of the tree with rocks and with the dogs soon killed it.

A few years ago I overheard a young man—rather inexperienced in such matters, talking of having spent the night with the brave old soldier, and he laughingly alluded to these two adventures, declaring, "Mr. Wylie Hill must have been a wonderful hunter in his time!—to kill a panther in the dark with a knife and a bear with rocks!" He was a stranger to us all and evidently thought these adventures rather *too* marvelous, but I assured him that I knew them to be positive facts, being an eyewitness—at least being present. It was too dark for *eye* witnesses when the panther was killed.

In going over these little experiences of our early times here I am reminded of a familiar old acquaintance of those days, who was famous for barbecuing meats and serving fine dinners. He had been complimented upon this faculty, till he felt very complacent upon the subject, and once triumphantly asserted that he had more experience in that line than anybody, adding, "I know I have prepared and superintended at least four hundred Fourth of July dinners!"

Along in those times it was reported among us that "a Mexican Lion" haunted Iron Mountain, on the head of Sandy Creek, and we were all anxious for an opportunity to kill it. Jonathan Thomas McGehee[4] had been over at Gonzales on business with a Mr. Bonner and was coming back through the hills at the head of Brushy Creek. He had a splendid rifle and was on the alert, and was much excited when he heard a roaring or growling, which he was sure came from the Mexican Lion. Venturing toward the noise he saw the

[4] Jonathan Thomas McGehee, the son of Sarah Milton (Hill) and John Gilmore McGehee, was born in Alabama on December 20, 1829. He married Emily Spencer in November of 1853. James Saunders, *Early Settlers of Alabama* (1899), 521–524.

animal, but it was so terrible he was afraid to shoot at it, and allowed it to go unmolested. Coming home, he met me first and said in some excitement, "I saw that Mexican Lion, John! Its tail was as long as that rail (ten feet), and its legs were as big around as my body!" I tried to persuade him to go back with me in search of the formidable creature, but he was compelled to go on home. As quickly as possible, my brother, Judge Eastland, and I, with dogs were upon the scene. Watch immediately struck the trail of the supposed Mexican Lion—treed it and I shot, killing it instantly, but it proved to be only a tremendously large panther. McGehee still believes that he saw the Mexican Lion, however.

When Colonel John S. Ford held his company of Rangers on the Rio Grande in 1858, he detailed a small squad of men under young Edward Burleson, Jr., to come in on the waters of the Nueces for the purpose, I think, of collecting money to defray the expenses of his company. Having attended to the business assigned them, they were on their way back to the Rio Grande, traversing an open country, when they discovered not very far away a band of Indians—a force about equal to their own. They advanced upon them, meanwhile trying to arrange or agree upon some plan for the impending fight. The Indians had only one or two guns and one of the Texans, James Carr,[5] a noted marksman, was appointed to do all the shooting, while his comrades were to load and hand him their guns. In this way they hoped to keep out of range of the enemy's arrows. As the little squad advanced, the Indians halted and prepared to meet their attack.

In excitement men sometimes forget or disregard everything, and instead of abiding by their decision or arrange-

[5] James Carr was born in Tennessee in 1807. He lived in Hays County and was still alive in 1885. *U.S. Census,* 1850, Hays County, 243; Sowell, *Early Settlers,* 165, 765.

ment there was wild confusion and disorder, for the instant
Carr dismounted, every man did likewise and made ready
to fight. Seeing this, the Comanches charged right in among
them, and a most terrible hand-to-hand struggle followed.
Bow and arrow, six-shooter, and rifle—all were wielded
with vigorous bravery, till finally all the Indians were killed
except three or four. We lost only one man killed, Baker
Barton, but all of our men were wounded except Warren
Lyons,* some of them receiving several wounds.⁶ James Carr,
who still lives, was wounded three times—first through the
thigh, then an arrow pinned his hand to the breech of his
gun, and finally an arrow struck him in the side, which would
have killed him had not a plug of tobacco in his roundabout
pocket broken its force. Seldom have men fought more desperately, and never were soldiers more sore, or more exhausted, than these were after the struggle.

Warren Lyons, the one Ranger who escaped unhurt, did
so by reason of his remarkable skill in dodging the arrows—
a skill acquired by long association with the Indians.

Lyons had quite a romantic and adventurous experience
in his early life which is very interesting. I think it was in the
fall of 1836 that Warren, a mere boy seven or eight years old,

⁶ This fight took place in December of 1850. Besides Baker Barton,
a ranger named William Lackey was killed. There were eight Texans
besides Burleson in the fight and some fifteen Indians. A runner was
sent to Ford, who sent an ambulance to pick up the men. They were
taken to San Antonio, where they remained until their wounds healed.
It was later discovered that the Indians had, less than twenty-four
hours before, been in a fight with Colonel Samuel Walker and his
rangers.
Warren Lyons was wounded in the battle but only slightly. When
the skirmish began, he abandoned his horse and began to take off his
boots. The men thought he was going to run away, but he was merely
preparing to fight. Sowell, *Early Settlers*, 399–400, 825–826; A. J.
Sowell, "Colonel Rip Ford and His Rangers Battle with Indians,"
Frontier Times, IV, 41–42; Wilbarger, *Indian Depredations in Texas*,
616–620.

accompanied his father to the field where he was plowing. A band of Comanches came suddenly upon them and killed the father and captured the son. Time rolled on, and nothing being heard from the boy he was almost forgotten, or at least seldom thought about. Nevertheless, the woman who was so suddenly bereft of husband and child watched and waited and hoped all along the dreary time, for surely nothing but positive proof could ever make a mother give up her child as dead.

Years afterward, when it was all "forgotten as a dream," a party of surveyors under William S. Wallace went out on the San Saba, and having worked up the river several days, a few of them—Wylie Hill, Richard Cheek, George Hancock,* James L. Jobe,* and perhaps one or two others— separated from the main party, with an appointed place of rejoining them. One evening as they were riding along they saw in the distance something bright and shining, that at first perplexed them, as it gleamed and glistened in the sunlight. Very soon, however, they recognized the shields of Comanches, and we may perhaps imagine their feelings when a nearer approach revealed fifty or sixty of these warriors standing and apparently watching them. As quickly as possible the little body of men secured a good position for self-defense, and by the time the Indians were in gunshot they were stationed in a thicket under a steep mountain, awaiting the attack. Instead of the anticipated charge, however, the Indians halted and signified that they wanted to talk, asking for the captain of the white men. George Hancock was appointed to act as captain and went out to meet their chief, although some violently opposed his going, as they feared foul play.

The old chief, dismounting, met him on "halfway ground," making many demonstrations of friendliness as he advanced, and gave him an earnest hugging when they met and declared him "Big Chief." Meanwhile all of the few whites came to the front in full view and prepared to fire at the slightest hostile movement. They soon realized their utter helplessness, though, for hearing a slight noise they looked around and were surprised to find that the brow of the overhanging mountain was almost covered with Indians, and thus they found themselves literally surrounded by a savage and hitherto merciless foe. No advantage was taken of the situation, however, and the chief proceeded to question Hancock very closely as to the number and whereabouts of the main body of surveyors, and at length proposed to accompany them on their way. So the little company of men found themselves riding along all mixed up with a large band of Comanches, and their sensations may have been somewhat peculiar as they realized the overpowering numbers of their volunteer traveling companions.

They accepted the situation as became brave men, and for a while proceeded upon their journey as if nothing unusual was transpiring. Darkness was fast coming on and the outlook was indeed a gloomy one, as no sign of Wallace and his company of surveyors cheered the hearts of our men. At length, hoping to receive an answer. Wylie Hill gave a keen, shrill halloo or whoop peculiarly his own. Seldom can the human voice make a sound which could be heard at so great a distance. I can hear him now in memory, and believe I would have recognized the signal as his own anywhere in the wide world.

It delighted and amused the savages greatly and they insisted on his repeating it at intervals all along, at the same time trying to imitate the sound. Thus they rode on, and at last, as night settled upon the crowd, the burden of suspense grew unendurable. Hill but spoke what was passing in every man's mind as he said, "Boys, they are going to kill us certain, and we had better take the main bulge on them."

Hitherto they had supposed that not one of the Comanches understood their language. Imagine their surprise when one of the warriors, speaking very good English, answered, "No, these Indians are not going to kill you!"

Turning in surprise Hill inquired, "Who are you? Where did you learn our language?"

Warren Lyons, for he it was, then gave them a brief account of his life among the Comanches—a life to which he had become not only reconciled, but even attached. So great is the power of habit and nature itself.

Finally Hill's halloo was heard and answered by Wallace and his men and guided by the sound all went into camp together. They collected about the same campfire, and "the lion and the lamb," as it were, lay down in peace together, although one man, Ben Heines, refused to trust either Providence or Comanches and sat up the whole night long.

In the course of the conversation the chief, pretending to be entirely ignorant of their business in those parts, asked "What do all these hacks or blazes on the trees mean? Why do you cut them?" Upon being told that they had been bee hunting, he, in a kind but somewhat threatening manner, advised them to leave the woods alone and go home, saying, "This is our hunting ground, and you had better leave at once."

Our men talked a good deal with Warren Lyons, who partially remembered his native tongue, but his long exile had dimmed all recollection of mother, home, and friends, and he seemed quite indifferent. Wylie Hill and others who knew his mother and relatives insisted on his at least making a visit home. The thought of leaving the Indians appeared to be a sad one to him; indeed, he would make no promise, and next morning went his way with the warriors, turning his back upon those of his own race without sign of hesitation or regret.

Not many months after this, Waymon Wells, a friend of
the family, met and recognized Warren Lyons with a band
of Comanches in San Antonio, and again every effort of
argument and persuasion was used to induce him to come
home. Pleading was more successful this time, and at last he
consented to accompany Wells to his mother. Wells described
their journey and the reunion of mother and son to me. As
they came in sight of his old home, Mrs. Lyons was sweeping
the front gallery, and the scene aroused emotion in the son,
as he exclaimed, "That is my mother now! I remember her
right there, sweeping in that way!"[7] Even then, however, in
the strange and intense joy of such a meeting, he seemed shy
and embarrassed, half-afraid of his own mother, as she gave
him the welcome which only a mother could.

And now he stayed a while with her at the home of his
infancy, settling, or trying to settle, into a new life, which
was entirely out of harmony with his taste and habits as
formed by his long and intimate association with the savages.
Soon mother and son went into La Grange together, he clad
in his Indian garb, which she replaced with a suit of clothes.
He could not take all on at once, however, for out in the
street, finding his new shoes not altogether comfortable, he
took them off and resumed his moccasins.

Thus it was with regard to his later life. He could not all
at once settle from a Comanche warrior into an American
citizen, and for some time his life was a struggle between
nature and habit. Once the power of habit prevailed, and he
went back to the Comanches, but amid their wildest scenes of
sport and strife, and in the calm night hours, I think the face
of his mother would constantly come to his mind, until the
warrior grew homesick and once more, this time of his own

[7] Upon reaching home he saw his mother on the porch of the house
and shouted, "Dar me mudder! Dar me mudder!" Wilbarger, *Indian
Depredations in Texas*, 215.

accord, came home, living in Texas ever afterward as a good soldier and an honored citizen.

In the case of Thomas Coleman, who was captured at the time of the Battle of Brushy Creek in 1839, the power of association prevailed, and strange to say he grew up to love a life among the people who had murdered his own mother and brother. His family spared no effort to recover him, and securing the celebrated chief of the Delawares, John Connor, as guide, his cousin looked all through the Indian Nation, till finding him, they almost forced him to come home. He could never, however, adapt himself to civilized life, and soon returned to his wild companions for good.

CHAPTER XIV

In Conclusion

THE HISTORY of our state since 1847 has, it is true, been a checkered one, and recalling our many trials and dangers and losses from annexation on through the Confederate War, one might feel tempted to indulge in egotism in regard to personal experience, for every true soldier was more or less a hero in those trying times. So many still live, however, who were shoulder to shoulder in those struggles both of state and nation, that I forbear entering into further details.

Suffice to say that my life has been almost entirely that of a Texas soldier. Entering service at thirteen years old, against Mexico, I have tried to be faithful to Texas throughout her troubles. I belonged to the very first company of Rebels who left Bastrop for the Confederate War in 1861, and marched home with the last band of troops after engaging in the last skirmish of the war, which occurred on Texas soil at what is called Palmito Ranch, about fifteen miles below Brownsville, on the east side of the Rio Grande.[1]

General James E. Slaughter was *called* commander, but

[1] John Jenkins enlisted in Captain M. B. Highsmith's Bastrop Cavalry, 26th Brigade, Texas State Troops, in July, 1861. His name also appears on a list of the officers and men in Company D, Twelfth Texas Cavalry, William H. Parson's brigade. In October, 1861, Jenkins and John J. Moncure were detailed by Colonel Parsons to obtain from Bastrop County one hundred swords and scabbards. In compliance with this order the county issued bonds to pay N. B.

John S. Ford in reality led and ordered our force of nearly eight hundred Confederates. The Federals had evacuated Brownsville and had gone out to Brazos Island, where they had a considerable force with a good position, well-fortified, holding two or three gunboats in readiness for action. In May, after Lee's surrender, though this was not known to our men at that time, a great deal of cotton was coming into Brownsville, and Ford still held his force there, probably intent upon saving what cotton he could, and when the Yankees entered the place once more, capturing the picket posts and several of our men, he determined to drive them back to the island. So mustering his force and taking four pieces of artillery he advanced upon the Yankee force, which was comprised of about one thousand men.

Ford managed to carry on light skirmishing until he could secure a good position, masking his artillery with his cavalry. When everything was ready the cavalry moved aside and all of the pieces of artillery were discharged at once and unexpectedly to the Yankees, it seemed, who commenced retreating after two or three volleys, and were finally driven back to the island. We captured in all about one hundred and twenty of them— no Confederates were killed, but several were wounded. It was then learned from the Yankee prisoners that the war was over.[2]

After the war I settled down to the quiet life of a farmer,

Tanner, who was operating an arms factory at Bastrop, for making the swords.

In 1863, Jenkins joined Colonel John S. Ford's Volunteers at San Antonio and remained with this group until the close of the war. General Services Administration, National Archives and Records Service, Washington, D.C.; Police Court Records, Bastrop County, Book B, 115.

[2] The skirmish took place on May 13, 1865. Clement Evans (ed.), *Confederate Military History* (1899), XI, 127–129; Dudley G. Wooten, *A Comprehensive History of Texas, 1685–1897* (1898), II, 551–561.

though there were still many exciting camping trips and bear hunts, a few of which I will give in this concluding chapter of my reminiscences.

I owned a pack of the very best trained dogs ever known. For bear hunting they positively could not be surpassed. If I were gifted in the art of making pen portraits, I would like to call them up before us here and show them as I would tell of their respective merits. Ah, they are before my memory now, ready for Mr. Bruin. Here they are—Watch, Caesar, Hector, Brindle, and Florida. No matter what difficulties or complications might occur on a hunt, I could always depend on my faithful dogs. Watch was the most intelligent animal that I have ever seen. He was famous for his wonderful sagacity and had warm friends among all classes everywhere. I could tell by their first bark what game the dogs had struck, and when Watch was in sight I could tell even on a cold trail the size of the bear they were after; he would run along and smell the bushes on either side, just as high as the bear in his flight had touched them, and I could make him attack anything anywhere. I could make him understand what I intended him to do first—indeed to mere animal instinct he added a vast amount of knowledge, reason, and forethought. He would show that he noted many things in our lives. Cold weather, he learned, was most suitable for bear hunting, and sometimes in the night, when everything was freezing, he would come to my bed and in the most eloquent and impressive dog language beg me to take him hunting.

There were two noted localities for bear near us then— Hornsby's Bend, twelve miles below Austin, and the other in the Eblin Bottom, twelve miles below Bastrop. Although bear was abundant in these places, few hunters tried to enter the almost impenetrable tangle of dogwood and greenbrier, of which the dense thickets were composed. A few of us were ready for almost anything of that kind, however, and I can recall exciting times in those old thickets. I remember two bear hunts with Jonathan T. McGehee, which will serve as specimens of many others we enjoyed in those times. First, we camped the night before the hunt within about a mile of the Eblin thicket. Next morning, a cold and frosty one, we entered the thicket on foot, followed by Watch, with his faithful fellows. Instantly he started a bear. There was a fine race through the thicket which stood on the banks of the Colorado and into that, bruin, who had the hounds at his heels, plunged and crossed before I could shoot. The river was quite wide at this point, probably more than a hundred yards. McGehee went around to find a ford while I stood to watch and cheer on the dogs, which had the bear "bayed" on the opposite side. I stood at my post for a considerable time, growing more and more impatient, listening every instant to hear the report of his gun. At last I could stand it no longer, and determined to cross then and there at all hazards, so I cut a couple of green grapevines, and rolling two dead chunks into the water, I tied them together with the vines, thus making me a raft. Then I undressed and put my clothes and gun on my impromptu raft. I plunged into the ice-cold water, and shoving my raft before me, I swam as if it were for dear life. When once across I drew on my clothes, grabbed my gun, and soon joined the dogs in the contest. They already had him up a tree. I shot him out and had him dressed before McGehee came upon the scene.

Another time we entered the terrible thicket in Hornsby's Bend. That was the most dense and impenetrable tangle of brush and brier I have ever seen. After a few sniffs around, Watch struck his trail, where he had been to water in the river, and of course had taken refuge in the thicket. We went into the brush well-clothed, at about nine o'clock, and had about four hours of constant running and struggle before we could get the slightest chance for a shot. Finally, however, I fired at a venture, guessing the whereabouts of the bear by the bend and break and crash of the bushes. The ball went through both thighs of the bear and passing on killed my dog Hector, greatly to my sorrow. Although wounded, the bear again made for the river, but while yet in the open bottom the dogs treed him, whereupon we soon killed him—and a fine, fat bear he was. Poor bear meat is the very poorest, most unpalatable meat in the world, but bear liver, on the other hand, is always good.

When I came out of the brush in Hornsby's Bend the small amount of clothing left on me was in tatters; indeed, no part of the pants and shirt survived except waist band and collar. Besides this my flesh was most terribly torn and scratched. I even had thorns in my head.

I would risk life itself once on a chase. This was the last bear ever seen in that thicket, which is now under cultivation. When bear could not be found near home, I have taken my dogs and gone a hundred miles to find them, and now, even after sixty years of the best hunting, I believe I would ride twenty-five miles to see a fresh bear track.

Biographical Notes

Biographical Notes

CHRISTOPHER B. ACHLIN was a member of Jack Hays's Texas Ranger company, which he joined in 1840. He was wounded in the Battle of Bandera Pass in 1841, served as orderly sergeant during Woll's invasion, was wounded three times in the Nueces Canyon fight in 1844, three times soon afterward in a personal encounter with Indians, and several more times in the fight on the Frio River in 1845. He served as captain of Company B in Hays's regiment during the Mexican War. After the war he moved to California with Hays.

Achlin was wounded more often than any other Texas Ranger, yet lived to die a natural death, though the exact date is not known. Henderson, *Colonel Jack Hays, Texas Ranger,* 21, 39, 57, 59, 64, 71; Sowell, *Early Settlers,* 58; Traylor, "Benjamin Franklin Highsmith," *Frontier Times,* XV, 316; Wilbarger, *Indian Depredations in Texas,* 78.

AMOS R. ALEXANDER, his wife Hannah, and two sons, Lyman W. and Amos, Jr., came to Texas from Pennsylvania in the spring of 1833. They settled at Bastrop where, after returning to New York for supplies, they opened a store and hotel.

In April of 1835 Amos and Amos, Jr., went to the coast to get a supply of goods they had ordered. They hired another man and his young brother to help them haul the goods. On June 1, just as they reached Pin Oak Creek, about thirty-five miles from Bastrop, they were attacked by a party of Indians. Amos Alexander was killed instantly and Amos, Jr., who was riding a horse, was shot through the body. He turned and rode full speed back toward Moore's Fort at La Grange until he met the other wagon driven by the two brothers. They started together for Moore's Fort, but after going about a mile, Amos, Jr., died from his wound. He was put under a tree and covered with leaves and moss.

The teamsters reached John H. Moore, who raised a party of men, commanded by Burleson, which went out and buried Amos and his father. The old man had been scalped and his body badly mutilated. The Indians were so close that the powder from their guns scorched the clothes of the Alexanders when they were ambushed. The Indians had plundered the wagon, taking everything they could carry and destroying everything else.

Alexander had approximately two leagues of land in Texas and a 12-acre farm lot and a building lot in Bastrop. Alexander's wife Hannah died in November of 1849 and Lyman Alexander was appointed administrator *de bonus non* of Alexander's estate. E. H. Alexander, "Amos Alexander and His Son Killed by Indians," *Frontier Times*, IV, 40–41; Probate Records, Bastrop County, File A-1; Register of Spanish Archives; Wilbarger, *Indian Depredations in Texas*, 207–208.

EDWARD BLAKEY came to Texas in 1832 from Kentucky with his parents, John and Nancy Blakey. John Blakey died of fever only a few weeks after reaching Brazoria. Undaunted, Mrs. Blakey made her way with her family to Bastrop, settling two miles west of the town on her headright league and labor. During the Runaway Scrape, Edward Blakey returned with Jenkins on furlough and stayed with his mother and sisters, but his brother, Lemuel Stockton Blakey, remained with Billingsley and was one of the nine Texans killed at the Battle of San Jacinto. His two sisters married Jonathan Burleson and Noah Smithwick. After the death of Edward Blakey, the last man of the family, Captain Jonathan Burleson and his wife moved to the Blakey league, so as to protect his mother-in-law. Mrs. Blakey died in 1852, leaving no one to carry on the Blakey name. Dixon and Kemp, *Heroes of San Jacinto*, 160, 455; Smithwick, *Evolution of a State*, 133, 156–157; Sowell, *Early Settlers*, 17–18; Sowell, *Rangers and Pioneers*, 57; C. R. Wharton, *San Jacinto, the Sixteenth Decisive Battle* (1930), 130–131.

JONATHAN BURLESON, a brother of Edward Burleson, was born in Tennessee in 1808. He moved to Texas in 1832 and settled in Travis County below Austin. He participated in the Siege of Bexar and was detailed to guard the baggage at Harrisburg during the Battle of San Jacinto. He married Nancy B. Blakey in 1833 and settled on his mother-in-law's league two miles west of Bastrop. He was in the Battle of Brushy Creek in 1839 and served as a captain of the Texas Rangers until 1845. He died December 3, 1879, and was buried on his property near Bastrop. His wife died ten years later. Brown, "Annals of Travis County," V, 44–47; L. W. Kemp, Harrisburg Roll.

JULIAN C. CALHOUN, born in Tennessee in 1815, moved to Texas and settled first at Bastrop, but later moved to his 640-acre farm in Fayette County. He was a gunsmith and farmer by profession. His wife Jeanette was born in 1818. They had six children, one of whom was born in Arkansas in 1836. Burlage and Hollingsworth, *Abstract of Land Claims; U.S. Census,* 1850, Fayette County, 162.

JAMES CAMPBELL received a league of land in Lavaca County on November 27, 1832. He was instrumental in laying out the town of Walnut Springs in 1838 and served under Burleson in the Cordova Rebellion. Brown, *Indian Wars,* 62–65; Burlage and Hollingsworth, *Abstract of Land Claims,* 610; Sowell, *Early Settlers,* 115, 131.

HUGH M. CHILDRESS was born in Tennessee about 1801. He received title to a league of land in Williamson County on October 31, 1832. He was a member of Tumlinson's Rangers and was wounded in the leg during the Hibbans fight. He returned to Bastrop after the Runaway Scrape and served on the jury of the first meeting of the County Court in May of 1837. A Methodist minister, he was also a proficient fiddler, dancer, hunter, and Indian fighter. Preachers who could do nothing but preach and pray found themselves without a job in early Texas. He was still living in Bastrop in 1838, but is listed as living in Burleson County in the 1850 census. Jesse Billingsley Papers (Archives Collection, University of Texas Library) ; Brown, *Indian Wars,* 90; Burlage and Hollingsworth, *Abstract of Land Claims,* 610; Police Court Records, Bastrop County, A, 10; Ray, *Austin*

BIOGRAPHICAL NOTES

Colony Pioneers, 307–308; Smithwick, *Evolution of a State,* 155, 207; *U.S. Census,* 1850, Burleson County, 432.

WILLIAM A. CLOPTON was born in Tennessee in 1815. He moved to Bastrop, Texas, in 1837. He and his wife Mary had a son, William A. Clopton, Jr., in 1840. They also had a daughter who later married Charles Cottingham. Clopton was second lieutenant in Company B during the Mier Expedition. He was released on September 16, 1844. Bastrop County Scrapbook (Archives Collection, University of Texas); *U.S. Census,* 1850, Bastrop County, 172; Wade, *Mier Expedition,* I, 123.

SAMPSON CONNELL and his wife Sarah J. Connell settled at Bastrop in an early day. He served in Jesse Billingsley's Mina Volunteers and participated in the Battle of San Jacinto. In 1838 he paid L. C. Cunningham $5.00 for preparing a "government paper," probably his donation certificate for 640 acres of land for his army services. He received his title to the land on September 14, 1838. He was granted more land in Caldwell County, but died in Washington County in 1847. His son, Sampson, Jr., was made administrator of his estate on March 29, 1847. Burlage and Hollingsworth, *Abstract of Land Claims,* 164; L. C. Cunningham Papers (Archives Collection, University of Texas Library); Dixon and Kemp, *Heroes of San Jacinto,* 163; Kemp, San Jacinto Roll; Smithwick, *Evolution of a State,* 134.

JOHN COOKE and his partner Isaac Hughes were Old Three Hundred settlers. On December 15, 1830, however, the title to their land was taken away from them because they had done nothing to improve the land since their arrival in 1824. John Cooke then received a league of land in Austin's Little Colony on April 4, 1831, in Fayette County. A John Cook was killed in the Alamo, who may or may not have been the same man. E. C. Barker, "Minutes of the Ayuntamiento of San Felipe de Austin," *Southwestern Historical Quarterly,* XXIII; Bugbee, "The Old Three Hundred," *Quarterly of the Texas State Historical Association,* I, 117; Gulick and others (ed.), *The Papers of Mirabeau Buonaparte Lamar,* IV, pt. 1, 39–40.

JAMES CRAFT came to Texas early in 1835, enlisted in the Mina Volunteers and was elected second lieutenant. He and his brother, Russell B. Craft, were both in the Battle of San Jacinto and were discharged at Bastrop on June 2, 1836. Russell built the first jail in Bastrop in 1840. James died in 1847, John S. Craft being appointed administrator of his estate. Comptroller's Military Service Records (Texas State Library), #3177; Dixon and Kemp, *Heroes of San Jacinto,* 163; Minutes of the Corporation of Bastrop, April 4, 1840; Probate Records, Bastrop County, File C-1.

LEANDER CALVIN CUNNINGHAM, ninth child of James and Margaret Cunningham, was born on the family farm in eastern Tennessee on July 10, 1810. The family moved to Alabama Territory in 1815 and it was here that young Cunningham studied law and was admitted to the bar, in 1832. Leander and two of his brothers emigrated to Texas in 1833. He settled in the then thriving town of Bastrop, where he began his practice of law. When Travis sent his famous letter from the Alamo in March, 1836, Cunningham and a few others tried to go to his aid, but could not get through the Mexican forces that surrounded the Alamo. Cunningham then joined the Mina Volunteers under Jesse Billingsley and fought in the Battle of San Jacinto.

In 1838 he married Mrs. Ann Sloan Slaughter, who had recently come to Texas from Kentucky. He ran for representative from Bastrop to the Second Texas Congress, receiving sixty-four votes to Jesse Billingsley's ninety, and took his seat in Congress when the first session opened. Billingsley protested that the election was illegal because thirteen of Cunningham's votes were from a company of Texas Rangers, who did not have the right to vote in such an election. Cunningham pointed out that ten of these had enlisted only as volunteers and had never taken the oath as soldiers. This still gave him a majority of one vote over Billingsley. Billingsley then showed that all thirteen names appeared on the muster roll of Company C and that they were therefore technically members of the company. The issue was put to vote in the House of Representatives; Billingsley won, thirteen to eleven, and took his seat the next day. However, in the same year Cunningham was elected County Judge of Bastrop

County and in 1841 Mayor of Bastrop. His home was even used as a courthouse for a short period of time in 1839.

He moved away from Bastrop in 1860, first to Alleyton, then successively to Columbus, Waelder, and finally, in 1895, to Seguin, where he died on December 24, 1896. He was buried at Waelder, next to his wife, who had died on June 19, 1895. Bastrop County History, Historical Records Survey (Archives Collection, University of Texas Library), 4; Brown, "Annals of Travis County"; L. C. Cunningham Papers (Archives Collection, University of Texas Library) ; Dixon and Kemp, *Heroes of San Jacinto*, 163–164; *Journal of the House of Representatives of the Republic of Texas, Second Congress, First Session, 1837* (1838), 25–27; Kemp, San Jacinto Roll; McDowall, "Journey," 30–31; *Monuments Erected . . . to Commemorate the Centenary of Texas Independence*, 171; Police Court Records, Bastrop County, A, 7–8, 25; Register of Spanish Archives, XVI, 410; Lewis Publishing Company, *Twentieth Century History of Southwest Texas* (1907), II; *U.S. Census*, 1850, Bastrop County, 19.

James Curtis, a participant in the Battle of San Jacinto, was born in Alabama in 1780. As one of Austin's Old Three Hundred he received a league of land in Burleson County, but moved to Bastrop County in 1831. He was the oldest man at the Battle of San Jacinto, which he entered to avenge the death of his son-in-law, Wash Cottle, who had fallen at the Alamo. He accompanied each shot at the Mexicans with the words, "Alamo! You killed Wash Cottle!" He died in 1849.

Curtis had three sons and two daughters by a first wife who died before 1830. He was married again, to a woman named Sarah, from whom he separated in 1838. He left his property to his children. Bugbee, "The Old Three Hundred," *Quarterly of the Texas State Historical Association*, I, 112; Dixon and Kemp, *Heroes of San Jacinto*, 164; Kemp, San Jacinto Roll; Smithwick, *Evolution of a State*, 126–128, 132, 207.

Matthew Duty, son of Solomon Duty, settled near Webberville, Travis County, with his brothers about 1830. Early in 1837 he and Billy Hornsby had an encounter with Indians which shows the courage and heroism of some of the early frontiersmen. They were out with a group of men, all of whom were mounted except Billy. When the Indians fired on them, all of the party ran off, not giving a thought to young Hornsby. Matthew Duty, however, wheeled his horse and put himself between Billy and the Indians. He presented his gun but knowing that once he fired the Indians would be on him before he could reload, he did not shoot. The bluff worked on the Indians perfectly. Every time he presented his gun the Indians fell back. Billy reached his home finally and Duty fired his gun at one of the Indians and entered the house in safety. Mrs. Hornsby watched helplessly the whole race, expecting every minute to see her son killed.

Matthew was riding a horse known as the "Duty roan," on which he was killed a few weeks later. The horse was ridden by Joseph Duty after Matthew's death and was captured by Indians, who shot at Joseph but only succeeded in wounding the Duty roan, while his rider escaped unharmed. In the Battle of Plum Creek in 1840 one of the Burlesons shot an Indian, whose horse turned out to be none other than the Duty roan. It was then kept and ridden by the Burlesons in many Indian fights. Brown, "Annals of Travis County," V, 19; *Handbook of Texas,* I, 528; Smithwick, *Evolution of a State,* 224, 226.

NICHOLAS W. EASTLAND was born in Woodford County, Kentucky, in 1803. He moved to Tennessee with his family, where he grew up. Eastland then preceded his brother, William M. Eastland to Texas. He received a league of land in Bastrop County on February 16, 1836. Jenkins tells the rest of his life in his sketch. Burlage and Hollingsworth, *Abstract of Land Claims,* 620; *U.S. Census,* 1850, Bastrop County, 191.

JAMES EDMONDSON was in Tumlinson's Rangers during the Texas Revolution and was then about sixteen years old. He was one of the men under Mark B. Lewis who recaptured the archives from Smith and Chandler in 1842. Edmondson went to California during the gold rush and lived nearly to the turn of the century there; the exact date of his death is not known. Smithwick, *Evolution of a State,* 124, 207; Hope Yager, "Archive War in Texas" (Master's Thesis, University of Texas, 1939).

JOHN EDWARDS received land in April, 1831, in either Fort Bend or Montgomery County, but lived for some time in Bastrop. Edward's horse and rifle were taken by the Indians in this encounter in 1836 described by Jenkins. Burlage and Hollingsworth, *Abstract of Land Claims*, 20; Wilbarger, *Indian Depredations in Texas*, 231.

STEPHEN V. R. EGGLESTON received two free building lots from the town commissioners of Bastrop. These lots were given to every "artist" who might settle in the town. This is the only intimation as to Eggleston's profession, but there is no record of what type of "artist" he may have been. He built the first two-story house in the town and it was used as a meeting house, courthouse, and dance hall.

Although Wilbarger says it was John Eggleston who was killed and Smithwick says it was James, the probate records of Bastrop County prove that Stephen died in 1839 and that he was survived by John and James. Probate Records, Bastrop County, File E-1; Ray, *Austin Colony Pioneers*, 318, 340; Smithwick, *Evolution of a State*, 202; Wilbarger, *Indian Depredations in Texas*, 88.

NATHANIEL W. FAISON was one of the original thirteen men who left La Grange with Captain Dawson on September 16, 1842. He was captured during the Dawson Massacre, one of the fifteen spared from death. After the battle he was the only prisoner who had any funds, about two dollars, of which he was soon relieved. His gold ring was also demanded, but he pretended that it wouldn't come off. A Mexican came up with a knife, evidently about to cut off Faison's finger. Then, however, Faison discovered that the ring would come off with ease.

He was taken to Perote Prison, where he was confined until his release on March 24, 1844. Faison was a merchant by trade. Chabot, *The Perote Prisoners*, 54, 82, 112, 297, 309; Weyand and Wade, *An Early History of Fayette County*, 151–161, 176.

DR. JAMES FENTRESS was born in Tennessee on May 7, 1802. He came to Texas in an early day and married Mary Ophelia Hardeman, who was born on June 8, 1822, also in Tennessee. He played the fiddle, and along with Rev. Hugh M. Childress

247

BIOGRAPHICAL NOTES

and Noah Smithwick often kept dances and parties in a lively mood all night long. Fentress participated in the Battle of Plum Creek, as well as the Cordova fight. In one of these encounters he cut off the head of an Indian he had killed and took it home with him for medical observation.

He and his wife settled near Prairie Lea, Caldwell County, where he died on July 7, 1872, and his wife on July 13, 1888. Fentress, a town with a population of 250, now stands on the site of his home. D. W. C. Baker, *A Texas Scrapbook* (1875), 579; Traylor, "Benjamin Franklin Highsmith," *Frontier Times,* XV, 314; *Monuments Erected ... to Commemorate the Centenary of Texas Independence,* 171; Smithwick, *Evolution of a State,* 155.

GREENLEAF FISK is listed as having been detailed to guard the baggage at Harrisburg during the San Jacinto battle. "Left at Harrisburg" was the term used for all Texan soldiers who were on official duty during the Battle of San Jacinto, even though some were on other army service.

Fisk was born in New York, May 19, 1807, and came to Texas in 1834. He settled at Bastrop and served in Billingsley's Mina Volunteers in 1836. He was Clerk of the District Court at Bastrop in 1837, Mayor of Bastrop in 1840, and Chief Justice of Bastrop County from 1841 to 1844. He served as a member of the Third Congress of the Republic of Texas and participated in the Mexican War. Moving to Brown County, he taught school and in 1862 was made first Chief Justice of that county. In 1870 he donated land upon which the town of Brownwood was built. Fisk died January 26, 1888, father of fifteen children, seven by Mary A. Manlove and eight by Mary Hawkins. *Biographical Directory of Texas Conventions and Congresses,* 84; Burlage and Hollingsworth, *Abstract of Land Claims,* 621; Kemp, Harrisburg Roll; Minutes of the Corporation of Bastrop, November 1839; Police Court Records, Bastrop County, A, 11; Probate Minutes, Bastrop County, A, B, C; Ray, *Austin Colony Pioneers,* 348.

TUCKER FOLEY was the son of an eccentric but wealthy planter, W. G. L. Foley, who gave up two other sons for Texas. Arthur Foley was killed in the Goliad Massacre in 1836 and James

248

BIOGRAPHICAL NOTES

Foley was killed by Mexicans in 1839. Boethal, "History of Lavaca County, 1685–1930" (Master's Thesis, University of
Texas, 1932), 23; Brown, *History of Texas,* I, 168n.

CHARLES FURNASH, popularly known as Jehu, was born about
1780. He was one of Austin's Old Three Hundred and received title to a sitio of land in present Burleson County on
August 19, 1824. He and his wife Sally had five sons, Charles,
Jr., John, Robert, Conrad, and Jehu, and two daughters, Lu-
cinda and Eliza Ann. The family moved to Washington County,
where many stories are told about Jehu, but it is not known
whether the stories are about old or young Jehu Furnash. Burlage and Hollingsworth, *Abstract of Land Claims;* Rena Green
(ed.), *The Swisher Memoirs* (1932), 9; *Handbook of Texas,* I,
657; Ray, *Austin Colony Pioneers,* 99.

JAMES GILLELAND was born September 8, 1798. He married a
sixteen-year-old girl named Diana on October 11, 1821, and a
week later they moved to Texas. His wife was the first white
woman to cross the Brazos River. In the 1830's they settled on
their headright league on Gilleland Creek, to which they gave
their name. It was then part of Bastrop County—later it became
part of Travis County. In the spring of 1834 he organized the
first Methodist Church in Austin's Little Colony. Services were
held in the incompleted storehouse of Jesse Halderman.

In the Brushy Creek battle Gilleland was shot in the neck, the
ball going down through his lungs. He was survived by his wife,
several daughters, and one son. His wife died in Waco in 1895.
Brown, "Annals of Travis County," V, 35; Korges, "Bastrop
County, Texas: Historical and Educational Development"
(Master's Thesis, University of Texas, 1933), I, 167–168; Per-
kins, "The Local History Approach . . . Bastrop" (Master's
Thesis, University of Texas, 1954), 174; Ray, *Austin Colony
Pioneers,* 314; Sowell, *Early Settlers,* 17.

JAMES H. GILLESPIE (or Gillaspie) was born in Virginia on
January 5, 1805, the son of William and Elizabeth Gillespie, and
emigrated to Texas in 1835. On January 14, 1836, at Nacogdoches, he enlisted in the volunteer auxiliary corps and served as
first lieutenant and captain in J. L. Bennett's company, commanding it in the Battle of San Jacinto.

Gillespie married Susan Faris, daughter of one of the men in his company, in Walker County near Huntsville. They were the parents of seven children. Gillespie died on October 3, 1867. For further details see Comptroller's Military Service Records (Texas State Library), #6575; Dixon and Kemp, *Heroes of San Jacinto*, 405; *Handbook of Texas* I, 689; Kemp, San Jacinto Roll; Probate Minutes, Bastrop County, A, B, C, D.

JAMES GOACHER, a native of Alabama, settled on Rabb's Creek in Lee County in 1828. Early in 1835 he and his family moved to Bastrop County where he opened a large cotton plantation In February of 1837 the family was attacked by Indians; Goacher, his son, and his son-in-law, Jane Crawford's husband, were killed while cutting wood.

One of Mrs. Jane Crawford's little sons was caught by an Indian while running away from the house. He grabbed the Indian's thumb with his teeth and bit it so hard and long that the Indian beat him over the head with a ramrod. Once, while Mrs. Crawford was a captive, the Indians took her little daughter and threw her into a stream to drown. Mrs. Crawford jumped in and saved her, whereupon the Indians grabbed the child and threw her in again. This continued for some time, Mrs. Crawford retrieving the child each time she was pitched into the water. Finally the savages tired of the game and one of them started to stab the girl when Mrs. Crawford picked up a log and hit the Indian over the head, knocking him out. This amused the rest of the tribe and they laughed loudly at their fallen comrade. They finally gave the child to her mother, saying, "Squaw too much brave. Damn you, take your papoose and carry it yourself—we not do it."

Mrs. Crawford and her children were taken to Holland Coffee's trading house on the Red River to sell. Charles Spaulding, a trader, bought them for 400 yards of calico, some blankets, a quantity of beads, and other articles. He married Jane Crawford and they moved to Bastrop, where in 1850 the family consisted of five Spaulding children and two Goacher boys aged 21 and 25.

The name Goacher was pronounced "Got-cher" by the early settlers and has been variously and incorrectly spelled Gotier, Gocher, Goucher, and Gotcher. Brown, "Annals of Travis County," IV; DeShields, *Border Wars*, 212–215; Korges, "Bas-

250

trop County, Texas: Historical and Educational Development"
(Master's Thesis, University of Texas, 1933), I, 72–73, 130;
Sowell, *Rangers and Pioneers,* 24; *U.S. Census,* 1850, Bastrop
County, 194; Wilbarger, *Indian Depredations in Texas,* 15–19.

DANIEL M. GRADY was born in Alabama in 1822. He served
under Colonel Thomas Howard in 1842 and was 2nd lieutenant
in Company C under Captain Thomas Green. Grady was captain of a company of Texas Rangers in the 1870's. He lived in
Bastrop County. Henderson, *Colonel Jack Hays, Texas Ranger,*
64, 78; Sowell, *Early Settlers,* 809; *U.S. Census,* 1860, Bastrop
County, 70.

FREDERICK W. GRASSMEYER was born in Germany in 1801. He
arrived in Texas a bachelor merchant in March of 1831 and
established a ferry on his quarter league where the Bastrop–
Fayette County line crosses the Colorado. This ferry was probably the flat boat used to carry the goods to La Grange. Grass-
meyer also received three-quarters of a league in Bastrop
County from the Mexican government, and bought half of the
S. A. Pugh league in 1831. He was the first German to own land
in Fayette County. Grassmeyer served in the Texas Revolution.
In 1850 he was living on the farm of James Sorrell and owned
real estate valued at $15,000. He died in La Grange in 1887.
Burlage and Hollingsworth, *Abstract of Land Claims,* 623;
Ray, *Austin Colony Pioneers,* 307–308; Register of Spanish
Archives, IV, 606; *U.S. Census,* 1850, Bastrop County, 194;
Weyand and Wade, *An Early History of Fayette County.*

JESSE HALDERMAN (spelled Holderman by most of the old settlers, but Halderman by himself) was born in Kentucky about
1801. He came to Texas from his native state in 1831 and on
December 3, 1832, received title to one-quarter league in Austin's Fourth Colony, situated in present Washington County.
In 1835 he owned a store in Bastrop, in which James Gilleland
organized the first Bastrop County Church.

He joined the Texas Army with his brother David in 1836
and served in Jesse Billingsley's Mina Volunteers from February
28 to May 20. They donated two teams and wagons loaded
with flour to the army. David was furloughed because of his

rheumatism during Houston's retreat, but Jesse participated in the Battle of San Jacinto, for which service he later received a donation certificate for 640 acres of land. In May of 1837 Jesse served on the first jury in Bastrop County. He and his brother received the first two marriage licenses issued in the county and were married in a double wedding on the Fourth of July, 1837—David to Candace Thompson and Jesse to Candace's stepsister, Harriet Campbell. On October 1, 1838, Jesse received a bounty warrant of 320 acres of land in Bastrop County for his services during the Texas Revolution. He died in 1850 in Bastrop. The administrator of Halderman's estate, Campbell Taylor, soon afterward married his widow. Burlage and Hollingsworth, *Abstract of Land Claims*, 627; Jones, *Bastrop* (1936), 13; Kemp, San Jacinto Roll; McDowall, "Journey," 59; Police Court Records, Bastrop County, A, 13; Register of Spanish Archives, A, 34; *U.S. Census*, 1850, Bastrop County, 151.

GEORGE DUNCAN HANCOCK, whose nativity and date of birth is as much a mystery as that of Walker Wilson, is listed by Dixon and Kemp as born in Adams County, Mississippi, on April 22, 1809. Baker in his list of members of the Texas Veterans Association, gives Hancock as a native of Tennessee. The 1850 census states that Hancock was born in Virginia in 1811.

It is definitely known that Hancock served in Kimbro's company at San Jacinto and soon afterward became a merchant at La Grange. He joined Company E under Fisher on the Mier Expedition, but was left on the camp guard detail during the Battle of Mier and hence was not captured. In 1845 he moved to Austin and served a term in the state legislature from Travis County. He married Laura Lewis in 1855 and had several children. Hancock died on January 6, 1879, at Austin. Baker, *A Texas Scrapbook*, 599; Dixon and Kemp, *Heroes of San Jacinto*, 429–430; Kemp, San Jacinto Roll; *U.S. Census*, 1850, Travis County, 38; Wade, *Mier Expedition*, I, 125.

THOMAS MONROE HARDEMAN was born at Bolivar, Tennessee, in 1814. He came to Texas in 1835 and fought in the Battle of Gonzales on October 2 of that year. He participated in the Battle of San Jacinto under Captain William Heard. Hardeman was captain of a company at Plum Creek and was in the Vasquez campaign in 1842. He married Susan Burleson, General Burleson's niece. Commissioned as a major, he joined the Confederate Army in 1862. He died at Knoxville, Tennessee, on September 14, 1862, while en route to join his command. Dixon and Kemp, *Heroes of San Jacinto,* 210–211; Kemp, San Jacinto Roll.

ANDERSON J. HARRELL, born in Tennessee in 1823, was the oldest son of Captain Jacob M. and Mary Harrell. The family came to Texas in 1833 and were living at Nashville, Texas, in 1836. In 1838 they moved to Waterloo, and built the first house where Austin now stands. He served in Hays's Texas Rangers and was wounded in the fight on the Hondo River. He was with Mark Lewis in the Archive War. Harrell was County Clerk of Travis County in 1845, Chief Justice in 1846, and later he was a clerk in the General Land Office. Harrell married prior to 1847, when he and his wife were listed as members of the Baptist Church in Austin. He died in the early 1870's. Brown, "Annals of Travis County," VI, IX, 7, X, 32–34; Hardy, "A History of Travis County, 1832–1865" (Master's Thesis, University of Texas, 1938), 26, 113; Sowell, *Early Settlers,* 28; *U.S. Census,* 1850, Williamson County, 23; Hope Yager, "Archive War in Texas" (Master's Thesis, University of Texas, 1939).

JOHN HARVEY was born in Tennessee in 1810 and came to Texas in 1834, settling at Nacogdoches. He served in Captain Hayden Arnold's company from March 6 to May 30, 1836, and participated in the Battle of San Jacinto. He married Polly Reed on October 15, 1837, in a double wedding with his brother James and Polly's sister Jane.

John and Polly Harvey moved to Bastrop in 1838, where he was engaged in many surveying expeditions. That same year he and twenty inexperienced men went on such an expedition out on the San Saba River. One day while encamped near a creek Harvey went to get some water and was captured by a group of Waco Indians. The Indians had stolen a Comanche pony and had eaten half of it. They made Harvey carry the other half on his back all day long, and near sunset they were surrounded by the Comanches. The Indian who had stolen the horse was given three hundred lashes on the back with a rawhide whip. The Wacoes were then asked who was responsible for taking Harvey prisoner and this man was given the same flogging. Harvey was then given a knife and told to kill the chief. He refused and was told to cut off the savage's ears. He still refused, and expected to be killed for disobeying the order, but for some reason he was returned to his camp safely and throughout the rest of the expedition the Comanches considered the band of Texans under their special protection. This was a rare and possibly unique incident of kindness towards Texans by the Comanche tribe.

Harvey died at his home in Salado, Bell County, in 1885. DeShields, *Border Wars*, 260–261; Dixon and Kemp, *Heroes of San Jacinto*, 345–346; Kemp, San Jacinto Roll; Ray, *Austin Colony Pioneers*, 116.

SARAH (CREATH) HIBBANS suffered more at the hands of Indians than any other woman in the history of Texas. She first married John McSherry and with him moved to Texas. McSherry was killed by Indians about the time she gave birth to John, Jr. After a few years she married John Hibbans and settled on the Hibbans league on the east side of the Guadalupe River.

In 1835 she took John McSherry, Jr., and a newborn child by Hibbans to visit her family in Illinois. She returned by boat early in 1836 with her brother, George Creath. In February Hibbans met them at Columbia on the Brazos with an oxcart, in which they were to journey home. While camping on Rocky Creek in Lavaca County, only fifteen miles from their house, they were attacked by thirteen Indians. Hibbans and Creath were killed and Mrs. Hibbans was captured.

The facts given by Jenkins are substantiated by all other known accounts, except that upon her escape Mrs. Hibbans first went into the house of Jacob Harrell, where she sat down in a chair. The Harrells were given quite a shock because they had entered the house and had been in the room for some time before they discovered her. She was too exhausted to speak for a while, but finally recovered enough to tell her story to Harrell who at once took her to Reuben Hornsby's house, where Tumlinson and his rangers were camping. After the recovery of her son, she lived with the Hornsbys and went with them on the Runaway Scrape. Soon afterward she married Claiborne Stinnett, a member of the Convention of 1832. He was killed by two runaway slaves in 1837, while sheriff of Gonzales County. In 1839 she was married a fourth and last time, to Philip Howard. They survived two more severe Indian attacks on their home, but suffered no more deaths in the family.

After the fight between Tumlinson and the Indians, the barrel of Josiah Wilbarger's gun was found on an Indian. The stock had been broken. Brown, *Indian Wars,* 88–91; Smithwick, 118–123; Wilbarger, *Indian Depredations in Texas,* 14, 220–221.

ABRAHAM WILEY HILL, the son of Sarah McGehee and Thomas Hill, was born in Georgia in 1816. In 1835 he and his brothers, Thomas and Middleton, joined a volunteer company in Montgomery, Alabama, and came to Texas to fight in the Revolution. Upon reaching Texas, the three brothers decided to settle permanently in Bastrop County, and bought the Edward Burleson league near Smithville. On July 7, 1835, Wiley bought the east half of the Jenkins league from Sarah Jenkins. He did not participate in the Battle of San Jacinto, for he was assisting his mother's family, the McGehees, on the Runaway Scrape. He returned to Georgia and in January, 1837, married Evaline Hubbard. They moved immediately to Bastrop County.

About 1854 Wiley Hill built a large, southern-type mansion on his half of the Jenkins league. It still stands. In 1850 Hill's real estate alone was valued at $14,925—which was then a large amount. Hill and his wife had six children. He died in 1887. Bastrop *Advertiser,* August 29, 1935; Korges, "Bastrop County, Texas: Historical and Educational Development" (Master's Thesis, University of Texas, 1933), I, 88; James E. Saunders, *Early Settlers of Alabama* (1899), 451, 530; *U.S. Census,* 1850, Bastrop County, 192; Wilbarger, *Indian Depredations in Texas,* 284–285.

JOSEPH HORNSBY was the same age as John Jenkins, both having been born in 1822. Joe was the son of Reuben and Sarah Hornsby and lived in Austin. It is not known when he died. Hardy, "A History of Travis County, 1832–1865" (Master's

Thesis, University of Texas, 1938), Appendix E, 238–241; Ray, *Austin Colony Pioneers,* 354.

ELIJAH INGRUM was in Texas as early as 1829, when he served in Captain Abner Kuykendall's company during the pursuit of some Indian robbers. He had a league and labor of land in Williamson County and received a bounty warrant for one year's ranger service. Burlage and Hollingsworth, *Abstract of Land Claims;* for Ingrum's Indian encounters see Brown, *Indian Wars,* 88–91; DcShields, *Border Wars,* 48–49; Smithwick, *Evolution of a State,* 227–228.

WILLIAM A. J. JENKINS was born in Marengo County, Alabama, May 16, 1828. He served in Highsmith's company in 1847 under Colonel Jack Hays, but as his service was confined to the frontier section of the state he did not participate in the Mexican War. He was, however, in many battles with Indians. He served as a teamster in the Confederate Army. After the war he farmed in Bastrop, Caldwell, and Frio counties and in 1889 retired and moved to Smithville, Texas. Jenkins married Evaline Faith on September 6, 1849, and they had eight children. Lewis Publishing Company, *History of Texas,* XII, 726–727.

WILLIAM EDWARD JENKINS, the oldest son of John and Mary Jane Jenkins, was born in 1847. He served as sheriff of Bastrop County from 1876 to 1884, the period when the sheriff was the most important man in the county, and when gunfights were common. With his brothers Holland and Joe Jenkins as deputies, he earned a respect somewhat like that accorded Pat Garrett of New Mexico. Resigning as sheriff, he was immediately elected to the office of County Clerk, which he held for sixteen years. He married Martha Aldridge on December 27, 1888.

JAMES L. JOBE came to Texas in the early 1830's, settling on a 320-acre farm in Bastrop County. He and his brother were in Captain James Gillespie's company in 1842 when the Texans met at San Antonio to repel Vasquez's invasion. He died early in 1848, leaving an estate consisting of fifty-four head of cattle, six hogs, his land, and a chest of carpenter's tools. Sarah Ann Jobe, his wife, married a man named Jackson within a year of

Jobe's death. Brown, "Annals of Travis County," IX, 12–13; Burlage and Hollingsworth, *Abstract of Land Claims;* Probate Records, Bastrop County, File J-1.

WILLIAM LENTZ and his wife Sarah lived in Missouri prior to their emigration to Texas. While in Missouri they had three children, Henry C., born 1820, Eunice, born 1823, and Mary J., born 1827. In Texas they had Ann E., born 1833, Amanda, born 1835, and Thomas H., born 1837. In the autumn of 1842, while Henry C. Lentz had gone out to look for some oxen, William was surprised and killed by Indians. His wife survived him at least eight years. Brown, "Annals of Travis County," IX, 24; Korges, "Bastrop County, Texas: Historical and Educational Development" (Master's Thesis, University of Texas, 1933), I, 73; *U.S. Census,* 1850, Bastrop County, 189.

JOHN L. LYNCH lived in Bastrop County in 1838, where he was paid a debt of $187.75 on October 15, 1838, by L. C. Cunningham. He was in the battle with Vicente Cordova on March 29, 1839, and in July of that year was a proprietor of the town of Montopolis, now a part of Austin. He was killed while leading a charge in the battle with Young Bowles and the Egg on December 25, 1839. Brown, *Indian Wars,* 68; L. C. Cunningham Papers (Archives Collection, University of Texas Library); Hardy, "A History of Travis County, 1832–1865" (Master's Thesis, University of Texas, 1938), 43; Ray, *Austin Colony Pioneers,* 307–308; Sowell, *Early Settlers,* 12–13; *Telegraph and Texas Register* (Houston), April 7, 1839; Wilbarger, *Indian Depredations in Texas,* 173.

WARREN LYONS was born in Ohio in 1826. He was captured by the Indians during the summer of 1837. Eleven years later, in 1848, he returned. His hair had been cut short on one side— punishment and disgrace, he said, because he had run in a fight between the Indians and some Mexicans. He resumed civilized life, married Lucy Boatwright, and raised a family. He died in Johnson County on August 11, 1870. DeShields, *Border Wars,* 228–231; Captain D. W. Roberts, "The Restoration of Warren Lyons," *Frontier Times,* IV, 24; *U.S. Census,* 1850, Fayette County, 85.

257

HUGH KING MCDONALD, who lived on a 500-acre farm at Hills Prairie, was born on February 8, 1816, in North Carolina. At the age of five he moved with his father, John McDonald, and family to Maury and Giles counties in Tennessee.

In 1851 McDonald moved to Texas and ran a ferry and a saw mill at Bastrop until 1861. During the war he bought cattle and supplies for the Confederate Army. During the Reconstruction period he was forced to sell first his ferry and then his saw mill. In 1868 he moved to his land at Hills Prairie, where he lived with his wife, Elizabeth (Gill) McDonald, and their seven children. His wife died in 1881 and his children went their separate ways, leaving the old man alone on his land until his death in the 1890's. Lewis Publishing Company, *History of Texas* (1893), XII, 766–767; *U.S. Census,* 1860, Bastrop County, 508.

WILLIAM HARRISON MAGILL (often spelled McGill) was born in Madison County, Kentucky, on January 3, 1813, and came to Texas in 1834. On September 16, 1834, with his partner William Redmond, he received one-half league of land located in Wharton and Goliad counties. He joined Jesse Billingsley's Mina Volunteers and was elected second sergeant, the position he held at the Battle of San Jacinto on April 21, 1836. In 1837 Magill was administrator of the estate of his friend Conrad Rohrer, who had been killed by Indians. He married Rebecca Pensana in Bastrop County on May 27, 1838. He served on a jury at Bastrop in August, 1838, was in the battle with Cordova on March 29, 1839, and participated in the Battle of Plum Creek under Burleson on August 12, 1840.

Magill moved to Burnet County in the early 1850's. He was married a second time on December 21, 1854, to Elizabeth Alice Hedrick while visiting in Kentucky. His first wife had evidently just passed away, for he had seventeen children by her between May 27, 1838, and December 21, 1854. In November of 1855 Magill was on a committee giving a Know-Nothing Party Ball in Travis County. Other committee members were John S. Ford, Edward Burleson, Jr., and Dr. James W. Robertson. His 13-year-old son Billy killed an Indian in an affray at Burnet in 1859. Magill commanded a company of Home Guards from Burnet County in the Confederate Army. He died in 1878 at the age of sixty-five. Brown, *Indian Wars*, 62–65; Hardy, "A History of Travis County, 1832–1865" (Master's Thesis, University of Texas, 1938), Appendix C, 235; Kemp, San Jacinto Roll; Police Court Records, Bastrop County, A, 31; Probate Records, Bastrop County, File R-1; Register of Spanish Archives; Smithwick, *Evolution of a State*, 313, 329.

BARTHOLOMEW MANLOVE was born in Delaware about 1776. In 1832 he came to Texas from Arabella, Kentucky. Later his wife, Aberilla, a native of Maryland, and their children joined him and they settled on their league near the mouth of Cedar Creek. In May, 1835, he was a member of the Committee of Safety and Correspondence at Mina, the first step toward organized resistance against Mexico. The committee consisted of Manlove, D. C. Barrett, John G. McGehee, Edward Burleson, and Samuel Wolfenbarger. Manlove was elected a delegate to the Consultation of 1835. He went to Columbia, where the session was supposed to have been held, but the meeting place was changed to San Felipe. He returned home without attending any of the meetings, disgusted at having been made to travel all the way to Columbia in vain.

In October of 1837 he was serving as first Mayor of Bastrop, though there were only a few families there. The town had been sacked and burned by Mexicans during the Texas Revolution and raided several times by Comanche Indians during the Runaway Scrape. Most of the settlers did not return to the settlement until 1838. In November he bought a lot in Bastrop from the estate of Richard (Big Dick) Andrews, who was killed in the Battle of Concepción on October 28, 1835. Manlove opened a hotel in the town and was elected mayor again in 1838, 1842, and 1845. In the census of 1850 he was listed as a farmer with a 200-acre farm valued at $2,407. He was still living in 1858.

Manlove prided himself on his horses, among which were the best work horses and some of the fastest horses in Austin's Colony. Once two favorites were stolen by Comanches who, being hotly pursued, placed one warrior in the rearguard position on Manlove's biggest horse, thinking it to be the fastest. Burleson got Chief Placido, who lived with his Tonkawa tribe on Burleson's farm, to send several of his men to recapture the horses. They soon overtook, killed, and scalped the rear Indian, who instead of being on Manlove's fastest horse, was riding his best, but slowest, work horse. The Tonkawas returned home and held a scalp dance over him. They placed the flesh from the Comanche's body in a large pot with corn and potatoes. Then they cooked their "stew" and every member of the tribe came around the pot and ate part of the meat of the dead Comanche. Afterward the men formed a circle and danced around the pot. A squaw would then present one of them with an arm or leg of their foe, which would be snatched and shaken in their teeth as a dog shakes a bone. This was repeated until the warriors were forced to desist from sheer exhaustion. This ceremony was witnessed and later recorded by Noah Smithwick. Placido's son later recovered Manlove's other horses.

Another tale is told about this enormous work horse. It was stolen again one evening by Indians, and Manlove ran to the door just as the savage rode off. He became so indignant and excited that he promised his daughter Dolly to a young suitor if he could get back the horse. The man, who had been trying for some time to gain Manlove's consent to marry Dolly, took out after the Indian, rode all night, and finally killed the Indian and recaptured the horse. He returned it to Manlove and was given Dolly's hand in marriage. What Dolly had to say about being traded for a horse is not known. Jesse Billingsley Papers (Archives Collection, University of Texas Library); *Biographical Directory of Texas Conventions and Congresses,* 134; Brown, *History of Texas,* I, 296; Burlage and Hollingsworth, *Abstract of Land Claims,* 38; Grace Fitzwilliam, "Early Election Held in Bastrop in 1831," *In the Shadow of the Lost Pines,* 42; Korges, "Bastrop County, Texas: Historical and Educational Development" (Master's Thesis, University of Texas, 1933), I, 74; Perkins, "The Local History Approach . . . Bastrop, Texas" (Master's Thesis, University of Texas, 1954), 53; Ray, *Austin Colony Pioneers,* 349; Smithwick, *Evolution of a State,* 245–246; Sowell, *Early Settlers,* 54, 311–312; *Telegraph and Texas Register* (Houston), October 31, 1835; *U.S. Census,* 1850, Bastrop County, 170; Wilbarger, *Indian Depredations in Texas,* 231.

JAMES MANOR was born in North Carolina in 1805. He and

his brother Joseph settled at Webber's Prairie, where they opened a saloon, or what was then termed a "grocery." Once a man referred to it as "Hell's Half Acre," and the "Half Acre" part stuck. It became famous during ante-bellum days. The town of Manor, ten miles east of Austin, is named for him. Brown, "Annals of Travis County," XI, 9–10; Hardy, "A History of Travis County, 1832–1865," (Master's Thesis, University of Texas, 1938), 88, 143–144; *U.S. Census*, 1850, Travis County, 21.

ALSEY S. MILLER was from Gonzales. An experienced Indian fighter, he served in many campaigns against the savages and was a participant in the Battle of Plum Creek. When news of Woll's invasion reached him he set out to join his old comrade-in-arms, Ben McCulloch. He first joined Jesse Billingsley's company, but when Billingsley decided it was useless to attempt to reach the Texas forces encamped on Salado Creek, Miller switched over to Dawson's company. He was immediately sent forward as a scout to locate Colonel Caldwell. Returning, he was attacked by three Mexican skirmishers, killed one of them, and made his report to Dawson, who determined to fight. Brown, *History of Texas*, II, 180, 212, 226–228; Sowell, *Early Settlers*, 25, 313, 414; Weyand and Wade, *An Early History of Fayette County*, 157–159.

JOHN HENRY MOORE was born in Rome, Tennessee, on August 13, 1800. He ran away to Texas in 1818 but was caught and returned home by his father. In 1821 he returned to Texas and settled on the upper Colorado River. He formed a partnership with Thomas Gray as one of Austin's Old Three Hundred. They received title to a league in Brazoria County and a labor in Colorado County on August 16, 1824. About 1827 he married Eliza Cummins and in 1828 he either built or bought from James J. Ross the twin blockhouse which became known as Moore's Fort. It was located on the site of the present city of La Grange, which Moore laid out, named, and received title to on May 17, 1831.

Moore built a home and plantation eight miles north of La Grange in 1838, where he raised his family, and where he died on December 2, 1880. For details see *Handbook of Texas*, II,

261

BIOGRAPHICAL NOTES

229–230; also see Brown, *Indian Wars,* 83–84; Burlage and
Hollingsworth, *Abstract of Land Claims,* 638; *Telegraph and
Texas Register* (Houston), August 17, 1842; *Texas Sentinel*
(Austin), November 14, 1840; Weyand and Wade, *An Early
History of Fayette County* (1936).

SARAH JENKINS NORTHCROSS. A year or so after Edward
Jenkins' death, Sarah Jenkins remarried. Her new husband,
James Northcross, was a Methodist preacher. Born in Virginia
in 1802, he had been living for some time in Alabama before
he arrived in Texas in August of 1829 and settled in the town
of Bastrop. On September 16, 1834, the Ayuntamiento of the
Municipality of Mina granted him a four-acre building lot in
Bastrop for four dollars. It was stated that he already had a
house built on that lot. On April 22, 1835, he was granted a
league of land in Milam's Colony in Travis County. He joined
the Texas Army and was killed in the Alamo on March 6, 1836.
His estate consisted of a horse, a league and labor of land, 640
acres of donation land, and an account on James Smith (the
man who married Rousseau's widow) for fifteen dollars. Northcross and Sarah had a son, James C. Northcross, whose guardian John Holland Jenkins was made in 1846. Sarah died in
1840. James C. Northcross died in January of 1852, while
living with Jenkins.

Jenkins makes no mention of his stepfather or stepbrother
in his reminiscences but named one of his sons James Northcross Jenkins, proving his respect for Northcross Jenkins' ideal
was always Edward Burleson, however, as the memoirs plainly
show. Bastrop *Advertiser,* August 29, 1935; Burlage and Hollingsworth, *Abstract of Land Claims,* 645; Probate Minutes,
Bastrop County, Book A; Probate Records, Bastrop County,
File N-1; Register of Spanish Archives; *U.S. Census,* 1850, Bastrop County, 191; Williams, "A Critical Study of the Siege of
the Alamo and of the Personnel of Its Defenders," *Southwestern Historical Quarterly,* XXXVII, 274.

CLAIBORNE OSBORN was born in 1826 in Matagorda, Texas, the
son of Benjamin and Leah (Stark) Osborn. His mother died in
1828 and the family moved to Austin's Little Colony, where his

father died in 1829. He was evidently raised by his older sister, Mrs. Louisa Hamilton.

The scalping incident occurred in 1840 at Rice's Crossing on Brushy Creek in Williamson County. A party of ten, not three, left the house of William Hamilton. The party included Claiborne's brothers, John Lyle Osborn, a San Jacinto veteran, Alexander Hamilton, and James Hamilton. Alex Hamilton and Claiborne went in one direction and the rest of the party in another. They discovered a band of Indians and turned to run away, but Claiborne's horse was shot, leaving him on foot. Before he knew what had happened the Indians had caught him and stabbed him in the back with a skinning knife. He fainted, but soon returned to consciousness and heard the Indians arguing over possession of part of his scalp, a large, double curl on the crown of his head. Parts of his scalp had already been taken.

Hamilton, who had decided to try to rescue his friend no matter what the risk, rode into the midst of the Indians. Claiborne jumped up in back of Hamilton and the two reached the rest of their party. Osborn was taken to Noah Smithwick's at Webberville, where his wounds were treated. He recovered completely, married Almira Jane Leverett in 1854, had ten children, and lived fifty-nine years after his scalping. He died on March 6, 1899. Bastrop *Advertiser*, August 2, 1956; Brown, "Annals of Travis County," VII, 42; DeShields, *Border Wars*, 341; Register of Spanish Archives, IX, 137.

Levi Payne was born in Tennessee in 1820 and was living in Bastrop County, Texas, in 1838. A member of the Santa Fe Expedition, he was released with Bill Alsbury and John Morgan on June 14, 1842. In 1850 he was living on his 320-acre farm in Harris County. Brown, "Annals of Travis County," VIII, 14; Burlage and Hollingsworth, *Abstract of Land Claims; Northern Standard* (Clarksville, Texas), August 20, 1842; Ray, *Austin Colony Pioneers*, 308; *U.S. Census*, 1850, Harris County, 60.

Cicero Rufus Perry, better known as "Old Rufe," was born in Alabama on August 23, 1822. He emigrated to Texas with his parents in 1833, settling first at Bastrop, then in Washington County. He participated in the Siege of Bexar and served from July 1 to October 1, 1836, in Captain W. W. Hill's Texas

Ranger company. He was wounded in John H. Moore's defeat on February 12, 1839. Perry served under Samuel Highsmith and Thomas Green in 1841. He was a scout for General Edward Burleson and Mark B. Lewis at various times and was a member of the Somervell Expedition. He joined Jack Hays's Texas Rangers in 1844 and participated in many Indian fights in that force. In 1874 he was captain of Company D, Frontier Battalion. He died at Johnson City, Texas, on October 7, 1898. It was said he could point out twenty bullet, arrow, and spear wounds on his body. Brown, *Indian Wars,* 75; *Handbook of Texas,* II, 363; Muster Roll Book; Sowell, *Early Settlers,* 58, 148–154, 272–274, 642.

DR. JOEL PONTON was a son of William Ponton, who was killed by Indians in 1834, and a brother of Andrew Ponton, who was Alcalde and first Judge of the Municipality of Gonzales. Dr. Ponton was born in 1802 in Maine. He was County Judge of Lavaca County under the carpetbag rule of 1866–1867. He then returned to medicine and enjoyed a large practice. Boethal, "History of Lavaca County, 1685–1930" (Master's Thesis, University of Texas, 1932), 25, 104, 169; Brown, *History of Texas,* I, 168n.; Brown, *Indian Wars,* 78–79; Hallettsville *Herald,* October 17, 1907; Morrell, *Fruits and Flowers from the Wilderness* (1872), 126; *U.S. Census,* 1850, Lavaca County, 116, 639.

HUTCHINSON REED was born in South Carolina in 1808, and his wife Elizabeth was born in Alabama in 1816. They had five children. Reed was County Surveyor of Bastrop County for many years and in 1850 he possessed real estate valued at $7,960. He was a scout for Burleson during the Plum Creek Campaign. Brown, *Indian Wars,* 78–82; Ray, *Austin Colony Pioneers; U.S. Census,* 1850, Bastrop County, 178.

JOSEPH ROGERS, son of James and Rachael Rogers, came to Texas with his parents in 1831 from Tennessee. He was granted his own league in Travis County on October 30, 1832. He served as first lieutenant of Tumlinson's Rangers. In November of 1837 he and a Captain McCullom from Alabama were cutting timber on Captain James Rogers' farm when they were attacked by Indians. McCullom was killed but Rogers escaped, only to be killed a few days later in the encounter narrated by Jenkins. Rogers left a wife and several children. He was an uncle of Joseph B. Rogers, who was a ranger captain for many years. Brown, "Annals of Travis County," VII, 82; Brown, *Indian Wars*, 88–91; Burlage and Hollingsworth, *Abstract of Land Claims*, 651; DeShields, *Border Wars*, 236–237; Register of Spanish Archives, IX; Smithwick, *Evolution of a State*, 124; Wilbarger, *Indian Depredations in Texas*, 238, 261–262.

CONRAD ROHRER was wagonmaster for General Houston in the Texas Revolution. "General" Rohrer, as his friends nicknamed him, was ordered to confiscate all the work oxen he could find to pull the artillery during the retreat to San Jacinto. He took a yoke of oxen belonging to an old woman, Mrs. Mann, who lived on her farm on the Brazos River. He had not gone far when she rode up with a knife and pistol plainly visible under her skirts. Rohrer disregarded her request for the return of her team, cracked his whip over the oxen, and urged them on in the trail driver's colorful language. Mrs. Mann then unlimbered her pistol and a vocabulary to match Rohrer's. General Houston, although himself rather proficient in the art of swearing, had never heard anything like the oaths she poured forth and finally threw up his hands and told her she could take them back. Rohrer refused to dismount and unhitch the team, so she herself got down from her mount and released them, retiring in triumph. This was the only time Houston and Rohrer were ever known to have been defeated.

Rohrer joined Tumlinson's Rangers soon after the disbanding of the army. He was particularly active in the Hibbans fight. At one point, when an Indian was about to shoot Captain Tumlinson, Rohrer ran up to the savage, jerked the gun from his hands, and dealt a blow on his head so powerful that it crushed his skull. When he mistook Mrs. Hibbans' son for an Indian, he pulled the trigger twice, but the gun refused to fire. He drew a bead for the third time, but one of the men saw him and knocked up the gun just as Rohrer squeezed the trigger—it fired clear. The boy had been carefully wrapped in a buffalo robe and tied on his mule, thus giving him the appearance of an Indian. The mule was so frightened that it had to be shot in order to get the boy untied. Rohrer scalped the Indian he had knocked down and gave the trophy to Noah Smithwick. Marquis James, *The Raven, a Biography of Sam Houston* (1929), 243; Smithwick, *Evolution of a State,* 121–123, 209.

MOSES (or MOSEA) ROUSSEAU was born in 1794 and came to Texas in 1828 with his wife Sarah, their three children, Mary, James, and Lavinia, and a woman named Polly Childress. The family first lived in San Felipe, but moved to Bastrop County where he was chairman of the election of the Ayuntamiento of San Felipe de Austin, which was held at William Barton's house in 1830. In 1829 Sarah had died, and Rousseau then lived with Polly Childress for a period of two years, finally marrying her in December, 1831. No children were born to them after their marriage, but Polly bore two children before their marriage. Rousseau acknowledged these children and had them baptized as his own after he married Polly.

On April 4, 1831, Rousseau applied for and received a league of land in Bastrop County on the Colorado River. On November 7, 1831, he was elected Sindico (notary public and city attorney combined) by one vote over Jesse Tannehill.

In April, 1832, he and Edward Jenkins had an argument that developed into a knife fight in which Rousseau was wounded. He had his wound dressed, bought a quart of whiskey and a blanket from Dr. Thomas J. Gazley on April 23, 1832, and died from his wounds prior to April 30, when Matthew Duty billed his heirs for one coffin and some medicated salt. Rousseau's second wife, Polly, soon married James Smith, who had also been living with the Rousseau family. When Smith gained title to half of Rousseau's league after Polly's death in 1839, a suit arose between him and Rousseau's legitimate children. This finally reached the State Supreme Court in 1845, and the Rousseau league was ordered divided equally among Rousseau's five children. Barker, "Minutes of the Ayuntamiento of San Felipe de Austin," *Southwestern Historical Quarterly,* XXIII; Burlage and Hollingsworth, *Abstract of Land Claims,* 55; Fitzwilliam, "Early Election Held in Bastrop in 1831," *In the Shadow of the Lost Pines,* 42; Gulick and others (eds.), *The Papers of Mirabeau Buonaparte Lamar* (1940–1945), IV, pt. I, 40; Oliver C. Hartley (reporter), *Reports of Cases Argued and Decided in the Supreme Court of the State of Texas* (1851–1852), VII, 184;

BIOGRAPHICAL NOTES

Probate Records, Bastrop County, Texas, File R-1; Register of Spanish Archives.

MICHAEL SESSOM was born in Tennessee in 1811 and moved to Texas where he received a league of land in Robertson's Colony in Falls County on August 3, 1835. He lived in Bastrop, however, at least until 1845, when he was present at an auction of part of the estate of Joseph Weeks. He then moved to Hays County, where he built the second house in the town of San Marcos, where he was living in 1850. Jesse Billingsley Papers (Archives Collection, University of Texas Library); Burlage and Hollingsworth, *Abstract of Land Claims,* 652; *U.S. Census,* 1850, Hays County, 241.

BARTLETT SIMS was one of Austin's Old Three Hundred colonists. He received title to a sitio of land in present Wharton County on August 7, 1824. Two months later he became surveyor for the colony. He married Sally Curtis in January of 1825 and they had at least one son. In June, 1826, Sims was captain of a company on an expedition against the Waco and Tawakoni Indians and was elected a militia captain in March, 1829. He served in that capacity on the San Saba Expedition.

Moving to Bastrop, he surveyed much of the land in Austin's Little Colony. The Convention of 1832 appointed Sims a member of the subcommittee of safety and vigilance from Bastrop, as well as District Treasurer of Bastrop. He represented the Bastrop area at the Convention of 1833 and the Consultation of 1835. After service under Robert M. Coleman before and during the Siege of Bexar, Sims served in an advisory capacity to the General Council.

Sims was on several of John H. Moore's expeditions and participated in the Battle of Brushy Creek. He served as captain of an unattached company of volunteers on the Somervell Expedition in 1842. After 1843 Sims moved to Williamson County, where he was living in 1850. Brown, "Annals of Travis County," IV, 19–20; Bugbee, "Old Three Hundred," *Quarterly of the Texas State Historical Association,* I, 116; Gammel, *Laws of Texas,* I, 497, 503; Handbook of Texas, II, 614; Henderson, *Colonel Jack Hays, Texas Ranger,* 50; Ray, *Austin Colony Pioneers,* 211, 307–308.

FRENCH SMITH was a regular in the Texas Ranger force. He fought under Caldwell in the Cordova Rebellion and participated in the Battle of Salado. He was a member of Colonel Jack Hays's Rangers and rose to the rank of colonel in the Mexican War. He lived on Darst Creek, twenty-six miles from Gonzales and served on the first grand jury of Gonzales County. Brown, *Indian Wars*, 62–65; Henderson, *Colonel Jack Hays, Texas Ranger*, 12; Sowell, *Early Settlers*, 313, 416, 418, 420, 427, 437, 808.

TAYLOR SMITH emigrated to Texas from Georgia with his son Taylor, Jr., in the early 1830's. They settled in present Williamson County on their league and labor of land. Ray, *Austin Colony Pioneers*, 307–308; *U.S. Census*, 1850, Williamson County, 7; Wilbarger, *Indian Depredations in Texas*, 89–90.

JAMES STANDIFER was born in Tennessee about 1809, but moved to Alabama, where he married a girl named Sarah. In March of 1829 they moved to Texas with Standifer's widowed mother. At this time Standifer was 21 and his wife 19, and they had one daughter. On November 8, 1832, he and his mother received adjacent leagues on the dividing line between present Travis and Bastrop counties. Both later received labors of land in Bastrop County. Standifer was on the 1838 Bastrop tax roll but his mother was not. By 1850 James and Sarah had nine children and a farm valued at $3,750. Burlage and Hollingsworth, *Abstract of Land Claims*, 660; Ray, *Austin Colony Pioneers*, 307–308; Register of Spanish Archives, IX, 129; *U.S. Census*, 1850, Bastrop County, 190; Smithwick, *Evolution of a State*, 291–293; Wilbarger, *Indian Depredations in Texas*, 8.

JAMES MONROE SWISHER was born in Williamson County, Tennessee. He moved to Texas in 1833 with his father, James G., and mother, Elizabeth (Boyd) Swisher. They settled at Tenoxtitlan in present Burleson County. In 1835 Swisher joined Captain John York's company of volunteers and fought in the Siege of Bexar. He was Treasurer and County Clerk or Travis County and a member of the Texas Legislature in the 1870's. He died in 1907. Brown, "Annals of Travis County," VI, 67; Muster Roll Book.

BIOGRAPHICAL NOTES

JOHN TANNEY was born in Maryland in 1817. He escaped at Salado on February 11, 1843, and was recaptured. On March 25, 1844, he escaped again at the Castle of Perote and was again recaptured. Tanney was finally released on September 16, 1844. He was living in Travis County in 1850. Green, *Mier Expedition*, 442, 450; Smithwick, *Evolution of a State*, 272; *U.S. Census*, 1850, Travis County, 15; Wade, *Mier Expedition*, I, 133, II, 23, 31–32.

TUMLINSON. The murdered man was one of the Tumlinson brothers who settled in DeWitt's Colony in present Fayette County in 1828. It was probably Joseph or George Tumlinson who was killed since James Tumlinson was with Captain James J. Ross in 1829 when he attacked the Indians near his home, and John Tumlinson was a famous ranger captain in later years. Brown, *History of Texas*, I, 143; DeShields, *Border Wars*, 47; Sowell, *Rangers and Pioneers*, 23.

DICK VAUGHN at this time was serving as first sheriff of Bastrop County. He was born in Virginia in 1800 and came to Texas prior to 1835. As a member of Captain J. B. Chance's company, he served in the Texas Revolution and was stationed at Harrisburg during the Battle of San Jacinto. It is not known when he died. Burlage and Hollingsworth, *Abstract of Land Claims*, 664; Kemp, Harrisburg Roll; Police Court Records, Bastrop County, 1837, A, 13.

WILLIAM SIMPSON WALLACE came to Texas from Tennessee in 1836. He settled at Bastrop and was elected county surveyor in 1837. He served under Burleson in the Cordova Rebellion and on May 14, 1837, killed Manuel Flores, a notorious Mexican whose gang had been terrorizing western Texas for some time. For this deed he was promoted from private to lieutenant colonel by President Lamar. The rifle and sword of General Flores were awarded to him by the Texans taking part in the battle. In 1841 he married Mary Ann O'Connell. Bastrop *Advertiser*, August 29, 1935; Jesse Billingsley Papers (Archives Collection, University of Texas Library).

JOHN B. WALTERS, about twenty-four years of age, came to

Texas in 1825 from Missouri. He first lived with the Hornsbys, but soon moved to his half league about two miles up the river from Wilbarger Bend. In 1831 and 1832 he did work for Moses Rousseau as a carpenter and gunsmith. He received 320 acres of land for three months' service as a ranger, but when he served is not known. He was shot in the head at Brushy Creek. Burlage and Hollingsworth, *Abstract of Land Claims,* 665; Probate Records, Bastrop County, File R-1; Register of Spanish Archives, IX, 53; Sowell, *Early Settlers,* 17.

MARTIN WELLS, born about 1776, married Sally Boyd in Tennessee, and in 1815 had a son, Wayman F. Wells. In 1817 the family moved to Marengo County, Alabama, where a second son, Martin Jones Wells, was born in 1819. His first wife died about this time, and when he emigrated to Texas in 1826, Wells had a second wife, Sarah, fifteen years younger than he. In January, 1830, he moved from Fayette County to Austin's Little Colony, where he received title to a league of land in Bastrop County. When his land was surveyed in 1832, he moved from his home at the site of Bastrop and settled at Wells's Pyramid, fifteen miles away. His home, which consisted of three small log cabins built close together, was used as a fort during Indian depredations. He died in 1836, leaving his wife and eight children, who were still living in Bastrop County in 1850. Brown, "Annals of Travis County," IV, 15; Burlage and Hollingsworth, *Abstract of Land Claims,* 66; Deed Records, Marengo County, Alabama; *Handbook of Texas,* II, 878; Probate Records, Bastrop County, File W-1; Ray, *Austin Colony Pioneers,* 338; *U.S. Census,* 1850, Bastrop County, 206; Clarence Carter, *Territorial Papers of the United States, Territory of Alabama, 1817–1819* (1952), 197.

GIDEON WHITE emigrated from Alabama to Texas in 1837. He returned to Alabama in 1838 and brought his family to Bastrop County. In 1839 he settled at Seider's Spring, adjoining Glen Ridge, near Austin. Paying no heed to the admonitions of his friends, he frequently traveled alone through the woods on foot. On October 25, 1842, he went out afoot to look for oxen which he had turned out to graze. He was attacked by mounted Indians and was killed only a few hundred yards from his cabin.

270

He had five daughters. Brown, "Annals of Travis County," IX,
15; Joseph C. McConnell, *The West Texas Frontier* (1939), I,
243; Wilbarger, *Indian Depredations in Texas*, 275–276.

HAMILTON WHITE was born in Virginia about 1808. Coming to
Bastrop prior to 1838, White engaged in farming and lumber
hauling. He and his wife Tabitha had had one child born in
Virginia and four others were born in Texas prior to 1850. The
1850 census lists White as a Bastrop County farmer having real
estate valued at $10,760. It is not known when he died. De-
Shields, *Border Wars*, 307; Ray, *Austin Colony Pioneers*, 307–
308; *U.S. Census,* 1850, Bastrop County, 183; *ibid.,* 1860, Bastrop County, 86; Wilbarger, *Indian Depredations in Texas,*
266–267.

JOHN L. WILBARGER, son of Josiah, was born November 29,
1829, in Matagorda, Texas. He was brought up in Bastrop
County and joined the ranger forces under Colonel John S.
(Rip) Ford while still a boy. In August of 1850 he received a
furlough and went to visit his family. After remaining there for
some time, he started back to join his command accompanied
by Sullivan and Neal (who may have been Adolphus D. Neill).
They were armed with two six shooters apiece, and so, when
Indians attacked them, they made a firm stand and evidently
killed a number of the savages. Wilbarger and Sullivan were
buried on the spot by the search party sent out when Neal
reached a settlement and told of the massacre. Some years later,
Harvey Wilbarger, a brother, removed Wilbarger's remains to
Fairview Cemetery in Bastrop, where they were placed near the
grave of his father. Bastrop *Advertiser,* January 23, 1897; Wilbarger, *Indian Depredations in Texas,* 615–616.

ROBERT MCALPIN WILLIAMSON was born in Georgia about
1804. When he was fifteen, he suffered an illness which left him
crippled. His right leg was drawn back at the knee and he wore
a wooden leg, which resulted in the nickname of "Three-Legged
Willie." *Handbook of Texas,* II, 917; Duncan W. Robinson,
*Judge Robert McAlpin Williamson, Texas' Three-Legged Wil-
lie* (1949) ; R. M. Williamson Biographical File (Archives Collection, University of Texas Library).

WALKER WILSON, according to the records available, was born in three different years and died in at least four different places on five different dates. The 1850 Bastrop County Census report shows first, that a Walker Wilson was born in Virginia in 1795 (p. 164) and second, that a Walker Wilson was born in Virginia in 1805 (p. 186), while L. W. Kemp in his San Jacinto Roll states that Walker B. Wilson was born in Richmond, Virginia, on November 17, 1801. The last is probably correct.

Wilson came to Texas about 1834 and on March 12, 1835, received title to a league of land on Bear Creek, Travis County. He was in the Siege of Bexar in December of 1835 and on February 28, 1836, joined Jesse Billingsley's Mina Volunteers. After being detailed with Jenkins, Fisk, and Blakey to remove the families, he somehow made his way back to the army and participated in the Battle of San Jacinto. Wilson received 640 acres of donation land on May 18, 1838, and is listed on the 1838 Bastrop tax roll.

According to the 1850 Census and to the probate records of Bastrop County, he married Jane Wilson (b. 1814 in Alabama), and they had three daughters, the oldest born in 1848. Kemp states that Walker Wilson married Mrs. Mima Eggleston Turner (b. 1825 in North Carolina; d. 1897 in Austin, Texas).

The Bastrop County Probate Records state that Wilson died in 1850, in which year his wife Jane was appointed administrator of his estate. Frank Brown estimates that Wilson died in 1840 on his land in Travis County. Kemp says that he died in 1878 at San Marcos, while a member of the Texas Veterans Association, O. A. Fisher, records that at 4:30 P.M. on September 8, 1876, Walker Wilson was buried by the San Marcos Grays. All state that he was a San Jacinto veteran. Brown, "Annals of Travis County," IV, 48; Burlage and Hollingsworth, *Abstract of Land Claims*, 665; Orceneth Asbury Fisher, Journal (unpub. Mss., property of Jesse N. Fisher) ; Kemp, San Jacinto Roll; Probate Records, Bastrop County, File W-1; Ray, *Austin Colony Pioneers*, 307–308; Register of Spanish Archives; *U.S. Census*, 1850, Bastrop County, 164, 186.

MONTE (or MONTRAVILLE) WOODS was born in Maryland in 1816 and came to Texas with his father, Zadock Woods, one of Austin's Old Three Hundred, in 1826. The family first settled in Matagorda County, but soon moved to Fayette County, where Monte was still living in 1860 on his own league and labor of land. Bugbee, "The Old Three Hundred," *Quarterly of the Texas State Historical Association*, I, 117; Burlage and Hollingsworth, *Abstract of Land Claims*, 15, 68; Gulick and others (eds.), *The Papers of Mirabeau Buonaparte Lamar*, IV, pt. 1, 39–40; *U.S. Census*, 1860, Fayette County, 374; Weyand and Wade, *An Early History of Fayette County*, 9, 14, 64, 97, 151–158.

MICHAEL YOUNG was born in Georgia in 1802 and came to Texas from Alabama in 1829 with two children. He was in the Battle of Anahuac in 1832, and in June, 1836, he joined Jesse Billingsley's company of Mina Volunteers. In 1842 he was living in Bastrop County, where he was wounded by Indians who came to his plantation. Encountering Young's eight-year-old son Perry, they threw a lasso around him. Perry slipped through the loop and escaped to give the alarm. Mike Young gathered fifteen neighbors, including Jenkins, and gave chase to the Indians. In the ensuing fight, which lasted some four hours, Young was wounded in the breast. For his military service he received bounty land in Bell County, to which he moved in his old age—still living there in 1874. In 1850 two farm workers and a school teacher lived on his plantation and his real estate was valued at $9,111. Burlage and Hollingsworth, *Abstract of Land Claims*, 669; *U.S. Census*, 1850, Bastrop County, 168; Clarence R. Wharton, *Wharton's History of Fort Bend County* (1939), 62–63.

Bibliography

Bibliography

UNPUBLISHED MATERIALS

Bastrop County History. Historical Records Survey, No. 11. Archives Collection, University of Texas Library.

Bastrop County Scrapbook. Archives Collection, University of Texas Library.

Billingsley, Jesse. Papers. Archives Collection, University of Texas Library.

Brown, Frank. "Annals of Travis County and the City of Austin from the Earliest Times to the Close of 1875." Transcript, Archives Collection, University of Texas Library.

Burleson, Aaron, II. Material Furnished by John Baptist Burleson's Son of Smithville in the Fall of 1937 to Mr. Kemp. Transcript, Texas History Collection, Baylor University, Waco, Texas.

Comptroller's Military Service Records. Archives Collection, Texas State Library.

Cunningham, L. C. Papers. Archives Collection, University of Texas Library.

Deed Records. Bastrop County, Texas, Office of County Clerk.

Deed Records. Marengo County, Alabama, Office of County Clerk.

Final Record of Superior Court of Cotaco County, State of Alabama, Held in Sommerville, 1819, III. Archives Division, Alabama State Library.

Fisher, Orceneth Asbury. Journal. Property of Jesse N. Fisher, Box 1298, Flagstaff, Arizona.

General Services Administration. National Archives and Records Service, Washington, D.C.

Grandrud, Pauline, and Kathleen Paul Jones. Alabama Records Survey. Archives Division, Alabama State Library.

Kemp, L. W. Harrisburg Roll. Archives Collection, Texas State Library.

———. San Jacinto Roll. Archives Collection, Texas State Library.

———. Monuments to Texas Veterans. Archives Collection, Texas State Library.

List of Civil and Military Appointments for Alabama Territory by Gov. Holmes, 1818. Archives Division, Alabama State Library.

McDowall, Mary Ann. "A Little Journey Through Memory's Halls," Historical Society, Bastrop, Texas.

Minutes of the Commissioner's Court. Bastrop County, Office of County Clerk.

Minutes of the Corporation of the City of Bastrop, 1837–1858. Transcript, Historical Society, Bastrop, Texas.

Muster Roll Book. Transcript, General Land Office, Austin, Texas.

Police Court Records. Bastrop County, Office of County Clerk.

Probate Minutes. Bastrop County, Office of County Clerk.

Probate Records. Bastrop County, Office of County Clerk.

Probate Records. Travis County, Office of County Clerk.

Register of Spanish Archives. General Land Office, Austin, Texas.

Smith, Ashbel. Papers, 1838. Archives Collection, University of Texas Library.

Travis, William B. Diary. Archives Collection, University of Texas Library.

U.S. Census, 1850, 1860. Transcript, Archives Collection, University of Texas Library.

Williamson, R. M. Biographical File. Archives Collection, University of Texas Library.

PUBLISHED MATERIALS

Books

Baker, D. W. C. A Texas Scrapbook, Made Up of the History, Biography, and Miscellany of Texas and Its People. New Orleans, A. S. Barnes & Co., 1875.

277

Bancroft, Hubert Howe. *History of Mexico*. New York, Bancroft Co., n.d. 6 vols.

Barker, E. C. (ed.). *The Austin Papers*. Washington, D.C., U.S. Government Printing Office, 1924, 1928; Austin, University of Texas Press, 1927. 3 vols.

Bastrop Historical Society. *In the Shadow of the Lost Pines, A History of Bastrop County and Its People*. Bastrop, Texas, Bastrop *Advertiser*, 1955.

Bedichek, Roy. *Karankaway Country*. Garden City, Doubleday & Co., 1950.

Biographical Directory of Texas Conventions and Congresses, Austin, 1941.

Brown, John Henry. *History of Texas from 1685 to 1892*. St. Louis, Bectold & Co., 1892. 2 vols.

———. *Indian Wars and Pioneers of Texas*. Austin, L. E. Daniell, n.d.

Burlage, John, and J. B. Hollingsworth (eds.). *Abstract of Valid Land Claims Compiled from the Records of the General Land Office and Court of Claims of the State of Texas*. Austin, John Marshall & Co., 1859.

Burleson, Georgia Jenkins. *The Life and Writings of Rufus C. Burleson, D.D., L.L.D.* Privately printed, 1901.

Carroll, H. Bailey. *The Texan Santa Fe Trail*. Canyon, Texas, Panhandle-Plains Historical Society, 1951.

Carter, Clarence. *Territorial Papers of the United States, Territory of Alabama, 1817-1819*. Washington, D.C., U.S. Government Printing Office, 1952.

Chabot, Frederick C. (ed.). *The Perote Prisoners, Being the Diary of James L. Truehart*. San Antonio, Naylor Company, 1934.

Clark, Joseph L. *A History of Texas, Land of Promise*. Dallas, D. C. Heath and Company, 1939.

DeShields, James T. *Border Wars of Texas*. Tioga, Texas, Herald Co., 1912.

———. *Tall Men with Long Rifles*. San Antonio, Naylor Co., 1935.

Dixon, Sam Houston, and L. W. Kemp. *The Heroes of San Jacinto*. Houston, Anson Jones Press, 1932.

Dobie, J. Frank, *John C. Duval, First Texas Man of Letters*. Dallas, Southwest Review, 1939.

BIBLIOGRAPHY

————. *Tales of Old-Time Texas.* Boston and Toronto, Little, Brown & Co., 1955.

Evans, Clement (ed.). *Confederate Military History.* Atlanta, Confederate Publishing Co., 1899. 12 vols.

Fisher, O. C. *It Occurred in Kimble.* Houston, Anson Jones Press, 1937.

Frantz, Joe B. *Gail Borden, Dairyman to a Nation.* Norman, University of Oklahoma Press, 1951.

Gammel, H. P. N. *The Laws of Texas, 1822–1897.* Austin, The Gammel Book Co., 1898. 8 vols.

Green, Rena (ed.). *The Swisher Memoirs.* San Antonio, Sigmond Press, 1932.

Green, Gen. Thomas J. *Journal of the Texian Expedition Against Mier.* New York, Harper & Brothers, 1845.

Gulick, Charles, and Katherine Elliot, Winnie Allen, and Harriet Smither (eds.). *The Papers of Mirabeau Buonaparte Lamar.* Austin, Texas State Library and Historical Commission, 1940–1945. 6 vols.

Haley, J. Evetts. *Fort Concho and the Texas Frontier.* San Angelo, San Angelo *Standard-Times,* 1952.

Hartley, Oliver C. (reporter). *Reports of Cases Argued and Decided in the Supreme Court of the State of Texas.* Galveston, Civilian Book Office; St. Louis, Gilbert Book Co., various dates. 19 vols.

Henderson, Harry M. *Colonel Jack Hays, Texas Ranger.* San Antonio, Naylor Company, 1954.

Houston, Andrew Jackson. *Texas Independence.* Houston, Anson Jones Press, 1938.

James, Marquis. *The Raven, a Biography of Sam Houston.* New York, Blue Ribbon Books, Inc., 1929.

Johnston, William Preston. *The Life of Gen. Albert Sidney Johnston.* New York, D. Appleton & Co., 1878.

Jones, Margaret Belle. *Bastrop.* Bastrop, Texas, Bastrop *Advertiser,* 1936. (pamphlet).

Journal of the House of Representatives of the Republic of Texas, Fifth Congress, First Session, 1840–1841. Austin, 1841.

Journals of the House of Representatives of the Republic of Texas, Seventh Congress, 1842–1843. Houston, 1843.

Kemp, L. W. *Signers of the Texas Declaration of Independence.* Houston, Anson Jones Press, 1944.

Kendall, George Wilkins. *Narrative of the Texan Santa Fe Expedition.* New York, 1844; Austin, The Steck Company, 1936.

Lewis Publishing Company. *History of Texas Together with a Biographical History of Milam, Williamson, Bastrop, Travis, Lee and Burleson Counties.* Chicago, 1893. 12 vols.

———. *Twentieth Century History of Southwest Texas.* Chicago and New York, 1907. 2 vols.

Linn, John J. *Reminiscences of Fifty Years in Texas.* New York, Sadler & Co., 1883; Austin, The Steck Company, 1936.

McConnell, Joseph Carroll. *The West Texas Frontier.* Palo Pinto, Texas, Texas Legal Bank and Book Co., 1939. 2 vols.

Monuments Erected . . . to Commemorate the Centenary of Texas Independence. Austin, The Steck Company, 1939.

Morrell, Z. N. *Fruits and Flowers from the Wilderness.* Boston, Gould & Lincoln, 1872.

Pickrell, Anne Doom. *Pioneer Women in Texas.* Austin, The Steck Company, 1929.

Ray, Worth S. *Austin Colony Pioneers.* Austin, Published by Author, 1949.

Red, William Stuart. *The Texas Colonists and Religion, 1821–1836.* Austin, E. L. Shettles, 1924.

Richardson, Rupert. *Texas, the Lone Star State.* New York, Prentice-Hall, Inc., 1943.

Robinson, Duncan W. *Judge Robert McAlpin Williamson, Texas' Three-Legged Willie.* Austin, Texas State Historical Association, 1948.

Rose, Victor M. *The Life and Services of General Ben McCulloch.* Philadelphia, Pictorial Bureau of the Press, 1888.

Saunders, Col. James Edmonds. *Early Settlers of Alabama.* New Orleans, L. Braham & Son, Ltd., 1899.

Seguin, Juan N. *Personal Memoirs.* 1842.

Smithwick, Noah. *The Evolution of a State.* Austin, Gammel Book Co., 1900; Austin, The Steck Company, 1935.

Sowell, Andrew Jackson. *Early Settlers and Indian Fighters of Southwest Texas.* Austin, Ben C. Jones & Co., 1900.

———. *Rangers and Pioneers of Texas: With a Concise Account of the Early Settlements, Hardships, Massacres, Battles and Wars, by Which Texas was Rescued from the Rule of the Savage and Consecrated to the Empire of Civilization.* San Antonio, Shepard Bros. & Co., 1884.

BIBLIOGRAPHY

Tevis, Dean, and J. Holmes Jenkins. *Texana.* San Antonio, Naylor Company, 1936.

Thrall, Rev. Homer S. *A Pictorial History of Texas.* St. Louis, N. D. Thompson & Co., 1879.

Tyler, George W. (edited by Charles W. Ramsdell). *The History of Bell County.* San Antonio, Naylor Company, 1936.

Wade, Houston. *Notes and Fragments of the Mier Expedition.* La Grange, Texas, La Grange Journal, 1937, 2 vols.

Webb, Walter Prescott. *The Texas Rangers.* Boston, Houghton Mifflin Company, 1935.

———, and H. Bailey Carroll (eds.). *The Handbook of Texas.* Austin, The Texas State Historical Association, 1952. 2 vols.

Weyand, Leonie L., and Houston Wade. *An Early History of Fayette County.* La Grange, Texas, La Grange Journal, 1936.

Wharton, Clarence R. *San Jacinto, the Sixteenth Decisive Battle.* Houston, Lamar Book Store, 1930.

———. *Wharton's History of Fort Bend County.* San Antonio, Naylor Company, 1939.

Wilbarger, J. W. *Indian Depredations in Texas.* Austin, Hutchings Printing House, 1889; Austin, The Steck Company, 1935.

Williams, Amelia W., and Eugene C. Barker (eds.). *The Writings of Sam Houston, 1813–1863.* Austin, University of Texas Press, 1938. 8 vols.

Wooten, Dudley G. (ed.). *A Comprehensive History of Texas, 1685–1897.* Dallas, William G. Scarff, 1898. 2 vols.

Yoakum, H. K. *History of Texas.* New York, Redfield, 1855. 2 vols.

Newspapers

Advertiser, Bastrop, Texas, 1884–1890, 1897, 1935, 1956.
American, Austin, Texas, 1939.
City Gazette, Austin, Texas, 1841, 1842.
Daily Telegram, Temple, Texas, 1936.
Herald, Halletsville, Texas, 1907.
Morning Star, Houston, Texas, 1839.
News, Galveston, Texas, 1857.
Northern Standard, Clarksville, Texas, 1842, 1846.

Telegraph and Texas Register, Houston, Texas, 1835, 1839, 1840, 1842, 1844.

Texas Gazette, San Felipe de Austin, Texas, 1830.

Texas National Register, Washington-on-the-Brazos, Texas, 1845.

Texas Sentinel, Austin, Texas, 1840.

Periodicals

Alexander, E. H. "Amos Alexander and Son Killed by Indians," *Frontier Times*, IV.

Bacarisse, Charles A. "Baron de Bastrop," *Southwestern Historical Quarterly*, LVIII.

Barker, Eugene C. "Minutes of the Ayuntamiento of San Felipe de Austin," *Southwestern Historical Quarterly*, XXIII.

Bastrop Historical Society. "Counties Embracing Area Once Large as States," *In the Shadow of the Lost Pines*, 21.

Bugbee, Lester G. "The Old Three Hundred," *Quarterly of the Texas State Historical Association*, I.

Erskine, Blucher. "Andrew N. Erskine," *Frontier Times*, IV.

Fitzwilliam, Grace. "Early Election Held in Bastrop in 1831," *In the Shadow of the Lost Pines*, 42.

———. "From Bastrop to Mina to Bastrop, 1832–1837," *ibid.*, 41.

Gunn, Jack Winton. "Ben McCulloch, A Big Captain," *Southwestern Historical Quarterly*, LVIII.

Morgan, H. L. "John Day Morgan," *Frontier Times*, IV.

Rabb, John. "Story of an Indian Experience in the Early Settlement of Texas," *Texas Monument*, August 27, 1841.

Roberts, D. W. "The Restoration of Warren Lyons," *Frontier Times*, IV.

Smither, Harriet. "The Alabama Indians of Texas," *Southwestern Historical Quarterly*, XXXVI.

Sowell, A. J. "Colonel Rip Ford and His Rangers Battle with Indians," *Frontier Times*, IV.

Terrell, Alexander W. "The City of Austin from 1839 to 1865," *Quarterly of the Texas State Historical Association*, XIV.

Traylor, Maude Wallis, "Benjamin Franklin Highsmith," *Frontier Times*, XV.

———. "Captain Samuel Highsmith, Ranger," *ibid.*, XVII.

BIBLIOGRAPHY

Williams, Amelia. "A Critical Study of the Siege of the Alamo and of the Personnel of its Defenders," *Southwestern Historical Quarterly,* XXXVII.

Winkler, E. W. "The Cherokee Indians in Texas," *Quarterly of the Southwestern Historical Association,* VII.

Theses

Benavides, Ilma M. "General Woll's Invasion of San Antonio in 1842." Master's Thesis, University of Texas, 1952.

Blake, Gertrude Burleson. "The Public Career of General Hugh McLeod." Master's Thesis, University of Texas, 1932.

Boethal, Carl. "History of Lavaca County, 1685–1930." Master's Thesis, University of Texas, 1932.

Goldman, Pauline Scott. "Letters from Three Members of Terry's Rangers, 1861 to 1865." Master's Thesis, University of Texas, 1930.

Hardy, Aloise Walker. "A History of Travis County, 1832–1865." Master's Thesis, University of Texas, 1938.

Korges, William Henry. "Bastrop County, Texas: Historical and Educational Development." Master's Thesis, University of Texas, 1933.

Perkins, Lucile Jackson. "The Local History Approach to Teaching Social Studies: A Compilation of Historical Data of Bastrop, Texas." Master's Thesis, University of Texas, 1954.

Yager, Hope. "Archive War in Texas." Master's Thesis, University of Texas, 1939.

Index

Index

286

INDEX

Bacon, Sumner: preaches in
Bastrop, 26
Bahalle, Carra: in Texas Revolu-
tion, 155
Baker (near Onion Creek): In-
dians visit home of, 76
Bandera Pass, Battle of: Neill
participates in, 155n.; Dunn
wounded in, 196n.; Achlin
wounded in, 239
Barber, James: killed in Battle of
Mier, 134
Barnett, Dr. George W.: joins
Coleman at Parker's Fort, 23n.
Barrett, Don Carlos: member of
Mina Committee of Safety and
Correspondence, 258
Barton, Baker: killed by Indians,
225–226
Barton, Benjamin: moves to Texas,
3n.
Barton, Elisha: moves to Texas,
3n.; after Second Runaway
Scrape, 49
Barton, Parthenia: courtship of,
208–209
Barton, William: moves to Texas,
3n.; talks with Comanches, 9;
Grumbles buys home of, 202n.;
election at home of, 265
Barton, William, Jr.: chased by
Indians, 72–73; on Vasquez
campaign, 166; on buffalo hunt,
206–207
Barton Creek (Travis County):
Shuff killed on, 162n.
Barton Springs: Shuff killed near,
162; Black killed near, 165–166
Barton's Prairie: Indians grow
troublesome in, 18
Bastrop, Baron de: aids Stephen
F. Austin, 5n.
Bastrop, Texas: establishment and
naming, 5n.; citizens lose horses,
19–20; Sumner Bacon preaches
in, 26; evacuated in Runaway
Scrape, 42–45; armed squads
protect citizens, 46–47; men
killed in, 55; organizes company

to protect townspeople, 59n.;
Eggleston killed in, 60; sends
volunteers to fight Comanches,
61n.; Burleson raises men in,
63; cannon used as warning
signal, 71; Hill's company
marches through, 193; Gazley
runs store in, 213–214; during
War between the States, 232–
233; Alexanders operate store
and hotel in, 239; Childress a
preacher in, 241; Craft builds
first jail in, 243; Eggleston's
house used as meeting place,
246; McDonald runs ferry and
sawmill at, 257; Manlove first
mayor of, 258
Bastrop County, Texas: first sermon in, 19; men from, in Mier
Expedition, 107; during War
between the States, 232n.; William Jenkins sheriff of, 255;
Reed county surveyor of, 263;
Vaughn first sheriff of, 268
Battle Island, Texas: Indians
attacked on, 161
Baylor, John R.: serves as gov-
ernment agent, 176
Baylor, Nicholas: killed by In-
dians, 80–82
Bazley (surveyor): killed by
Indians, 80–82
Bell, William: killed by Indians,
166–167
Bell County, Texas: Taylors at-
tacked in, 182–183; Harvey dies
in, 253; Young moves to, 272
Belton, Texas: Bird attacked near,
179; Taylors attacked near, 182
Bennett, J. L.: Gillespie in com-
pany of, 248
Berry, Andrew Jackson: in Second
Runaway Scrape, 47n.
Berry, John: in Second Runaway
Scrape, 47n.
Berry, John Bate: captures Caddo
Indian, 21–22; in Second Run-
away Scrape, 47; on Mier Ex-
pedition, 118

Berry, Joseph: in Second Runaway Scrape, 47n.; on Mier
Expedition, 117–118

Bexar, Siege of (1835): Burleson
in command during, 31n.; Mina
Volunteers at, 36n.; Alexander
participates in, 131n.; Jonathan
Burleson in, 241; Perry takes
part in, 262; Sims serves at, 266;
Swisher fights in, 267; Wilson
takes part in, 271

Bibb, Jack: in Vasquez invasion,
220

Big Prairie, Texas: battle fought
near, 63; Indian fight in, 70

Billingsley, Jesse: commands
company in Texas Revolution,
36–37; in Woll's invasion, 100–
101; runs for Congress against
Cunningham, 243

Biloxi Indians: join with Cordova,
84–85

Bird, John: killed by Comanches,
178–181

Bird's Creek: Bird killed on, 179

Black, John R.: killed by Indians,
165–166

Black Bean Episode (1843): 113–
114

Blakey (from Bastrop): escapes
Indians, 29

Blakey, Edward: serves in Texas
Revolution, 41; in Runaway
Scrape, 43n.; killed in Brushy
Creek fight, 59; biographical
sketch, 240

Blakey, John: moves to Texas, 240

Blakey, Lemuel S.: killed in Battle
of San Jacinto, 240

Blakey, Nancy: in Runaway
Scrape, 43n.; settles near Bastrop, 240

Blakey, Nancy B.: marries Jonathan Burleson, 240–241

Blanco River: Indian chase near,
88

Bliss (in raid led by Coleman):
wounded by Indians, 23

Boatwright, Lucy: marries Warren Lyons, 256

Bonnell, George W.: in Mier
Expedition, 117

Bonnell, Mount (Austin, Texas):
named after George W.
Bonnell, 118

Bonner (friend of J. T. Mc-
Gehee): sees wild panther,
224–225

Boone, Daniel: granddaughter
captured, 61n.

Bowie, James: in Indian fight, 178

Bowie, Rezin P.: in Indian fight,
178

Bowles (Cherokee Indian Chief):
leads Indians against Burleson,
13–17

Bowles, Young (son of Bowles):
killed by Burleson,17

Boyd, Sally: marries Martin
Wells, 269

Brazoria, Texas: Blakey dies in,
240

Brazoria County, Texas: Moore
receives land in, 260

Brazos Island, Texas: Confederate battle near, 233

Brazos River: in Texas Revolution, 43–44; Santa Fe men
follow, 121; first white woman
to cross, 248

Brenham, Richard Fox: on Santa
Fe Expedition, 123

Bright, John: chased by Indians,
78–79; on buffalo hunt, 206–207

Bright, Tom: on buffalo hunt,
206–207

Brown, John Henry: tells of
Caddo band being caught, 22n.

Brown County, Texas: Fisk first
chief justice of, 247

Brownsville, Texas: Dunn killed
in, 196n.; Confederate battle
near, 232–233

Brownwood, Texas: Fisk donates
land for, 247

Brushy Creek: Wilbarger scalped
near, 26; battle fought near,

288

Brushy Creek—*Continued*
58–59; Indians camp on, 85;
Fort Kenney located on, 120n.;
panther hunt on, 224–225;
Osborn scalped on, 262
Brushy Creek, Battle of (1839):
58–59
Buckman, Oliver: kills Indian woman, 24; in ranger squad, 181
Buckner, Aylett C.: raises force
against Indians, 161
Buffalo Hump: visits Jenkins
settlement, 8–10; thought to be
on Linnville raid, 60; killed by
Texans, 179n.
Burleson, Aaron: in Brushy Creek
fight, 58n.; in Plum Creek
battle, 66n.
Burleson, Edward: settles in
Texas, 12–13; defeats Bowles,
13–17; makes first scouting raid,
21–22; leads force against Wacoes, 23–26; in command during
Siege of Bexar, 31n.; serves as
colonel in Texas Revolution,
36n.; acts as Jenkins' guardian,
41; family in Runaway Scrape,
43n.; chases Indians, 50; follows
Wacoes and Tawakonies, 53; in
Brushy Creek fight, 58–60; in
Plum Creek battle, 61–68; horse
stolen, 69; originates warning
system, 71n.; chases Webster
murderers, 81; in Cordova Rebellion, 84–85; during Woll's
invasion, 95–96; Caddoes seek
revenge against, 182–183; member of Mina Committee of Safety and Correspondence, 258
Burleson, Edward, Jr.: in Indian
fight, 225–226; member of
Know-Nothing Party, 257
Burleson, Elizabeth: wife of Jacob
Burleson, 58n.
Burleson, Jacob: killed in Battle
of Brushy Creek, 58–59; sketch
of life, 58n.; mistaken for brother, 66

Burleson, James: settles in Texas,
12; tells of Indian encounters,
13–17; family in Runaway
Scrape, 43n.
Burleson, John: in Battle of
Brushy Creek, 58n.; in Plum
Creek battle, 66n.
Burleson, Jonathan: serves as
scout, 16–17; in Runaway
Scrape, 43n.; horse leaps high
bluff, 53; mistaken for Jacob
Burleson, 58n.; seeks aid from
Placido, 61n.; chases Indian
thieves, 102–104; biographical
sketch, 240–241
Burleson, Joseph: home of, near
Smithville, 36n.; son in Plum
Creek battle, 67n.
Burleson, Joseph, Jr.: in Plum
Creek battle, 67
Burleson, Nancy (Gage): son
in Plum Creek battle, 67n.
Burleson, Susan: marries T. M.
Hardeman, 252
Burleson County, Texas: Jacob
Burleson settles in, 58n.; Bird
receives land in, 178n.; Hill
camps in, 194; Childress lives
in, 241; Curtis owns land in, 244;
Furnash resides in, 248; Swisher
settles in, 267
Burnet (surveyor): wounded by
Indians, 90
Burnet, David G.: as vice-presi-
dent, 170
Burnet County, Texas: Webster
massacred en route to, 82n.;
Magill lives in, 257
Burnham neighborhood (Fayette
County): Texas army retreats
through, 39–40

Caddo Indians: have council with
settlers, 10–12; killed by mistake
by pioneers, 21–23; defeated by
Delawares, 87–88; murder Bird,
178–181; attack Taylor family,
182–183

Coke, Richard: serves as governor, 168
Coleman, Albert: murdered by Indians, 56–57
Coleman, Alexander: in Indian encounter, 166–167
Coleman, Elizabeth: killed by Indians, 56–57
Coleman, James: escapes Indians, 57n.
Coleman, Robert M.: serves as alcalde, 5n.; emigrates to Texas, 19; leads raid near Navasota River, 23; commands Mina Volunteers, 36n.; company protects settlers, 49; commands Fort Colorado, 50; wife killed by Indians, 56–57
Coleman, Thomas: captured by Indians, 57n.; bought by white men, 60; returns to Indian life, 231
Collingsworth (wagonmaker): makes wagon for Jenkinses, 75–76
Collins, Tom C.: on pecan hunt, 202–203
Colorado City, Texas: Moore's fight near, 173n.
Colorado County, Texas: Moore receives land in, 260
Colorado River: Colemans killed near, 56–57; Hornsbys killed on, 143–144; Karankawas attack pioneers on, 160; Moore's fight on, 171–174; pecan hunt on, 202
Colt revolver: used by Hays's Rangers, 145–146
Columbia, Texas: Mrs. Hibbans meets husband in, 253; Manlove goes to, 258
Columbus, Texas: Cunningham lives in, 244
Comanche, Texas: horses stolen at, 75–76
Comanche Indians: kill Tumlinson, 6; visit Jenkins settlement, 8–10; murder John Edwards, 33; attack Hornsby family, 45–

46; steal horses, 54; raid Victoria and Linnville, 60–62; defeated at Plum Creek, 63–68; defeated at Council House Fight, 82–84; murder Hornsby, 143–144; Neill and Curtis surprised by, 157; kidnap Simpson children, 164–165; Moore defeats, 171–174; murder Bird's group, 178–181; raided by Howard, 188–191; wound Perry and Achlin, 195–197; defeated by Burleson, 225–226
Comanche Peak: Santa Fe men pass, 121
Concepción, Battle of (1835): Andrews killed in, 258
Connell, Sampson: serves in Texas Revolution, 38–39; biographical sketch, 242
Connor, John: acts as interpreter and guide, 151; finds Thomas Coleman, 231
Constitution of 1824 (Mexico): violated by Mexico, 35
Cook, William G.: on Santa Fe Expedition, 123
Cooke, John: warns settlers about Caddoes, 10–11; biographical sketch, 242
Cordova Rebellion (1838): 84–85
Corretto, Mexico: Santa Fe prisoners march through, 128–129
Cós, Martín Perfecto de: in Texas Revolution, 43
Cottingham, Charles: marries Clopton girl, 242
Cottle, Wash: Curtis avenges death of, 244
Council House Fight (1840): 82–84
Coushatta Indians: take horses by mistake, 10
Crabapple Creek: rangers camp on, 150
Craft, James A.: serves in Mina Volunteers, 36n.; chased by

298

INDEX

Live Oak Bayou: Cavinas killed near, 161n.
Llano River: Waco Indians camp on, 150–151; Howard force crosses, 190
Lloyd, Richard J.: marries Parthenia Barton, 208n.
Lockhart, Matilda: captive of Indians, 82–84
Lockhart, Texas: Indian battle near, 63–68
Los Moros Creek: Indian signs found on, 187
Loy (with supply boat): killed by Karankawas, 160
Luckett, Nolan M.: child killed, 167n.
Luckie, Samuel H.: wounded in Battle of Salado, 99
Lynch, John L.: killed by Indians, 17; biographical sketch, 256
Lyons, DeWitt: in Moore's Defeat, 186
Lyons, Warren: in Indian fight, 225–226; captured by Indians, 226–231; biographical sketch, 256

McClure, Mrs. (widow): gives horse to Morgan: 131
McClusky, Felix: in ranger service, 183–184
McCulloch, Ben: leads men against Comanches, 61n.; escapes capture, 219
McCulloch, Henry: marries widow McClure, 131
McCullom, Captain (from Alabama): killed by Indians, 263–264
McDonald (from Bastrop): killed by Indians, 29–30
McDonald, Hugh K.: land settled by James Neill, 20; biographical sketch, 257
McGehee, John Gilmore: family in Runaway Scrape, 43n.; son on panther hunt, 224–225

McGehee, Jonathan Thomas: on panther hunt, 224–225; on bear hunt, 235
McGehee, Sarah Milton (Hill): mother of J. T. McGehee, 224n.
Machochochomochouch (Comanche Indian chief): killed by Texans, 173n.
McKarnan, Tom: in Wren fight, 51
McLeod, Hugh: leads Santa Fe Expedition, 120
McNuner, William: killed by Comanches, 61n.
McSherry, John: marries Sarah Creath, 253
Magill, William: mistakes Smith Hornsby for Indian, 25; biographical sketch, 257–258
Magill, William, Jr.: kills Indian, 257
Manlove, Bartholomew: escapes Comanches, 33; horse stolen, 85–86; biographical sketch, 258–259
Manlove, Dolly: traded for horse, 259
Manlove, Mary A.: wife of Greenleaf Fisk, 247
Mann, Mrs. (widow): defeats Houston and Rohrer, 264
Manor, James: wounded in Moore's Defeat, 187n.; on buffalo hunt, 205–206; biographical sketch, 259–260
Manor, Joseph: settles in Travis County, 260
Manor, Texas: named for Manors, 260
Manshack Springs: Indian fight near, 71–72
Marea, Hosea: chief of Karankawas, 160
Martin, James: killed by Indians, 80–82
Martin, Joseph: scouts for Moore, 185; killed in Moore's Defeat, 187n.

Martin, Philip: killed in Wren fight, 51n.

Matagorda, Texas: Karankawas visit, 159–160; Indian fight near, 161; Osborn born in, 261

Matamoros, Mexico: Mier prisoners march through, 110; Morgan almost recognized in, 134; Hays's rangers pass through, 147–148; Mexicans in command in, 170

Mayfield, James L.: in Woll Invasion, 99

Mayhard Creek: Walker Wilson lives near, 86

Medina River: Woll camps on, 99; Somervell camps on, 107

Menardville, Texas: rangers camp near, 168

Mexican War (1848): 146–150

Mexico City, Mexico: Mier prisoners march toward, 110; Texans sent to, 114; Santa Fe prisoners marched to, 128; captured by Americans, 148–150

Mier, Battle of (1842): 108–110; 133–134

Mier, Mexico: invaded by Texans, 108–110; flag torn at, 132

Mier Expedition (1842): 106–118

Miller, Alsey S.: in Dawson Massacre, 98–99; biographical sketch, 260

Mina, Francisco Xavier: Mexican hero, 5n.

Mina, Municipality of: creation of, 5n.

Mina, Texas: see Bastrop, Texas

Mina Committee of Safety and Correspondence: members of, 258

Mina Volunteers: serve in Texas Revolution, 36n.

Mitchell, Asa: Hill's company organized at, 193

Monclova, Mexico: Mier prisoners march toward, 112

Moncure, John J.: detailed to get swords, 232n.

Monterrey, Mexico: Mier prisoners march through, 110

Montopolis, Texas: Smith cabin located in, 31n., 162n.; Lynch a proprietor of, 256

Moore, John H.: commands force against Indians, 23–25; in Woll Invasion, 99; leads Indian expedition, 171–174; defeated by Indians, 183–187; chases Alexanders' murderers, 239–240; biographical sketch, 260–261

Moore, Pat: in Moore's Defeat, 186

Moore, Thomas: Rohrer killed at home of, 46

Mordecai (from Victoria): killed by Comanches, 61n.

Morgan, John Day: in Mier Expedition, 107; on Santa Fe Expedition, 119ff.

Morrell, Rev. Z. N.: warns of Indian raid, 60n.

Morris, J. D.: Indian fight near home of, 48; house robbed, 53

Muguaro (Comanche Indian chief): in Council House Fight, 83n.

Nacogdoches, Texas: Cordova marches from, 84; Gillespie enters soldier force at, 248

Nash, Michael: killed by Indians, 104

Nashville, Texas: Taylors move to, 182n.; Harrells live in, 252

Navarro, Jose Antonio: on Santa Fe Expedition, 123

Navarro County, Texas: Houston killed in, 194n.

Navasota River: R. M. Coleman leads raid near, 23

Neal (friend of Morgan): on Mier Expedition, 136–139

Neal (ranger): scalped by Indians, 33–34, 270

INDEX

Perote Jalapo, Mexico: Santa Fe prisoners march through, 130

Perote Prison: Mier prisoners at, 114–117; Morgan passes through, 137–138; Twohig escapes from, 221n.

Perry (in Howard's force): raid against Comanches, 188

Perry, Rufus: in Indian fight, 145; wounded in Moore's Defeat, 187n.; in Hill's ranger force, 192–194; wounded by Indians, 195–198; biographical sketch, 262–263

Perry, William: chased by Indians, 72–73

Pin Oak Creek: Alexanders attacked on, 239

Pinta Trail: Indian fight on, 145–146; Howard force follows, 190

Pipkin (surveyor): chased by Indians, 91–92

Placido (Tonkawa Indian chief): assists Burleson at Plum Creek, 61–68; recaptures Manlove's horse, 258–259

Plum Creek: Indians fought on, 63; Neill and Curtis attacked near, 157

Plum Creek, Battle of (1840): 61–68

Ponton, Andrew: first judge of Municipality of Gonzales, 263

Ponton, Joel: attacked by Comanches, 60–62; biographical sketch, 263

Ponton, William: killed by Indians, 263

Ponton's Creek: men attacked near, 60n.

Prairie Lea, Texas: Fentress settles near, 247

Prayor, Jeff: distrusts Caddoes, 11

Prior: see Prayor

Puebla, Mexico: Santa Fe men march through, 130; Hays's rangers pass through, 146–147

Pugh, S. A.: Grassmeyer buys land of, 250

Putnam, James: marries Nash's widow, 104n.

Quenisaik (Comanche Indian chief): killed by Texans, 186

Rabb, John: tells of Caddo band being caught, 22n.

Rabb's Creek: Goachers settle on, 249

Raphael (Negro captive): confirms statement of Robison, 84n.

Redmond, William: moves to Texas, 257

Red River: Indians return Mrs. Coleman near, 249

Reed, Hutchinson: spies for Burleson, 53; wounded in Plum Creek battle, 65; biographical sketch, 263

Reed, Jane: marries James Harvey, 252

Reed, Polly: marries John Harvey, 252

Reno de Melone, Mexico: Mier prisoners march through, 135

Rice, William: killed by Indians, 80–82

Richardson, Varlan: killed by Comanches, 61n.

Ridgeby, Lieutenant: in Mexican War, 147

Rio Grande, Republic of: 109n., 170

Rio Grande River: Mier soldiers cross, 107, 132

Robbins, Nathaniel: operates ferry, 44n.

Robbins' Ferry: used during Runaway Scrape, 44

Roberts, Dan W.: in Indian fight, 169–170

Roberts, Jacob: in Mexican War, 147–148

Robertson, James W.: member of Know-Nothing Party, 257

Robertson, Joel W.: house raided by Indians, 56–57

302

303

near, 66; Indian encounter on, 88

San Saba Presidio: Moore carves name on ruins of, 173n.

San Saba River: Harvey surveys near, 90; rangers camp beside, 168; Bowie's fight near, 178; Moore defeated on, 185–187; surveying expedition along, 252–253

Santa Anna, Antonio Lopez de: invades Texas, 36n.; captured, 44; speaks of Texas soldiers, 111; frees Santa Fe prisoners, 128–130

Santa Fe, New Mexico: Santa Fe men head for, 123; Texans surrender in, 125

Santa Fe Expedition: see Texan Santa Fe Expedition

Santa Fe Trail: Texans follow, 121

Schriff: see Shuff

Scott, Winfield: in Mexican War, 146–150

Scurry, Richard: presents Burleson with horse, 69

Secqualtapan, Mexico: Texans pass through, 148

Seguin, Juan N.: joins Mexican army, 96; in Dawson Massacre, 98

Seguin, Texas: Cordova defeated near, 84–85; Texans march to 220; Cunningham dies in, 244

Seider's Spring: White settles near, 269

Seminole War (1813–1814): Eastland participates in, 152

Sessom, Mike: rides with Delaware Indians, 87–88; biographical sketch, 266

Shepherd (coffin-maker): keeps charge of cannon, 71n.

Shepherd, John Levi: killed on Mier Expedition, 114

Shoal Creek: White lives near, 163; Texans camp on, 165; pecan hunt on, 202

Shuff, Charles: in Moore's fight, 172–173

Shuff, Thomas: killed by Indians, 162

Silsbey, Albert: killed by Indians, 80–82

Simpson, Mrs. (widow in Austin): children kidnaped, 164

Simpson, Emma: kidnaped by Indians, 164–165

Simpson, Thomas: kidnaped by Indians, 164–165

Sims, Bartlett: attacked by Indians, 152; biographical sketch, 266

Sinnickson, Dr.: on Mier Expedition, 118

Slaughter, Ann Sloan: marries L. C. Cunningham, 243

Slaughter, James E.: leads Confederate troops, 232–233

Smith, French: kills Indian squaw, 66; biographical sketch, 267

Smith, James (of Austin, Texas): cabin located in Austin, 31; horse stolen, 76; killed by Indians, 162–163

Smith, James (of Bastrop, Texas): cattle collected at home of, 42; owes money to Northcross, 261; marries Polly Rousseau, 265

Smith, Taylor: wounded by Indians, 94; biographical sketch, 267

Smith, Thomas I.: archives recaptured from, 245

Smithville, Texas: Burleson home near, 36n.; William Jenkins retires in, 255

Smithwick, Noah: tells of Indian thievery, 20n.; in Texas Revolution, 43n.; in Wren fight, 51n.; marries Blakey girl, 240; keeps parties lively with dancing, 247; witnesses scalp dance, 259; Osborn taken to home of, 262; given scalp by Rohrer, 265

Somervell, Alexander: in Mier Expedition, 107–108; offers no

Tonkawa Indians: assist Burleson at Plum Creek, 61–68; cannibalistic traits of, 77–78; assist white men, 84–85; description of, 161–162; recapture Manlove's horse, 258–259

Toulon Singo, Mexico: Texans pass through, 148

Travis, William B.: dies in Alamo, 37n.

Travis County, Texas: Burleson settles in, 241; Dutys live in, 244; Harrell chief justice of, 252; Manors settle in, 261; Swisher county clerk of, 267

Trinity River: flooded during Runaway Scrape, 44; Santa Fe men cross fork of, 121

Tumlinson, John: raises company of rangers, 31; rescues Mrs. Hibbans, 32–33; details men to help Hornsbys, 45n.; leads force against Comanches, 61–62; Rohrer saves life of, 264

Tumlinson brothers: one killed by Indians, 5; biographical sketch, 268

Turkey Creek: Indian signs found on, 187

Turner, Mima Eggleston: marries Walker Wilson, 271

Turner, Winslow: in Brushy Creek fight, 50n.

Twohig, John: in Vasquez's invasion, 220–221

Tyler County, Texas: Indian fights in, 16

Urrea, Jose: leads Mexican army, 153

Uvalde, Texas: Indian signs found near, 187; Perry and Achlin wounded near, 196n.

Vanham, young travelers stop at house of: 217

Vasquez, Raphael: invades Texas, 95; captures Dunn, 196n.; captures San Antonio, 219–221

Vaughn, Richard: horse killed in Indian fight, 54; biographical sketch, 268

Vera Cruz, Mexico: officers sent to, 117; Santa Fe prisoners march through, 130; Morgan passes through, 138; Hays's rangers stop in, 146

Victoria, Mexico: Mier prisoners march through, 135

Victoria, Texas: raided by Comanches, 60–61

Waco, Texas: Indian village on site of, 121

Waco Indians: attacked by pioneers, 23; attack Wilbarger and party, 26–29; raid Ebbins neighborhood, 53; steal Manlove's horse, 85–86; killed by rangers, 151–152; attack pioneers, 217–218; Sims leads raid against, 266

Waelder, Texas: Cunningham lives in, 244

Walker, Samuel: in Woll's invasion, 101; in Indian fight, 145–146; Comanches fight with, 226n.

Walker County, Texas: Gillespie marries in, 249

Wallace (in raid led by Coleman): killed by Indians, 23

Wallace, William S.: leads surveying expedition, 90; encounters Comanches, 227–229; biographical sketch, 268

Waller's Creek: Indian fight near, 166–167; horses stolen near, 174

Walnut Creek: Fort Colorado established near, 50

Walnut Springs, Texas: Campbell lays out, 241

Walters, John B.: killed in Brushy Creek fight, 59; biographical sketch, 268–269

War between the States: Jenkins experiences in, 232–233